D1191342

THIS IS YOUR
ACCESS CODE

nelson 4256 XVBW

Enter your code in myNelson to access:

Nelson History 7
Student Book Online PDFs

Already a myNelson user?	New to myNelson?
ADD THIS PRODUCT TO YOUR DASHBOARD 1. Go to mynelson.com. 2. Log in using your email address and password. 3. Enter your code in the "Add new resource" field and click Submit. 4. Keep a record of your username and password.	**REGISTER** 1. Go to mynelson.com. 2. Follow the onscreen instructions to create an account. 3. Enter your code in the "Add new resource" field and click Submit. 4. Keep a record of your username and password.

For assistance, visit mynelson.com for tutorials and FAQs, contact Customer Support at inquire@nelson.com, or call Customer Support at 1-800-268-2222 from Monday to Friday, 8:00 a.m. to 6:00 p.m. EST.

Lochlan

NELSON

978-0-17-671052-1

NELSON HISTORY 7

AUTHOR TEAM

Theodore Christou, Ph.D., Queen's University

Rachel Collishaw, Ottawa Carleton DSB

Stanley Hallman-Chong, OISE, formerly Toronto DSB

Charlene Hendricks, Limestone DSB

CONTRIBUTING AUTHORS

Julia Armstrong, York Region DSB

Jan Haskings-Winner, Toronto DSB

Margaret Hoogeveen

Kelly-Ann Lee

Jennette MacKenzie

Margaret McClintock

NELSON

NELSON

Nelson History 7

Authors
Theodore Christou
Rachel Collishaw
Stanley Hallman-Chong
Charlene Hendricks

Contributing Authors
Julia Armstrong
Jan Haskings-Winner
Margaret Hoogeveen
Kelly-Ann Lee
Jennette MacKenzie
Margaret McClintock

Publisher, Social Studies and Business
Paula Smith

Managing Editor
Jennifer Hounsell

Product Manager
Jessie MacKinnon

Program Managers
Jackie Brown
Kimberly Murphy
Adele Reynolds

Consultants
Jennette MacKenzie
Janice Schoening

Developmental Editors
James Gladstone
Naomi Go
Margaret Hoogeveen
Jennifer Hughes
Sarah Jones
Evelyn Maksimovich
Jack Whelan

Editorial Assistant
Sarah Jones

Researchers
Hilary-Rosalind Ashe
Blythe Koreen

Fact Checkers
Marc-André Brouillard
Sarah Jones

Director, Content and Media Production
Linh Vu

Production Project Manager
Susan Lee

Content Production Editors
Nicole Boocock
Susan Lee

Copyeditor
Paula Pettitt-Townsend

Proofreaders
Linda Cahill
Shana Hayes

Indexer
Marilyn Augst

Design Director
Ken Phipps

Interior Design
Courtney Hellam

Cover Design
Courtney Hellam

Cover Image
Nine OK/Getty Images

Asset Coordinator
Suzanne Peden

Illustrators
Michael Borop
Crowle Art Group

Compositors
deboraH brock
Courtney Hellam
Cathy Mayer
Trinh Truong

Photo/Permissions Researcher
Kristiina Paul

Student Text
ISBN-13: 978-0-17-671053-8
ISBN-10: 0-17-671053-1

Student Text + PDF
ISBN-13: 978-0-17-671054-5
ISBN-10: 0-17-671054-X

Printed and bound in Canada
5 6 7 19 18 17

For more information contact Nelson Education Ltd., 1120 Birchmount Road, Toronto, Ontario M1K 5G4. Or you can visit our website at nelson.com.

NELSON HISTORY 7 Advisors and Reviewers

ADVISOR TEAM

Rachel Collishaw, Ottawa Carleton DSB

Jan Haskings-Winner, Toronto DSB

Stéphane Levesque, Ph.D., Associate Professor of History Education, University of Ottawa

Larry McKeigan, York Region DSB

James Steeves, Peel DSB

SPECIALTY REVIEWERS

Nancy Christoffer, *Bias*

Margaret Conrad, Ph.D., Professor Emerita at the University of New Brunswick, *Accuracy Consultant*

Monika Orzechowska, *First Nations, Métis, and Inuit*

CLASSROOM REVIEWERS

Christine Battagli, Niagara Catholic DSB

Julie Byvelds, Catholic DSB of Eastern Ontario

Anna Caravaggio, Peel DSB

Nicolina Custoza-Scanga, Durham DSB

Heidi Dee, Limestone DSB

Heather Delorenzi, Windsor Essex Catholic DSB

Judith Eaton, Hamilton-Wentworth Catholic DSB

Ronan Heffernan, London District Catholic SB

Andrea Higgins, Upper Grand DSB

Lisa Hoffman, York Region DSB

Blair Janzen, DSB of Niagara

Terri Klassen, Ottawa Carleton DSB

Karen Koop, Hamilton-Wentworth DSB

Lena LeFave, Kawartha Pine Ridge DSB

Janice Maggio, Halton DSB

Carolyn Martin, Toronto Catholic DSB

Kristen McDade, Simcoe Muskoka Catholic DSB

Adele McLeod, Upper Canada DSB

Melissa Monardo, York Catholic DSB

Nancy Murovec, Waterloo Region DSB

Judith Murphy, Hastings and Prince Edward DSB

Debbie Price, Greater Essex County DSB

Sonia Racco, York Catholic DSB

Lori Ramer, Simcoe County DSB

Leanne Rust, Halton DSB

Ramandeep Sarai, Toronto DSB

Steve Sheehan, Rainbow DSB

Shannon Simpson, Simcoe County DSB

Anna Tardella, Dufferin-Peel Catholic DSB

Marco Vispo, Ottawa Catholic SB

TABLE OF CONTENTS

USING THIS
RESOURCE

INTRODUCTION

In the Introduction, you will be introduced to the discipline of history, as well as the **inquiry skills** and **historical thinking concepts** you will be using throughout this resource. Use the Introduction as a reference that you can turn back to throughout this resource.

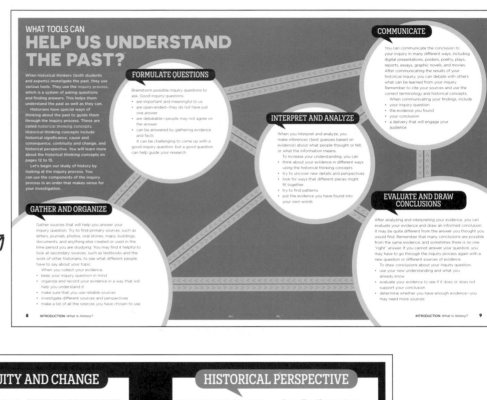

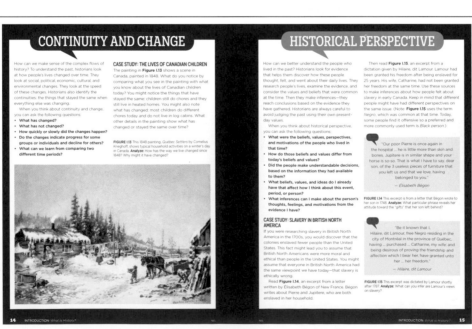

UNIT OPENER

There are two units in this book. Each unit has four chapters.

These bubbles contain questions from the viewpoints of the different **historical thinking concepts**. You will also see these bubbles throughout the chapters. Each colour always connects to the same thinking concept. PURPLE means Continuity and Change, ORANGE means Cause and Consequence, BLUE means Historical Perspective, and YELLOW means Historical Significance.

The timeline shows different events that occur throughout the unit.

The infographics reveal interesting information about the time period.

This is an introduction to the **Unit Challenge**, an activity that you will work on throughout the unit.

CHAPTER OPENER

The chapter opener introduces the theme and content covered in the chapter.

This is the main question that you will explore in the chapter.

These skills and ideas are covered in the chapter.

CHAPTER FEATURES

These questions represent the viewpoints of the different **historical thinking concepts**. Each colour always represents the same thinking concept.

Important words are highlighted and defined directly on the page.

The figure reference tells you what the figure (image, photo, source, map, diagram, graph, or table) is about.

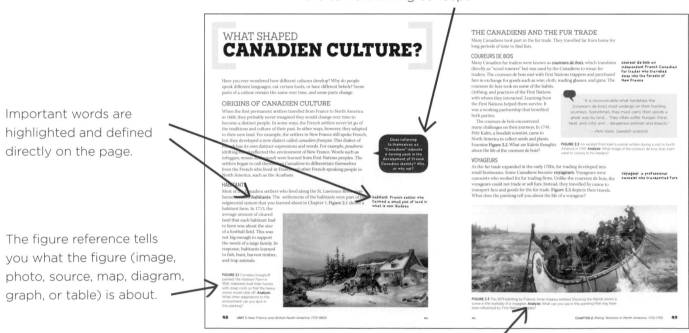

The **Analyze** question asks you to examine and interpret the figure (image, photo, source, map, diagram, graph, or table) in a different way.

Quotes provide evidence and additional perspectives on the topics, issues, and events that are covered in the chapter.

Transcriptions of letters, treaties, proclamations, and other sources are provided.

The **History at Work** features profile different careers related to history.

The **Connecting to Our Past** features profile young people who are actively connecting to Canada's history—to people and events from our past.

Use the **Check-In** questions and activities to assess your understanding. Each question or activity is labelled with the **historical thinking concept** or the **inquiry skill** that it covers.

CHAPTER FEATURES (CONTINUED)

Each **Focus On** feature will help you look more closely at a **historical thinking concept** or an **inquiry skill** and practise using it.

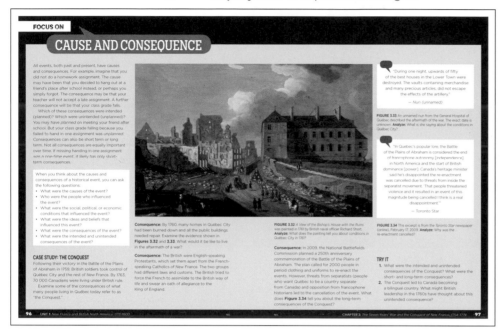

Activity pages appear in every chapter to help you read, analyze, and create different kinds of maps and graphs, and read and analyze primary and secondary sources.

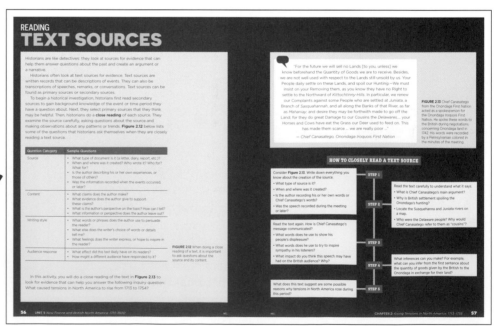

LOOKING BACK

You will have the opportunity to look back at what you have learned at the end of each chapter and each unit.

These questions and activities will help you apply your learning. Each question relates to a **historical thinking concept** or an **inquiry skill**.

These activities will help you summarize what you have learned in the chapter.

At the end of each chapter, you will complete a step in your **Unit Challenge**.

The timeline shows different events you learned about throughout the unit.

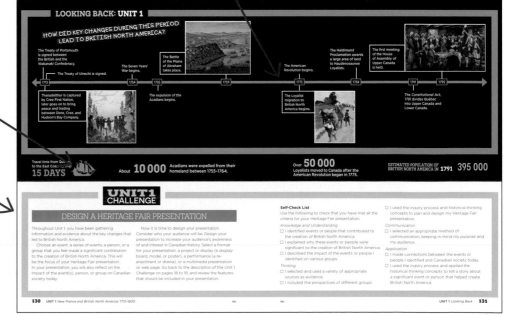

The infographics reveal interesting information about the time period.

These instructions will help you complete your **Unit Challenge**.

WHAT IS HISTORY?

WHY IS THE PAST STILL IMPORTANT TO US TODAY?

LEARNING GOALS

As you work through this introduction, you will
- reflect on why we study history
- think about how we know what we know about the past
- learn how the historical inquiry process works
- explore the concepts of historical thinking

Who are we? What came before us, and how have we changed? These questions are a part of the study of history. Although history is the study of the past, it helps us to make connections between the past and our lives today.

We tell stories about the past to help us remember and understand what has happened before. The role of a historian is to create those stories by examining and interpreting evidence.

In the photo on these pages, students are examining English artist Thomas Gainsborough's copy of the painting *Lords John and Bernard Stuart*. The original was painted around 1638 by Anthony van Dyck. Gainsborough painted his version around 1760 to 1770. Today, it hangs in an art museum. John and Bernard Stuart were brothers and were teenagers when the original painting was created. By looking at this painting, you can see what the brothers looked like and what clothes they wore. You can also tell that they seem like members of the English nobility. This painting is a historical source that we can use to learn about the past. How do you think future historians will learn about our lives and society today?

WHY STUDY HISTORY?

Everything we are and everything we do has roots in the past. Even your chair in the classroom has a history. For thousands of years, the only chairs with backs were large, imposing thrones made for lords, kings, and queens. It was only in the 1600s that woodworkers started making lighter, more practical chairs for everyday life.

LEARNING WHO WE ARE

People study history for different reasons. By looking at the lives of the people who came before us, we can better understand how the society we have today came to be. Why do we have the laws we do? Why does our country have the borders it does? Why do I speak this language and not another language? For example, the canoe is a part of Canada's cultural heritage. Look at **Figures I.1A** and **I.1B**. What can you learn about Canada by examining these images and the history of the canoe?

Some people study history because they want to find out more about what interests them, like the age of the sailing ship or the history of hockey. People also study history because they want to find out more about where they came from. Studying your personal roots by learning about your ancestors, family history, family traditions, and the history of your country can help you understand how you became the person you are today.

FIGURE I.1 (A) This photo shows a Canadian family canoeing in Obatanga Provincial Park in Northern Ontario in 2006. (B) This painting by Peter Rindisbacher shows an Aboriginal family canoeing on a lake in Manitoba about 200 years earlier, in the 1800s. **Analyze:** What similarities and differences do you see when examining these two images?

LEARNING WHO WE WANT TO BECOME

History can guide us to become the kind of individual or society that we want to be. By studying history, we can try to avoid the mistakes that people have made in the past. We can also be inspired by the actions of others.

Think about the brave actions of 17-year-old Ann Harvey. In 1828, the sailing ship *Despatch* was shipwrecked on the rocks near her home off the coast of Newfoundland and Labrador. The *Despatch* carried over 200 people. All the passengers could have drowned if not for Harvey, her father George, her 12-year-old brother, and her dog, called Hairy Man. They rowed in an open fishing boat through stormy weather to reach the survivors. Hairy Man swam out with a lifeline. Together, they saved around 160 people. The Harvey family were awarded a medal for their brave actions. George Harvey gave the medal to Ann since it was her determination that led them to rescue so many people.

Harvey's courage helped people in need. By knowing about the actions of Harvey and her family, you might be inspired to face your own challenges. Knowing and understanding history may help you become the kind of person you want to be.

Today, the Canadian Coast Guard uses different equipment than the Harvey family. However, like Harvey and her family, they do their best to help people who are lost and stranded at sea. In 1987, the Canadian government named the Coast Guard vessel in **Figure I.2** after Ann Harvey. The Newfoundland and Labrador town of Isle aux Morts has an annual festival, called Ann Harvey Days, to celebrate the Harvey family's heroic actions. One of Bruce Arnott's ancestors was a survivor of the *Despatch*. Read **Figure I.3**, a quote from Arnott where he reflects on the impact Harvey had on him and many others. How do you think knowing our history can help us become a better society?

"I and many others would never have been born but for Ann Harvey's courage in rescuing our ancestors from the wreck of the *Despatch* in 1828 ..."

— *Bruce Arnott*

FIGURE I.3 This quote is from Arnott, a descendant of a *Despatch* passenger. **Analyze:** How do you think Ann Harvey's actions affected the people and society of Newfoundland and Labrador?

HOW DO WE KNOW
WHAT WE KNOW ABOUT THE PAST?

All histories are rooted in sources. Historians examine relevant sources, apply their understanding of the time period, and then tell a story about what they think happened in the past.

USING PRIMARY SOURCES

A primary source is an account or a document that was created by someone who witnessed an event. It can also be an artifact created or used during the time period when the event happened. Everything we know about the past is based on primary sources. These sources can be tools, photos, paintings, diaries, eyewitness accounts, oral histories, even digital recordings.

In 1783, Hannah Ingraham and her family left the United States and moved to British North America. Read **Figure I.4**. It is a primary source because it is a recollection of an event by an eyewitness.

Follow the steps in **Figure I.5** to gather evidence from a primary source.

> "I was just eleven years old when we left our farm to come here....
>
> We had to live in tents ... It was just at the first snow then, and the melting snow and the rain would soak up into our beds as we lay....
>
> We came up the river at last in a [ship], and were nine days in getting to St. Anne's....
>
> [Father built our first house.] Oh, what joy to see our [new home]. There was no floor laid, no windows, no chimney, no door, but we had a roof at least."
>
> — *Hannah Ingraham*

FIGURE I.4 This is an excerpt from Ingraham's memoir about her personal experience in 1783. Her memoir was recorded when Ingraham was in her nineties. **Analyze:** This account was documented long after the events took place. Why is it still considered a primary source?

Gathering Evidence from Primary Sources

Step	Example
1. **Source** the primary source. Write down whatever you know about the origins of the source.	The caption for **Figure I.4** tells you who the speaker was and the year that she was talking about.
2. **Examine** the source in detail.	You might notice details like Hannah's delight with her new home.
3. **Consider the historical context.** What was happening in the world at that time in history?	You might know, for example, that 1783 was the first year that Loyalist settlers fled to British North America after the American Revolution.
4. **Make inferences** about the source; that is, draw conclusions based on evidence.	After reading Ingraham's quote, you might infer that starting a new life in British North America was hard work.
5. **Corroborate** your inferences. This means checking to see if other reliable sources confirm your inference.	For example, you might compare the source with the online information in **Figure I.6** on the next page.

FIGURE I.5 These five steps will help you gather evidence from primary sources.

USING SECONDARY SOURCES

A secondary source is an account about an event or time period created by someone who did not experience it first-hand. Secondary sources are created by gathering evidence from primary sources. For example, this book includes many primary sources, but it is a secondary source. The authors are telling a story about events that happened a long time ago.

Read **Figure I.6**, which gives more information about Ingraham and her family. It is a secondary source because it was written hundreds of years after the events took place. The website where **Figure I.6** originally appeared used Ingraham's memoir to gather information. Which type of source do you think is more valuable to historians?

Follow the steps in **Figure I.7** to gather evidence from a secondary source.

> "Like many Loyalists, Hannah Ingraham's family paid dearly for their loyalty to the British cause in the American Revolutionary War. Hannah was only four years old when her father joined the King's American Regiment in 1776, which resulted in American Patriots harassing the family and confiscating their farm.
>
> When the war ended, the Ingrahams had few options other than to start life over again in what remained of British North America. They left New York for New Brunswick in September 1783. As winter set in, the Ingrahams settled at St. Anne's Point, which had been renamed Fredericton when it was chosen as the capital of the colony in 1784."
>
> — *The Atlantic Canada Virtual Archives*

FIGURE I.6 This quote about Ingraham's family appears on a website created by the Atlantic Canada Virtual Archives. **Analyze:** What new information does this quote give you?

Gathering Information from Secondary Sources

Step	Example
1. **Source** the secondary source. That is, write down whatever you know about who made it, when, where, and why.	For example, the caption for **Figure I.6** tells you that the Atlantic Canada Virtual Archives (ACVA) is the website where the quote appeared.
2. **Check the reliability** of the source.	You might check online and find out that the ACVA is associated with the University of New Brunswick.
3. **Examine** the source in detail to gather new information.	Background information, such as the harassment that the family experienced, might explain why the Ingraham family had to flee their home in New York.
4. **Corroborate**, or double-check, the source against other primary or secondary sources.	You might notice that St. Anne's is mentioned in both **Figure I.4** and **Figure I.6**. This means that you can have more trust in the information.

FIGURE I.7 These four steps will help you gather information from secondary sources.

DOCUMENTING YOUR SOURCES

If you wrote a history of Hannah Ingraham, you might draw on the evidence that you gathered from the primary and secondary sources on these pages. If you did, you should say where you got your information. It gives your readers confidence in what you are telling them. For example, you might state the sources in your text, or you could use a bibliography to document where you found your information. A bibliography is a list of sources that usually appears at the end of a text.

WHAT TOOLS CAN HELP US UNDERSTAND THE PAST?

When historical thinkers (both students and experts) investigate the past, they use various tools. They use the inquiry process, which is a system of asking questions and finding answers. This helps them understand the past as well as they can.

Historians have special ways of thinking about the past to guide them through the inquiry process. These are called historical thinking concepts. Historical thinking concepts include historical significance, cause and consequence, continuity and change, and historical perspective. You will learn more about the historical thinking concepts on pages 12 to 15.

Let's begin our study of history by looking at the inquiry process. You can use the components of the inquiry process in an order that makes sense for your investigation.

FORMULATE QUESTIONS

Brainstorm possible inquiry questions to ask. Good inquiry questions

- are important and meaningful to us
- are open-ended—they do not have just one answer
- are debatable—people may not agree on the answer
- can be answered by gathering evidence and facts

It can be challenging to come up with a good inquiry question, but a good question can help guide your research.

GATHER AND ORGANIZE

Gather sources that will help you answer your inquiry question. Try to find primary sources, such as letters, journals, photos, oral stories, maps, buildings, documents, and anything else created or used in the time period you are studying. You may find it helpful to look at secondary sources, such as textbooks and the work of other historians, to see what different people have to say about your topic.

When you collect your evidence,

- keep your inquiry question in mind
- organize and record your evidence in a way that will help you understand it
- make sure that you use reliable sources
- investigate different sources and perspectives
- make a list of all the sources you have chosen to use

COMMUNICATE

You can communicate the conclusion to your inquiry in many different ways, including digital presentations, posters, poetry, plays, reports, essays, graphic novels, and movies. After communicating the results of your historical inquiry, you can debate with others what can be learned from your inquiry. Remember to cite your sources and use the correct terminology and historical concepts.

When communicating your findings, include
- your inquiry question
- the evidence you found
- your conclusion
- a delivery that will engage your audience

INTERPRET AND ANALYZE

When you interpret and analyze, you make inferences (best guesses based on evidence) about what people thought or felt, or what the information means.

To increase your understanding, you can
- think about your evidence in different ways using the historical thinking concepts
- try to uncover new details and perspectives
- look for ways that different pieces might fit together
- try to find patterns
- put the evidence you have found into your own words

EVALUATE AND DRAW CONCLUSIONS

After analyzing and interpreting your evidence, you can evaluate your evidence and draw an informed conclusion. It may be quite different from the answer you thought you would find. Remember that many conclusions are possible from the same evidence, and sometimes there is no one "right" answer. If you cannot answer your question, you may have to go through the inquiry process again with a new question or different sources of evidence.

To draw conclusions about your inquiry question,
- use your new understanding and what you already know
- evaluate your evidence to see if it does or does not support your conclusion
- determine whether you have enough evidence—you may need more sources

HISTORICAL INQUIRY
IN ACTION

You are asked to conduct a historical inquiry related to First Nations land claims. Let's look at how you might make your way through the inquiry process.

FORMULATE QUESTIONS

In your initial research, you see the photo in **Figure I.8**. It shows a blockade in Caledonia, Ontario, by the Six Nations people of the Grand River. They are opposing a 40-hectare housing development because they believe that the land really belongs

to them. You formulate an inquiry question that is meaningful to you, open-ended, debatable, and can be answered by gathering evidence: *Why do the Six Nations believe they have a claim to the land in Caledonia?* You use the inquiry process and historical thinking concepts to help you answer this question.

FIGURE I.8 This 2006 photo shows a blockade set up by members of the Six Nations of the Grand River. It blocks access to a construction site where houses are being built. **Analyze:** What inquiry questions can you develop, based on this photo?

GATHER AND ORGANIZE

Next, you gather information from reliable sources. Keeping your inquiry question in mind, you make the following notes, citing your sources:

- The Six Nations of the Grand River include the Mohawk, Seneca, Oneida, Cayuga, Onondaga, and Tuscarora nations.
- The Six Nations had fought as allies of the British during the American Revolution. Because of the war, the Six Nations lost their territories in the United States. To compensate them, the British gave them land in present-day southern Ontario.
- The Haldimand Tract was the 385 000 hectare piece of land granted by the British to the Six Nations of the Grand River in 1784.

You find a quote from the original Haldimand Proclamation (**Figure I.9**) and a map showing the original grant and the present-day land (**Figure I.10**).

> "I ... authorize and permit the ... Six Nation Indians ... to take possession of and settle upon the banks of the ... Grand River ... which them and their posterity to enjoy for ever."
>
> — *Haldimand Proclamation*

FIGURE I.9 This excerpt is from the 1784 Haldimand Proclamation, which granted land to the Six Nations of Grand River. **Analyze:** What other perspectives might help you understand the situation?

The Haldimand Tract, 1784–2001

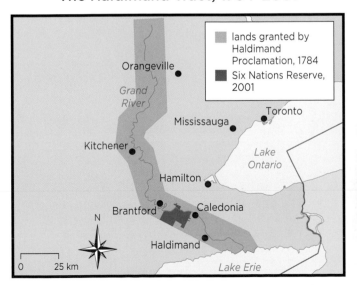

lands granted by Haldimand Proclamation, 1784

Six Nations Reserve, 2001

INTERPRET AND ANALYZE

You examine your evidence, including your notes, as well as primary and secondary sources you have gathered, such as the proclamation in **Figure I.9** and the map in **Figure I.10**. Look for ways that your information fits together, or doesn't. After looking at **Figure I.10**, you notice that the size of the Six Nations lands has shrunk over time. Now you have more questions. Did the Six Nations sell the land? Was it somehow taken from them? Who was involved in the events that led to this? Who were the decision makers? You decide that you need to gather more evidence.

EVALUATE AND DRAW CONCLUSIONS

You evaluate your evidence and use your new understanding to settle on this conclusion to your inquiry question: *The Caledonia land was part of the 1784 land grant, which was promised to the Six Nations forever. They are trying to get back their land that seems to have been taken from them.* You may have also generated new questions that you could continue to investigate in a new inquiry process.

COMMUNICATE

To communicate your conclusion, you consider a variety of options, from a digital presentation to writing a letter to the government calling for action. After thinking about what will interest your audience, you decide to create a podcast that you will play in class. As you write the script, you remember to state your inquiry question and conclusion clearly and to show how your evidence supports your conclusion.

FIGURE I.10 This map shows the Haldimand Tract as it was in 1784 and as it is today. **Analyze:** What might have accounted for the change you see on the map?

PRACTISING HISTORICAL THINKING

What additional questions do you have about the land claims of the Six Nations people of the Grand River? Write a new inquiry question, and research new sources to support your inquiry. Once you have examined your evidence and come to a conclusion, present your findings in a short opinion piece.

HISTORICAL SIGNIFICANCE

How do we decide what is important to learn when studying the past? As historians investigate the past, they make choices about what is significant enough to research. They try to choose events, people, issues, or developments that have had a major, long-lasting impact on many people. A war hero, for example, might fit those criteria. Historians also look for events, people, and developments that help us better understand an important issue. For example, knowing about the experiences of students in a one-room schoolhouse might help us understand how people learn.

When you think about the historical significance of various events, people, and developments, you can ask the following questions:

- **Did the event, person, or development create a long-lasting change?**
- **If so, how many people were affected, and were they affected profoundly or deeply?**
- **Was this the first time that an event such as this occurred or an idea such as this was introduced?**
- **Does this event, person, or development reveal something about the past that is different from the present?**
- **How did the significance of this event, person, or development vary for different people?**
- **Has the significance of this event, person, or development changed over time?**

CASE STUDY: JOHN GRAVES SIMCOE

The first Monday of August each year is a holiday for many Canadians. This holiday is known by different names across the country. In Ontario, it is known as Colonel By Day in Ottawa, Joseph Brant Day in Burlington, and Simcoe Day in Toronto. These differences can help us see how historical significance can vary from group to group. All three individuals whose names were used had a big impact on the people of Ontario, but their biggest impact was in the communities where they lived.

For example, John Graves Simcoe was Upper Canada's first lieutenant-governor. When he arrived in British North America in 1792, Simcoe had big plans for what he called his "dream province." He gave out land grants to attract settlers. He set up a government and made laws where there had been none. He built roads through the forest. He also moved the capital of Upper Canada to York (present-day Toronto) and built Fort York. The settlement and city of Toronto grew around the fort. Today, Fort York is a National Historic Site and holds a special celebration for Simcoe Day every year, as shown in **Figure I.11**. Simcoe had a long-lasting impact on all Ontarians, but especially on the millions of people who live in or near Toronto today. Do you know of anyone who is historically significant to your community?

FIGURE I.11 This photo shows Lieutenant-Governor of Ontario David Onley inspecting the guards at the annual Simcoe Day celebration at Fort York in 2013. **Analyze:** How does Simcoe meet the criteria for historical significance?

CAUSE AND CONSEQUENCE

Why do events happen, and what are their impacts? All events have causes that make them happen and consequences that result. To better understand a significant historical event, historians try to discover all the causes of the event, especially the causes that had the most influence. Historians also try to discover all of the consequences, including positive and negative, short-term and long-term, and intended and unintended (planned and unplanned) consequences.

When you think about the causes and consequences of a historical event, you can ask the following questions:

- **What were the causes of the event?**
- **Who were the people who influenced the event?**
- **What were the social, political, or economic conditions that influenced the event?**
- **What were the ideas and beliefs that influenced the event?**
- **What were the consequences of the event?**
- **What were the intended and unintended consequences of the event?**

CASE STUDY: GROSSE ÎLE

In 1832, officials in Lower Canada opened a quarantine facility (a building that isolates people who have been exposed to a contagious disease) where all immigrants to Lower Canada were screened for signs of illness. The facility was on Grosse Île, an island in the St. Lawrence River near Québec City, which was the main port of entry to Canada. Around 1830, about 30 000 immigrants arrived in Québec City every year.

Why was the quarantine facility opened? Cholera, a deadly disease, was sweeping through Canada. We now know that cholera is spread through contaminated water. At the time, however, no one knew what caused it or how to prevent it. Examine the flow chart in **Figure I.12**. Why do you think historians try to look at both the short- and long-term causes and consequences?

Long-term causes: Economic conditions in Scotland, Ireland, and England were poor in the early 1800s. Many people began immigrating to Canada. Most were Irish.

Short-term causes: A major cholera epidemic reached Britain in 1831. It killed tens of thousands of people. Many immigrants carried the disease to Canada.

The Event: In 1832, government officials opened a quarantine facility on Grosse Île to screen all immigrants.

Short-term consequences: All ships carrying immigrants began stopping at Grosse Île. Unhealthy immigrants were kept at Grosse Île for 3 to 15 days. Many did not survive.

Long-term consequences: Because screening methods were not effective, the facility did not slow the spread of the disease. By 1854, cholera had killed 20 000 people in Canada. Irish immigrants were blamed, and discrimination against them rose.

FIGURE I.12 This flow chart shows two causes and two consequences of the opening of the Grosse Île quarantine station. **Analyze:** What were the intended and unintended consequences of the quarantine facility?

CONTINUITY AND CHANGE

How can we make sense of the complex flows of history? To understand the past, historians look at how people's lives changed over time. They look at social, political, economic, cultural, and environmental changes. They look at the speed of these changes. Historians also identify the continuities: the things that stayed the same when everything else was changing.

When you think about continuity and change, you can ask the following questions:

- **What has changed?**
- **What has not changed?**
- **How quickly or slowly did the changes happen?**
- **Do the changes indicate progress for some groups or individuals and decline for others?**
- **What can we learn from comparing two different time periods?**

CASE STUDY: THE LIVES OF CANADIAN CHILDREN

The painting in **Figure I.13** shows a scene in Canada, painted in 1848. What do you notice by comparing what you see in the painting with what you know about the lives of Canadian children today? You might notice the things that have stayed the same: children still do chores and they still live in heated homes. You might also note what has changed: most children do different chores today and do not live in log cabins. What other details in the painting show what has changed or stayed the same over time?

FIGURE I.13 This 1848 painting, *Québec Settlers* by Cornelius Krieghoff, shows typical household activities on a winter's day in Canada. **Analyze:** How has the way we live changed since 1848? Why might it have changed?

HISTORICAL PERSPECTIVE

How can we better understand the people who lived in the past? Historians look for evidence that helps them discover how these people thought, felt, and went about their daily lives. They research people's lives, examine the evidence, and consider the values and beliefs that were common at the time. Then they make inferences—they reach conclusions based on the evidence they have gathered. Historians are always careful to avoid judging the past using their own present-day values.

When you think about historical perspective, you can ask the following questions:

- **What were the beliefs, values, perspectives, and motivations of the people who lived in that time?**
- **How do those beliefs and values differ from today's beliefs and values?**
- **Did the people make understandable decisions, based on the information they had available to them?**
- **What beliefs, values, and ideas do I already have that affect how I think about this event, period, or person?**
- **What inferences can I make about the person's thoughts, feelings, and motivations from the evidence I have?**

CASE STUDY: SLAVERY IN BRITISH NORTH AMERICA

If you were researching slavery in British North America in the 1700s, you would discover that the colonies enslaved fewer people than the United States. This fact might lead you to assume that British North Americans were more moral and ethical than people in the United States. You might assume that everyone in British North America had the same viewpoint we have today—that slavery is ethically wrong.

Read **Figure I.14**, an excerpt from a letter written by Élisabeth Bégon of New France. Bégon writes about Pierre and Jupitere, who are both enslaved in her household.

Then read **Figure I.15**, an excerpt from a dictation given by Hilaire, dit Lamour. Lamour had been granted his freedom after being enslaved for 25 years. His wife, Catharine, had not been granted her freedom at the same time. Use these sources to make inferences about how people felt about slavery in early Canada. Keep in mind that different people might have had different perspectives on the same issue. (Note: **Figure I.15** uses the term *Negro*, which was common at that time. Today, some people find it offensive so a preferred and more commonly used term is *Black person*.)

> "Our poor Pierre is once again in the hospital ... he is little more than skin and bones. Jupitere is in similar shape and your horse is so-so. That is what I have to say, dear son, of the 3 useless pieces of furniture that you left us and that we love, having belonged to you."
>
> — *Élisabeth Bégon*

FIGURE I.14 This excerpt is from a letter that Bégon wrote to her son in 1748. **Analyze:** What particular phrase reveals her attitude toward the "gifts" that her son left behind?

> "Be it known that I, Hilaire, dit Lamour, free Negro residing in the city of Montréal in the province of Québec, having ... purchased ... Catharine, my wife; and being desirous of proving the friendship and affection which I bear her, have granted unto her ... her freedom."
>
> — *Hilaire, dit Lamour*

FIGURE I.15 This excerpt was dictated by Lamour shortly after 1787. **Analyze:** What can you infer are Lamour's views on slavery?

UN

CONTINUITY AND CHANGE

How has life today changed compared to the time of the early settlers?

CAUSE AND CONSEQUENCE

What were the consequences of the conflicts of the 1700s on the people of North America?

HISTORICAL PERSPECTIVE

How did the British, the French, and First Nations view the development of British North America?

UNIT 1

NEW FRANCE AND BRITISH NORTH AMERICA: 1713–1800

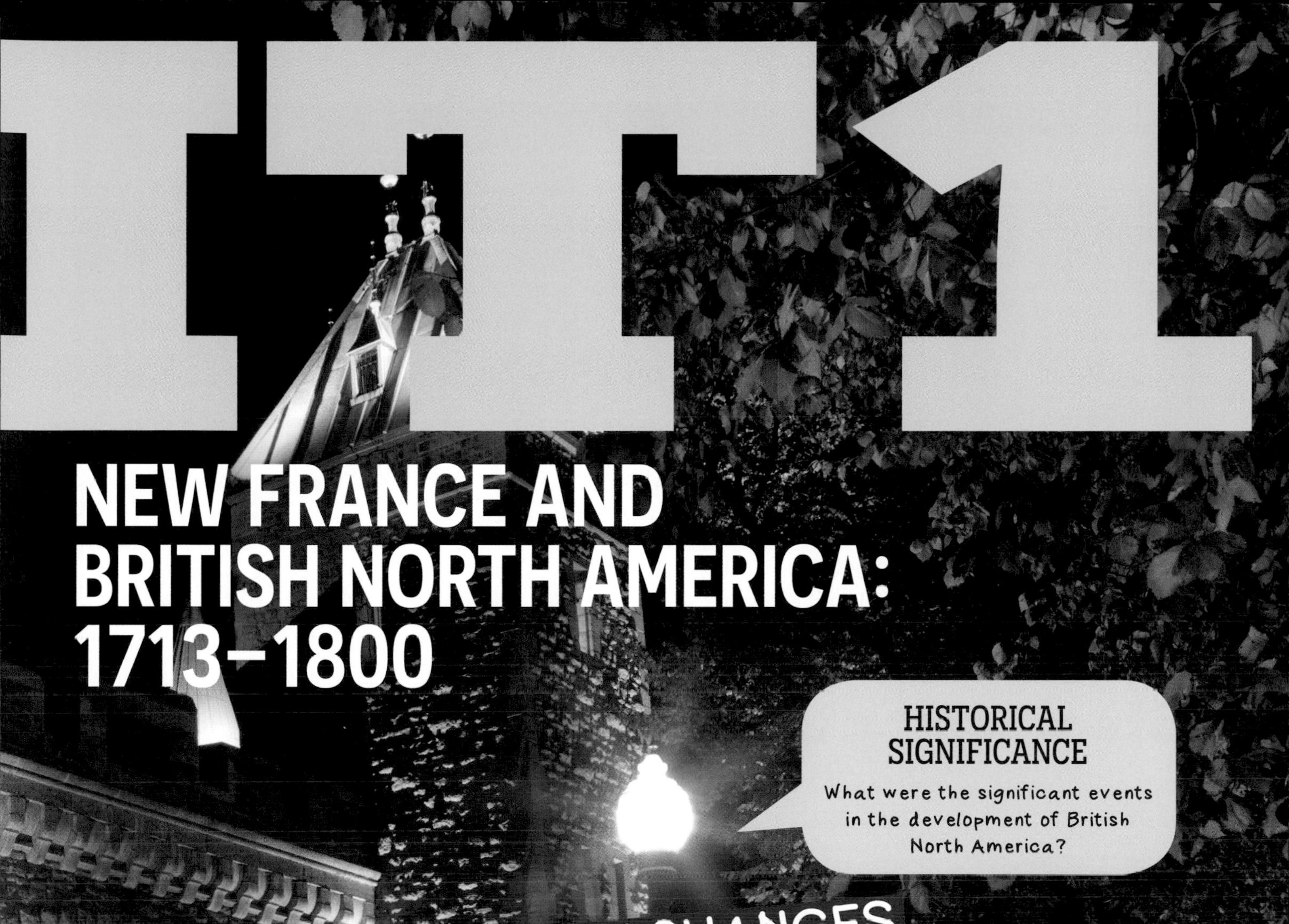

HISTORICAL SIGNIFICANCE

What were the significant events in the development of British North America?

HOW DID KEY CHANGES DURING THIS PERIOD LEAD TO BRITISH NORTH AMERICA?

At the beginning of the 1700s, the British and the French both controlled large areas of North America. As the colonies expanded and grew, conflicts between both groups and First Nations also grew. Valuable resources, such as furs, became a huge part of the expanding European presence.

In this photo, you can see the past and the present come together. During the 1700s, the walls of Québec City first defended the French and, after 1759, the British. Today Québec City is the only remaining walled city in North America. You can drive through the Porte Saint-Louis (St. Louis Gate), shown here, along the same path as in the 1700s.

In this unit, you will learn about the important changes during this period and how these changes affected the lives of different people and ultimately shaped the future of British North America.

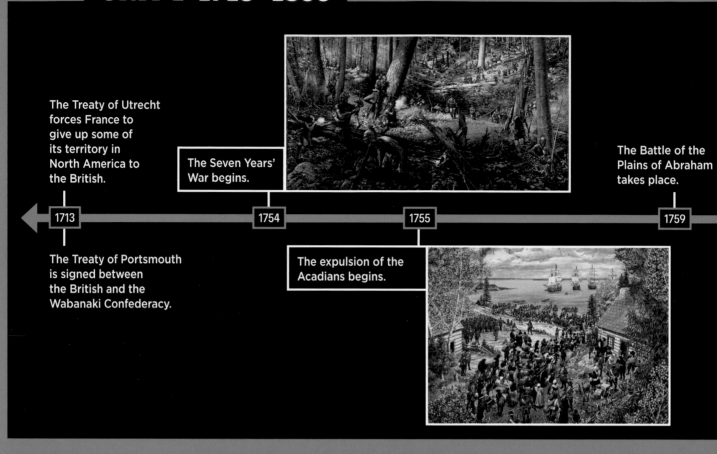

The Treaty of Utrecht forces France to give up some of its territory in North America to the British.

The Seven Years' War begins.

The Battle of the Plains of Abraham takes place.

| 1713 | 1754 | 1755 | 1759 |

The Treaty of Portsmouth is signed between the British and the Wabanaki Confederacy.

The expulsion of the Acadians begins.

ESTIMATED POPULATION OF BRITISH NORTH AMERICA IN **1750**

French 54 500
British 27 000
First Nations 200 000

DESIGN A HERITAGE FAIR PRESENTATION

In Unit 1, you will explore the changes that occurred in North America in the 1700s and led to a shift in power between the French, the British, and First Nations. You will examine the events that contributed to these changes, as well as the groups and individuals who played a central role.

As you work through Unit 1, you will learn how to identify important changes over time, determine the causes and consequences of those changes, and evaluate their impact on various groups of people. You will also learn how to use historical sources to interpret the past. At the end of the unit, you will respond to the Unit Big Question: *How did key changes during this period lead to British North America?* by designing a Heritage Fair presentation.

What to Consider

A Heritage Fair presentation tells a story about a significant aspect of our past. Your Heritage Fair presentation will focus on the events or people that contributed to the development of British North America.

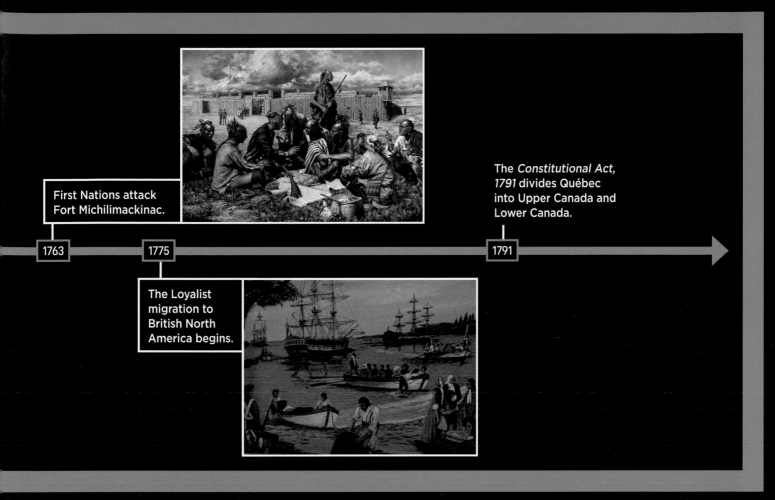

First Nations attack Fort Michilimackinac.

The *Constitutional Act, 1791* divides Québec into Upper Canada and Lower Canada.

1763

1775

1791

The Loyalist migration to British North America begins.

SOLDIERS IN THE SEVEN YEARS' WAR
(👤 = 5000 people)

BRITAIN 👤👤👤👤👤👤👤👤👤 42 000

FRANCE 👤👤 10 000

Number of beaver pelts sent to Europe in 1787
139 509

Your presentation should include the following features:

- **Purpose:** What is the focus of your presentation? What time period, events, or people will you consider?
- **Historical thinking:** Why are the events or people historically significant? What caused the events, and what were the consequences?
- **Research:** Which documents, images, and other sources will you use to gather information and evidence? How will you check the evidence you find?
- **Perspective:** Whose perspectives will you include? Why will you focus on these perspectives?

- **Conclusions:** What conclusions will you make about the impact of the events or people on the development of British North America? What evidence will you use to support your conclusions?

At the end of each chapter, you will identify the most significant events for the time period and assess the consequences of each event. You will also assess the contributions of key people or groups. You will record your findings in a log book. You will learn more about keeping a log book at the end of Chapter 1. At the end of Unit 1, you will choose a topic and create your presentation.

CANADIAN BEGINNINGS:
1713

HOW DID THE TREATY OF UTRECHT LEAD TO CHANGES IN NORTH AMERICA?

LEARNING GOALS

As you work through this chapter, you will

- identify the people who were living in North America in 1713 and why the land was important for different groups
- formulate questions about life in North America and examine the time period using continuity and change
- explain how the land was divided by the Treaty of Utrecht and how this division affected people's relationships and led to uncertainty in North America
- analyze maps to understand the changes in borders and the movement of people after 1713

Have you ever attended a Canada Day celebration? Why do we remember some events and consider them important, even if they happened a long time ago?

In 2013, the city of Utrecht in the Netherlands launched a year-long celebration of the anniversary of the Treaty of Utrecht, which was signed in 1713. There were concerts and parties, exhibits, plays, and fireworks. The Treaty of Utrecht ended the War of the Spanish Succession, which was a war between European countries. However, the treaty also affected North America. European powers redrew the map of North America and divided land between France and Britain.

The Treaty of Utrecht, by Turkish artist Semiramis Öner Mühüdaroğlu, was painted to celebrate the 300th anniversary of the signing of the treaty. The artist included the 24 diplomats who signed the treaty; four women to represent the city of Utrecht, peace, justice, and art; and one child holding the world as a symbol of the future. What does that tell you about who was included in the creation of the treaty and who was not included?

WHO WANTED
THE LAND, AND WHY?

Imagine that you are a young person living in North America in 1713. You might be living in a small but growing French colony in the St. Lawrence Valley, a British colony in what is now the United States, or an **Indigenous**, native, village along the fur trade route.

The land known as Canada today has gone through many changes over hundreds of years. Early French maps—as far back as the early 1500s—showed the land as both New France and Canada. The name Canada comes from the Iroquois word *Kanata*, which means "village" or "settlement." Early English maps did not give this land a single name. Those maps referred to the land by the different names of the different regions existing at that time. Historical maps would have looked very different, almost unrecognizable compared to those of Canada today, because Europeans had just begun to discover the vast land.

Indigenous native to the area; to do with the original inhabitants of Canada (First Nations, Métis, and Inuit)

disputed territory area of land that different groups claim belongs to them

Look at **Figure 1.1**, which is a map of part of North America, showing how it was divided before the Treaty of Utrecht in 1713. Some land was considered disputed territory. **Disputed territory** is land over which different groups are arguing and claiming ownership. Where does the map show disputed territories?

Who was claiming ownership of North America at that time?

North America before the Treaty of Utrecht, 1713

Hudson Bay

Rupert's Land

Newfoundland

NEW FRANCE

ACADIA

Louisiana

BRITISH COLONIES

ATLANTIC OCEAN

N

0   390 km

NEW SPAIN

NEW SPAIN

Gulf of Mexico

- British territory
- French territory
- Spanish territory
- disputed territory
- land undiscovered by Europeans

FIGURE 1.1 This map shows European territories in North America in 1713, before the Treaty of Utrecht. **Analyze:** How is this map similar and different to a map of North America today?

EUROPEAN INTEREST IN NORTH AMERICA BEFORE 1713

By 1713, Europeans had been coming to North America for over 200 years. They were competing with each other to claim the land, send goods back to Europe, and build settlements. Early explorers, such as Genoese explorer Giovanni Caboto (also known as John Cabot) arrived in 1497. The King of England had sent Caboto to explore and claim lands for England. French explorer Jacques Cartier arrived in North America in 1534. He claimed land for France.

Read the quote in **Figure 1.2**. It is an excerpt from a letter by Raimondo di Soncino, ambassador in England for the Duke of Milan. He recorded his experiences in several letters while sailing on the ship with Caboto. Now look at the drawing in **Figure 1.3**. Based on these two pieces of evidence, what value did European explorers see in the lands and waters of North America?

FIGURE 1.2 This excerpt is from a December 18, 1497, letter by Raimondo di Soncino reporting on Caboto's findings. **Analyze:** Why did the ambassador devote part of his letter to describing the huge numbers of fish in the ocean off the coast of North America?

> "... the sea is covered with fish ... will fetch so many fish that this kingdom will have no more need of [the fish around] Iceland."
>
> — *Raimondo di Soncino, ambassador to the Duke of Milan*

FIGURE 1.3 Nicolas de Fer drew this image in 1698. He was the official geographer for the kings of France and Spain. This image was copied and used on European maps of North America decades later. **Analyze:** What is the artist's main message in this image?

THE IMPORTANCE OF NATURAL RESOURCES

When arriving in North America, the Europeans saw the large amounts of resources such as fish, fur, and timber. Back in Europe, the demands of a large population left most fur-bearing animals and fish from local lakes close to extinction. The new land in North America offered jobs and wealth and a way to supply growing demands back home.

Fish, an important part of the European diet, was simple to cook and easy to preserve and transport. It took several weeks to preserve the fish with salt before it could be sent back to Europe for sale. During this time, the Europeans developed relationships with the First Nations peoples. First Nations taught Europeans how to build canoes and sleds and how to navigate the terrain. They began trading fresh food and fur to Europeans in exchange for metal pots, tools, and cloth. First Nations women provided Europeans with warm clothing such as mittens and leggings, and they helped to prepare fur for transport.

THE FUR TRADE

Fur was a necessity to survive in the winter climate, but it also became a popular European fashion in the 1500s. Over time, Europeans' desire for fur, especially beaver pelts, grew. Fur was used to make hats and other items for wealthy people. First Nations peoples did not fully understand why Europeans would choose to trade what they considered valuable everyday items in exchange for fur. But the trade was beneficial for both groups, so it continued. What does **Figure 1.4** tell you about the importance of fur to Europeans?

FIRST NATIONS TERRITORIES

Thousands of years before Europeans came to North America and claimed the land and resources, people were living in the land we now call Canada. First Nations lived throughout North America and had developed a variety of cultures. Each group had its own distinct language, ways of living on the land, ways of governing and organizing themselves, and beliefs and values. Peter Jones (also known as Kahkewaquonaby), a Mississauga Ojibwe chief, explains this idea in **Figure 1.5**. The quote uses the term *Indians*, which was common at that time. Today, a more preferred term is *First Nations*, or *Aboriginal peoples* when including Inuit and Métis.

FIGURE 1.4 This drawing by Wenceslaus Hollar shows an unnamed woman wearing a fur muff and cape in 1646. **Analyze:** What is the connection between a wealthy European woman dressed in fur and settlement in North America?

> "Each tribe or body of Indians has its own range of country, and sometimes each family its own hunting grounds, marked out by certain natural divisions ... all the game within these bounds are considered their property ... It is at the peril of an intruder to trespass on the hunting grounds of another."
>
> — *Mississauga Ojibwe Chief Peter Jones*

FIGURE 1.5 This excerpt is from an 1861 book called *History of Ojibway Indians* by Chief Jones. **Analyze:** What do Jones's words suggest about the importance of land for First Nations before Europeans arrived?

The map in **Figure 1.6** shows the territories of the First Nations of northeastern North America from 1650 to 1760. Settlements were strategically built close to a water source to access drinking water and transportation.

The Haudenosaunee (hoh-den-oh-shoh-nee) Six Nations are made up of several groups who speak the Iroquois language. The French called them the Iroquois Confederacy. The Huron (Wyandot) Nation shared land with the Haudenosaunee. These groups sustained themselves by farming crops of corn, squash, and beans. These crops made it possible for them to live in relatively large groups of over a thousand people in the same village. However, farmland could only support agriculture for about 20 years. After this, entire villages had to relocate to look for new farmland.

Many different nations make up the Algonquian (al-gong-kee-uh-n) peoples. These nations lived in areas surrounding the Haudenosaunee. The Algonquians needed even larger territories than the Haudenosaunee because they hunted and fished for their food. Since wildlife and fish require large areas of land and water to survive, the people who depended on them also needed large areas to roam. In order to sustain their food sources, they lived in small groups of about 50 people.

> How did the way people lived influence how much land they needed?

First Nations of Northeastern North America, 1650–1760

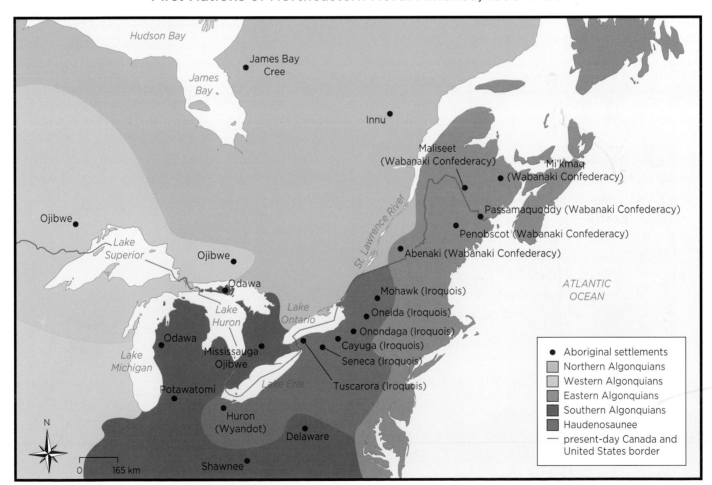

FIGURE 1.6 This map shows the different territories where various First Nations peoples settled. The dots on the map do not represent permanent settlements. Most First Nations peoples built homes that could be taken apart and rebuilt in a different location. **Analyze:** How do you think First Nations peoples' mobility affected these borders?

FORMULATE QUESTIONS

Asking questions about the past is one of the most important parts of studying history. A good inquiry question can help guide the exploration of a historical topic.

Good inquiry questions
- are important and meaningful to us
- are open-ended—they do not have just one answer
- are debatable—people may not agree on the answer
- can be answered by gathering evidence and facts

Brainstorming can help formulate a good question to lead an inquiry. Think about what you already know about your subject. Now decide what you might need to know and what you want to find out. A table like the one in **Figure 1.7** can help get your brainstorming activity started.

Who/Which?	Who owned the land in North America in the 1700s?
What?	What difficulties could Europeans encounter in North America?
Where?	Where might Europeans live in North America while gathering resources?
When?	When did First Nations begin trading with Europeans?
Why?	Why would Europeans find North American resources so valuable?
How?	How could the weather and land affect travel?
Other	Did First Nations peoples fight among themselves?

FIGURE 1.7 This table can help you brainstorm a variety of questions to focus your inquiry. **Analyze:** Which of these questions spark further questions for you?

CASE STUDY: FIRST NATIONS TRADING RELATIONSHIPS

First Nations peoples built shelters, gathered food, and made clothing from the resources available in their surroundings. Plants, trees, and animals could be used in many different ways including as medicine or for spiritual ceremonies. For certain items, such as rare stones (**Figure 1.8**), horses, buffalo hides, and bitter root, they traded with other First Nations. Some of the objects were essential for everyday life. Others were used for decoration, like making jewellery.

Trade between First Nations peoples was a respected activity that brought peace between nations. A ceremony would be held where trading nations would smoke a pipe to accept the responsibilities of the trade and to show goodwill. Gifts were also exchanged as a sign of friendship. Nations that did not speak the same language used a form of sign language to communicate.

Trading benefited First Nations peoples in many areas. Trade brought people the goods they needed and helped different nations engage with one another.

FIGURE 1.8 Volcanic glass called *obsidian* was traded between First Nations peoples. Obsidian could be broken easily to produce sharp edges. **Analyze:** What items do you think could be made with obsidian?

FIGURE 1.9 This early 1900s painting by Archibald Bruce Stapleton is entitled *Radisson & Grosseilliers Established the Fur Trade in the Great North West, 1662*. Radisson and Des Groseilliers are shown in the centre negotiating with First Nations people. **Analyze:** How do you think the goods being traded with Europeans changed life for First Nations peoples?

When Europeans arrived in North America, trade quickly developed with First Nations peoples. Examine **Figure 1.9**. The painting shows explorers Pierre-Esprit Radisson and Médard Chouart Des Groseilliers trading with First Nations people. How do you think Europeans trading with First Nations peoples would be different than First Nations trading among themselves? Radisson and Des Groseilliers were the first Europeans to extensively explore the interior of Canada. They eventually set up a trading post on Lake Superior, negotiating with the Cree to trade furs. Europeans depended on trade with First Nations peoples to help them survive in North America.

TRY IT

1. Work with a partner to develop an inquiry question on the topic of First Nations trading relationships. Write a question for each row in **Figure 1.7**.
2. Choose a topic relevant to life in North America in the 1700s. Write three possible inquiry questions using the criteria of a good inquiry question. Share your questions with one or two classmates. Ask them to offer suggestions for improvement. Revise your questions if necessary.

FRENCH AND ENGLISH SETTLEMENTS

In the early 1600s, France and England tried to make their claims on North America stronger. They did this by establishing permanent settlements. These settlements were built on land where First Nations peoples lived. Why did the French and English believe that they had the right to build on First Nations' land?

Read the quote in **Figure 1.10**. It is from a sermon about First Nations peoples, written by a preacher in 1609. A sermon is a speech on a religious or moral subject. Sometimes sermons were printed and published so that a wider audience could read them. The word *savage* is a racist term that both the English and the French used for Aboriginal peoples. Read the quote in **Figure 1.11** from historian Dr. Emma LaRocque, a Plains-Cree Métis. Why do you think Europeans used the word *savage* so freely?

"... it is likely to be true that these savages have no particular property in any part or parcel of that country, but only a general residency there, as wild beasts in the forest."

— *Preacher*

FIGURE 1.10 This quote comes from a preacher's sermon in 1609. The sermon was published at the time when Europeans began to make settlements in North America. **Analyze:** What does the language in this quote suggest about European attitudes toward First Nations peoples at that time?

"Europeans [called] themselves ... 'civilized' and Indigenous peoples ... 'savages,' the underlying assumption being that as savages, 'Indians' were at the bottom of human development."

— *Dr. Emma LaRocque, historian and First Nations expert*

FIGURE 1.11 Dr. LaRocque explains the use of the word *savage* in historical documents. **Analyze:** What reasons could there be for the Europeans to think of themselves as civilized?

The first English settlement was in Newfoundland. The English focused their settlements along the east coast of North America, south of the French, who lived mostly along the St. Lawrence River. As well, the English built three trading posts around James Bay. These trading posts put the English closer to some First Nations, making it easier to trade with them for furs.

The French relied on First Nations traders to bring them furs along the St. Lawrence River, which had the largest French settlements. First Nations came from the north to Montréal and other French trading posts to exchange furs for European goods. The river was the best way to move goods in New France.

In the early 1600s, France put in place the **seigneurial system** for its North American settlements. The seigneurial system was the way that land was divided among settlers in New France. A landlord, called a *seigneur*, rented out farmland to farmers for a small fee. Most of the farms in New France were located along the St. Lawrence River. **Figure 1.12A** shows the shape of the farms in New France in the 1600s and 1700s. **Figure 1.12B** shows farmland in the province of Québec today, from above. What similarities do you see?

seigneurial system the system used by the government to divide land among settlers in New France

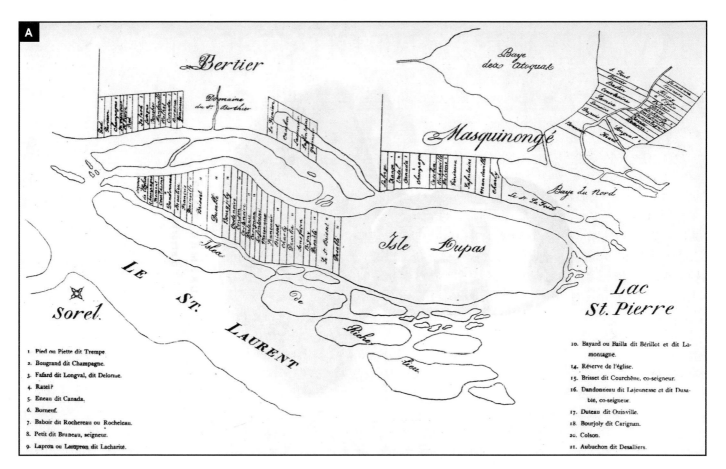

FIGURE 1.12 (A) This 1709 diagram by Gédéon Catalogne shows farms along the St. Lawrence River in New France. (B) This photo shows farms today along the St. Lawrence River in the province of Québec. **Analyze:** Why would people design settlements this way?

CHECK-IN

1. **GATHER AND ORGANIZE** What was the significance for both Europeans and First Nations of the arrival of Europeans in North America and their use of resources? Create a t-chart to explain what European arrival in North America and Europeans' use of resources reveals about Europeans' and First Nations' values.

2. **CONTINUITY AND CHANGE** How did land use change with the arrival of Europeans in North America? How did land use stay the same?

3. **HISTORICAL PERSPECTIVE** Why did Europeans want to own different parts of North America? How did Europeans try to claim ownership of the land? Would this method work today?

HOW DID THE LAND CHANGE
AFTER THE TREATY OF UTRECHT?

Borders within countries and between countries are not always permanent. Even though it may seem unlikely, there is a possibility that the borders within or around Canada may change again one day. The 1700s were a time when the borders in North America were constantly changing.

In 1700, the King of Spain, Charles II, died without an heir to take over his throne. France took this opportunity to try to seize Spain and its territories. This started the War of the Spanish Succession in Europe. The **United Kingdom of Great Britain**, also known as Britain, formed in 1707 when England and Scotland united. It was ruled by Queen Anne, and joined many European countries in fighting against France. Peace talks followed the war and led to the Treaty of Utrecht in 1713. A **treaty** is a formal agreement between countries, often signed to end a war. A treaty may also define borders and identify the ownership of different pieces of land. France was forced to give up some of its territory as part of the terms of the treaty. Read excerpts from the Treaty of Utrecht in **Figure 1.13**. What parts of North America changed hands, according to these excerpts?

French and British colonies in North America had little to do with the war in Europe. However, the treaty had consequences for North America.

United Kingdom of Great Britain the kingdom of Great Britain, or Britain, was formed when England and Scotland united in 1707

treaty an agreement signed between different countries, in which promises are made

FIGURE 1.13 These images and excerpts are from the Treaty of Utrecht. **Analyze:** Based on the excerpts of the treaty, did more lands in North America now belong to France or Britain?

X: The said most Christian King [the French King] shall restore to the kingdom and Queen of Great Britain, to be possessed in full right for ever, the bay and straits of Hudson [Hudson Bay], together with all lands, seas, sea-coasts, rivers, and places situate in the said bay and straits, ...

XII: The most Christian King [the French King] shall take care to have delivered to the Queen of Great Britain, ... the island of St. Christopher's ... to be possessed alone hereafter by British subjects, likewise all Nova Scotia or Acadie [Acadia], with its ancient boundaries, as also the city of Port Royal, now called Annapolis Royal, and all other things in those parts, ...

XIII: The island called Newfoundland, with the adjacent islands, shall from this time forward belong of right wholly to Britain ...

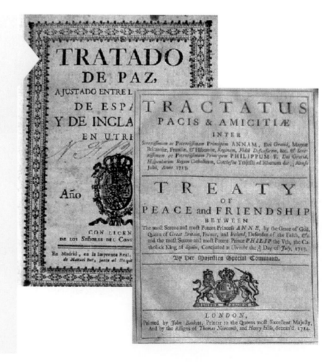

FRENCH AND BRITISH TERRITORIES AFTER 1713

Today, New Brunswick is the only Canadian province that is officially bilingual. This means that both English-speaking and French-speaking citizens have equal status, rights, and privileges. The area that is now New Brunswick was once a French colony. It was known as Acadia, which included parts of present-day Nova Scotia and Prince Edward Island. The Treaty of Utrecht handed this area over to the British, eventually leading to English settlement in the region.

After British Queen Anne, French King Louis XIV, and the other European leaders agreed to the Treaty of Utrecht, the terms of the treaty had to be carried out. The first step was to create new maps of North America showing the new boundaries. Look back at **Figure 1.1** on page 22. This map shows the North American territories claimed by France, Britain, and Spain before 1713. **Figure 1.14** shows the territories after 1713—after the Treaty of Utrecht had been signed. The French had agreed to give the British large amounts of land, including Newfoundland and parts of Acadia. What did the loss of this land mean to France?

Despite the treaty, some land was still considered disputed territory. Where do you see disputed territories after the treaty was signed?

> How does the bilingual nature of New Brunswick show Canada's connection to its past?

North America after the Treaty of Utrecht, 1713

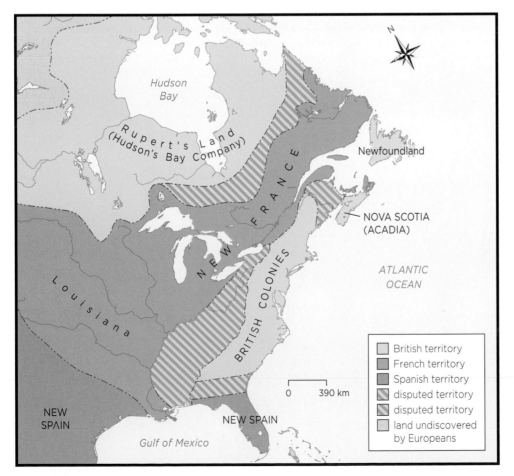

FIGURE 1.14 This map shows the North American territories claimed by European countries after the 1713 Treaty of Utrecht. **Analyze:** How much land did France lose to Britain because of the treaty?

CONTINUITY AND CHANGE

One of the ways historians learn about the past is by examining how the lives of people changed, or did not change, over a period of time. Think about the past five years. What changes have you gone through? What aspects of your life have stayed the same or almost the same?

Sometimes changes are rapid, with a lot of events occurring over a very short period of time, such as the many interactions during a war. Other times, changes take place almost too slowly to see them happening, such as when glaciers melt naturally over 100 years. And sometimes, things remain unchanged, even as everything else alters around them, such as a national historic site set aside by our federal government.

When you think about continuity and change, you can ask the following questions:
- What has changed?
- What has not changed?
- How quickly or slowly did the changes happen?
- Do the changes indicate progress for some groups or individuals and decline for others?
- What can we learn from comparing two different time periods?

CASE STUDY: ACADIA

As you read through the history of Acadia, consider what changed immediately, what changed gradually, and what did not change at all for Acadians.

Before the Treaty of Utrecht was signed, Acadia was part of New France. After the treaty was signed, the same territory belonged to Britain, and the Acadians became British citizens. The French government encouraged the Acadians to move to the French colony of Île Royale (present-day Cape Breton), and the British offered to transport them.

Read the quote in **Figure 1.15**. Father Felix Pain explains to the French governor of Île Royale the Acadians' position on relocating. How does Father Pain justify the Acadians' choice to stay?

"[To move] would be to expose us manifestly to die of hunger burthened as we are with large families, to quit the dwelling places and clearances from which we derive our usual subsistence, without any other resource, to take rough, new lands, from which the standing wood must be removed. One fourth of our population consists of aged persons, unfit for the labour of breaking up new lands, and who, with great exertion, are able to cultivate the cleared ground which supplies subsistence for them and their families."

— *Father Felix Pain*

FIGURE 1.15 Father Pain summarizes for the French governor of Île Royale the Acadians' reasons for refusing to be removed from their farms. **Analyze:** According to this quote, what continuity do the Acadians desire?

Consider the Acadians' claim in **Figure 1.15** that a quarter of the population was made up of "aged persons." Acadian families had an average of six or seven children, and few died in childhood, so 75 percent reached adulthood. The population grew from 2500 in 1711 to 14 000 in 1755. How do you think the British felt about a growing population of French-speaking colonists within their new borders?

Over the decades, Acadians continued to speak French and attend Catholic church. They became prosperous through trade. They began to supply agricultural goods to the British and to French military forts. The British did not like the Acadians supplying their enemy. How do you think this growing issue changed the lives of the Acadians?

FIGURE 1.16 Lewis Parker painted *Acadians Building Dykes and Aboiteaux at Grand Pré* in 1989. **Analyze:** What skills and knowledge would the Acadians have to pass on to maintain their way of life?

Acadians had great ties to their land. They drained the salt marshes using a system of dikes (walls built to control water and prevent it from covering an area of land). The annual task of making and maintaining the dikes is illustrated in **Figure 1.16**. How would this routine affect the Acadian community? The salt marshes were very fertile, allowing the Acadians to grow a rich variety of crops. Fruit grew in orchards on the higher lands surrounding their farms. Most families also kept farm animals, such as cows, goats, and chickens.

TRY IT

1. Create a t-chart to compare examples of continuity and change in Acadia.
2. Use one example of continuity and one of change to explain how the two co-existed in Acadia. Would you consider your examples to have positive or negative consequences for the Acadians?

FRENCH AND BRITISH DISPUTED TERRITORIES

Before the Treaty of Utrecht was signed, the French and British disagreed over who owned what land. Did the treaty settle these land disputes, or did the French and the British still disagree over who owned what land? Look again at the maps in **Figures 1.1** and **1.14**. Both of these maps—before and after the treaty was signed—show disputed territory. Both the French and the British claimed ownership of land that was disputed. Why would the French and the British argue over the ownership of land after they had signed a peace treaty? Consider the words in the treaty that you read in **Figure 1.13** and the term *ancient boundaries*, used in section XII. Read what historian John G. Reid says about this phrase in **Figure 1.17**. According to Reid, the phrase *ancient boundaries* meant nothing. No one—neither the French nor the British—knew what the ancient boundaries were, so some land remained in dispute after the treaty was signed.

FIGURE 1.17 In 1994, John G. Reid comments on the phrase *ancient boundaries* in the Treaty of Utrecht. **Analyze:** What might be some of the problems with using a phrase like *ancient boundaries*?

"... its ancient boundaries is a conveniently high sounding phrase that meant nothing, as there was no clearly understood notion of where boundaries lay."

— John G. Reid, historian

EUROPEAN EXPLORATION

Another reason why some land remained in dispute after the treaty was that the French and the British did not know exactly what land they were claiming. It took a lot of work for Europeans to explore and map out North America. By 1713, only some of this work was done. The French had only recently sent explorers to search the territory beyond the Great Lakes, in the middle of the continent. Louis Jolliet was a North American-born explorer chosen by the administrative official of New France, Jean Talon, to explore the continent. **Figure 1.18** is a representation of one of these voyages. In 1673, Louis Jolliet and Father Jacques Marquette were the first non-Aboriginal people to travel to the upper reaches of Louisiana and create a map of that part of the continent. There were vast amounts of land that no European had ever seen. As explorers discovered more of North America after 1713, this created more disputes over territory.

FIGURE 1.18 This illustration was created in the 1800s by A. Russell. It depicts a scene in the 1600s. In the first canoe, we see Louis Jolliet (sitting) with Father Jacques Marquette (standing) and their First Nations guides. **Analyze:** What does the illustration suggest to you about the relationship between European explorers and First Nations in the 1600s?

EUROPEAN AND FIRST NATIONS RELATIONS

Europeans negotiated and signed the Treaty of Utrecht. They did not consult First Nations about their claims to the land or about the terms of the treaty. However, part of the treaty, such as section XV, referred to First Nations. Read that section of the treaty in **Figure 1.19**. What was the relationship between First Nations and Europeans supposed to be like, according to this section of the treaty?

FIGURE 1.19 These words from the Treaty of Utrecht speak of creating peace among all the nations living in North America. **Analyze:** Why was it important for the French and the British to have peace with each other and with First Nations?

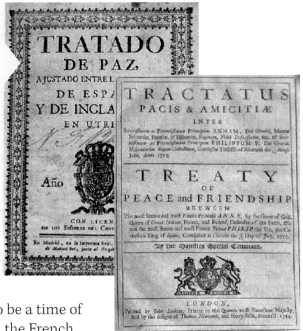

XV: The subjects of France inhabiting Canada, and others, shall hereafter give no hinderance or molestation to the ... Indians [First Nations], subject to the Dominion of Great Britain, nor to the other natives of America, who are friends to the same. In like manner, the subjects of Great Britain shall behave themselves peaceably towards the Americans who are subjects or friends to France [including First Nations]; and on both sides, they shall enjoy full liberty of going and coming on account of trade ...

TRADING RELATIONSHIPS

The treaty had been signed, and it was considered by some to be a time of peace among the French, British, and First Nations. However, the French and the British were back in competition for the fur trade. How did this competition affect First Nations?

The British wanted to strengthen trading relationships with some First Nations peoples after the Treaty of Utrecht. Many First Nations peoples believed that trading with the British would benefit their people. This belief led to the expansion of trading relationships between First Nations and the British.

In **Figure 1.20**, historian Peter Schmalz writes about how the fur trade affected the Ojibwe First Nation during the first half of the 1700s. Schmalz is one of the first historians to write a history of First Nations using **oral history**. Oral history is one method used by First Nations Elders to pass history and knowledge of their people through the generations. How did the French and the British treat the Ojibwe people, according to Schmalz?

oral history a method of obtaining information about the past by gathering and interpreting voices and memories from people, communities, and past participants in events

"With the advantages of competitively priced European goods, gifts from their allies ... the Ojibwe were in an enviable position ... As long as the French were pitted against the English [in the fur trade], the Ojibwe were treated with respect and sought as friends in trade ..."

— *Peter Schmalz, historian*

FIGURE 1.20 In 1991, Peter Schmalz describes the benefits that the Ojibwe experienced after 1713. **Analyze:** What caused the French and the British to treat the Ojibwe well after 1713?

ANALYZING
FLOW MAPS

Maps are graphic or visual representations of what is happening on Earth. They can be used to show the borders of countries or the locations of cities or towns. They can also be used to show the movement of people or the change in settlement patterns. Maps use colour, symbols, and labels to tell a story.

Maps can be primary or secondary sources. A map that was created during and about a period of time is a primary source for that period. A map that was created recently, based on information collected from primary sources of the 1700s, is a secondary source. Maps do not need to be old, however, to be primary sources. For example, a current map of Canada is a primary source map for what Canada looks like today.

One type of map is a flow map, which shows the movement of people or goods using arrows. Each arrow begins at the source of the movement and ends at the destination. By reading a flow map, you can determine the distance and directions of movement and assess any patterns in the movement.

Figure 1.21 shows the movement of the Ojibwe, Odawa, and Haudenosaunee nations around 1713. In what directions were these nations moving?

FIGURE 1.21 This map shows the movement of three First Nations around 1713. These nations had lived on their territories for thousands of years.

Movement of Ojibwe, Odawa, and Haudenosaunee Nations around 1713

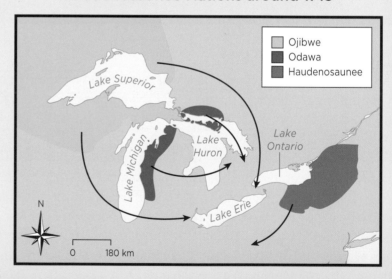

HOW TO READ A FLOW MAP

Examine **Figure 1.21**. Identify the title of the map. What is the location being shown on the map?

STEP 1

STEP 2 Read the legend. Identify the colours on the map.

Investigate if the map is a primary or secondary source. Justify your choice.

STEP 3

STEP 4 Look for patterns you can see on the map. What factors might explain these patterns?

CLAIMING FIRST NATIONS LAND

As Europeans settled the east coast of North America during the 1600s and 1700s, they forced many First Nations people from their homes. Europeans, including the British, also killed First Nations people or sold them into slavery. **Figure 1.22** is an image of a First Nations person who was sold into slavery. What beliefs, held by many Europeans at that time, might have caused them to enslave First Nations peoples?

Now that the treaty had given the British control of the East Coast, the British wanted First Nations land that was in this area. Nation by nation, the First Nations of the East Coast were either chased away or killed by British settlers who were seeking land. Like other east coast Algonquians, the Abenaki (ah-buh-nah-kee) were forced to flee their territory. The Abenaki Nation was part of the Wabanaki (wah-buh-nah-kee) Confederacy. The Wabanaki Confederacy was made up of five distinct groups of First Nations peoples who lived in Acadia, including the Mi'kmaq (meeg-mah or mick-mac) and Maliseet (MAL-uh-seet). Some Abenaki relocated to New France. They joined their French and First Nations allies in both regions. The Abenaki wanted to fight the British. Read the quote in **Figure 1.23** from French missionary (person engaged in a religious mission) Father Loyard. Father Loyard's words suggest that he thought the Abenaki could help the French defend New France from future attacks by the British.

FIGURE 1.22 This 1732 painting by an unknown artist is entitled *Slave of Fox Indians*. This young First Nations man was sold as a slave in North America. **Analyze:** How did the artist depict the First Nations slave?

> "... of all the savages of New France ... the greatest services are the Abenaki. This nation is composed of five villages, which in all make five hundred men bearing arms ... It is this which renders their situation so important as regards Canada, of which they are the strongest defences ..."
>
> — *Father Loyard*

FIGURE 1.23 In this quote from 1722, Father Loyard is commenting on the Abenaki. **Analyze:** What did he think the Abenaki could do for New France, which he refers to as *Canada*?

The French urged the Abenaki to move from British territories and settle in New France. The Mi'kmaq and the Maliseet were the largest group on the East Coast in terms of population in 1713. They remained in that area and continued to fight against British control. Governor General Vaudreuil of New France gave out huge payments to the nations of the Wabanaki Confederacy. He wanted to ensure their loyalty to New France. Why would the French want the loyalty of the Wabanaki Confederacy?

CHECK-**IN**

1. **CONTINUITY AND CHANGE** What changed after the Treaty of Utrecht for the French, the British, and First Nations? What stayed the same?

2. **CAUSE AND CONSEQUENCE** Look back at **Figure 1.19**. According to the treaty, how were the British supposed to treat First Nations? How did the British treat the Abenaki people?

HOW DID THE TREATY OF UTRECHT AFFECT RELATIONS IN NORTH AMERICA?

Have you ever strongly disagreed with a person and then decided to come to an agreement despite your differences? If you still had to be around that person every day, would it be easy or uncomfortable?

The Treaty of Utrecht was also called the Treaty of Peace and Friendship. By signing this treaty, France and Britain agreed to stop fighting one another. As you learned earlier in the chapter, valuable land changed hands from French to British. There were also disputed territories without clear ownership. How would these factors affect the relationships among the different groups living there? Was this really a period of peace or was it a state of uncertainty?

By 1713, there had been many years of conflict among the French, the British, and First Nations peoples living in North America. Although the French and the British had established peace, First Nations had been left out of that process. Read the excerpt from a letter written by a Jesuit missionary in **Figure 1.24**. Jesuit missionaries were members of the Society of Jesus, a Roman Catholic religious order. They lived among First Nations to learn their cultures and languages. The Jesuits also taught First Nations peoples about Jesus and attempted to convert them to Christianity. In the letter, the missionary speaks about the Abenaki reaction after the British began settling in former French territories. What were the concerns of the Abenaki people?

> What was the significance of the Treaty of Utrecht for First Nations?

> "They [the Abenaki] asked the English by what right they had thus settled in their territory.... The answer that was given them— that the King of France had ceded [given] their country to the King of England—threw them into the greatest alarm; for there is not one savage Tribe will patiently endure to be regarded as under subjection to any Power whatsoever."
>
> — *Jesuit missionary*

FIGURE 1.24 This reaction of the Abenaki to British settlement was recorded by a Jesuit missionary in 1722. **Analyze:** What does the missionary mean by "under subjection"?

After ending the war with the French, the British wanted to continue to explore and expand their territory. To help gain more land and create stability, the British needed to repair relationships with First Nations in Acadia, particularly the Wabanaki Confederacy. The French and the Wabanaki Confederacy had an **alliance**, cooperated together, to fight against the British.

alliance a type of agreement between people or groups to achieve a common goal

CREATING THE TREATY OF PORTSMOUTH

The British wanted to end the alliance between the Wabanaki Confederacy and the French and take control of the land. In July 1713, the British and the Wabanaki Confederacy came together in Portsmouth on the eastern coast of North America to reach an agreement.

The British agreed to not build on Wabanaki land any further, to conduct trade at a neutral location, and to exchange gifts as part of Wabanaki tradition. In return, the Wabanaki Confederacy agreed to stop attacks on the British, give back settlements and lands taken from the British, and allow any future disputes to be decided on by the British government.

The treaty was written in English and was read aloud to nation members of the Wabanaki Confederacy by interpreters. What misunderstandings do you think could happen with the treaty being written only in English? The document in **Figure 1.25** is a page with signatures from the Treaty of Portsmouth. How do you think this treaty would establish peace between the British settlers and the Wabanaki Confederacy?

Just like the anniversary of the Treaty of Utrecht, the 300th anniversary of the Treaty of Portsmouth was celebrated with several exhibits. Copies of the original treaty were put on display. Read the quote in **Figure 1.26** by Charles B. Doleac about the 300th anniversary of the Treaty of Portsmouth. What headlines do you think he is referring to?

> "The issues discussed in Portsmouth in 1713 have a direct connection with ideas concerning the Rights of Indigenous People that are in the headlines today."
>
> — Charles B. Doleac, chairman of the 300th anniversary of the Treaty of Portsmouth

FIGURE 1.26 This quote is from the 2013 chairman of the 300th anniversary of the Treaty of Portsmouth. **Analyze:** What do you think he means by "direct connection"?

FIGURE 1.25 The last page of the Treaty of Portsmouth, 1713, shows the signatures of all the people who were present. **Analyze:** What do you notice about the signatures?

DAVID KAWAPIT: YOUTH ON A MISSION

David Kawapit is an 18-year-old Cree youth with a mission. His mission is to spread the message of unity and equality to all Canadians. In January 2013, he set out on a walk from his home in Whapmagoostui (Waup-mag-stoo-ee or Waup-ma-GOO-stoo-ee), Québec, to Parliament Hill in Ottawa. Six others joined him, forming a group called the Nishiyuu (Nish-you) walkers. Over the course of two months, they walked more than 1500 km along traditional Cree and Algonquin trading routes. They were accompanied by a police escort and other support vehicles to assist them on their journey. Strangers also stopped during the trek to show their support.

Kawapit was inspired to take action by a vision he once had. His vision showed a wolf and a bear. The wolf represented the First Nations peoples and the bear represented the Canadian government. While a bear can easily kill a wolf, many wolves, banded together, can take down a bear. This image of strength in unity served as the driving force behind Kawapit's activism. Kawapit and the six walkers (**Figure 1.27**) highlighted the importance of protecting their lands and their traditional ways of life for future generations.

> "IT FEELS REALLY GOOD THAT A LOT OF PEOPLE ARE PAYING ATTENTION TO WHAT'S GOING ON."

When the Nishiyuu walkers arrived in Ottawa in March 2013, thousands had gathered to welcome them. They spoke with the aboriginal affairs minister about the necessity of fair and equal treatment of Canada's First Nations people. Kawapit's work brought attention to Aboriginal rights. His group inspired many other Canadians to consider the importance of the historical origins of the relationships between First Nations and the rest of Canada.

Kawapit's efforts were sparked by one important vision that inspired hundreds of others to think and take action as well. He said, "It feels really good that a lot of people are paying attention to what's going on." In the end, the relationships he built during his journey were the gifts that he took away from the experience. "I'm going to miss all these guys. The memories we shared—I won't forget them," he said of his fellow Nishiyuu walkers and the hundreds who joined them along the way. For Kawapit and his group, this walk was just the beginning of their efforts to create meaningful change for all First Nations people living in Canada.

FIGURE 1.27 David Kawapit (front, centre) was one of seven Nishiyuu walkers who walked from Whapmagoostui First Nation in northern Québec to Parliament Hill in Ottawa. The walk was to support the Idle No More movement.

A CALL TO **ACTION**

1. What inequalities is the Idle No More movement trying to deal with?

2. How can you and your classmates take action to support a current movement in your community?

FIGURE 1.28 Henri Beau painted this portrait of Philippe de Rigaud de Vaudreuil in 1923. Vaudreuil served as a captain for the New France military as well as the governor general of New France. **Analyze:** What sentiment is the artist trying to portray about Vaudreuil?

> "[W]e treat our Indians [First Nations] as allies, and not as subjects ..."
>
> — *Governor General Vaudreuil*

FIGURE 1.29 This comment was made by Vaudreuil in a public statement, in 1721. **Analyze:** What does Vaudreuil mean by "subjects"?

> "... by uniting the Abenakis and the Mi'k Maqs, we should be in a position to recover ... all we have lost in the East by the Treaty of Utrecht."
>
> — *Governor General Vaudreuil*

FIGURE 1.30 Vaudreuil tells his King, in a 1724 report, that the French needed to unite the Wabanaki Nations. **Analyze:** Would this goal benefit the Wabanaki Confederacy? Why, or why not?

FRENCH AND FIRST NATIONS ALLIANCES

Philippe de Rigaud de Vaudreuil, pictured in **Figure 1.28**, wanted to preserve the relationship between the French and the Wabanaki Confederacy. Vaudreuil was the governor general of New France from 1703 to 1725. Vaudreuil gave out payments to the Wabanaki to encourage them to settle in New France. What does Vaudreuil say about the Wabanaki First Nations in **Figure 1.29**? A subject is a person or nation under the rule of another person or nation. Allies are people or nations with a common cause. Vaudreuil was seeking to ally New France with the Wabanaki First Nations. What common cause might the French and Wabanaki have had?

By stating that the Wabanaki First Nations were allies, not subjects, Vaudreuil was saying that the Wabanaki Confederacy was a separate nation and was not subject to the Treaty of Utrecht in the same way that the French were. He was claiming that much of the land that the British thought was part of Acadia was Wabanaki land. Wabanaki land was not part of the treaty and did not belong to the British. For the French, this meant that they would have the right to use this land after 1713. The British took a different position. Since the Wabanaki Confederacy had allied themselves with the French, they were subject to the Treaty of Utrecht just as the French were. That is, the Wabanaki First Nations had lost their right to the land in Acadia.

STRENGTHENING TIES

Vaudreuil not only wanted to ally New France with the Wabanaki, he also wanted to unite all the Wabanaki Nations of the Confederacy. Read the quote in **Figure 1.30** where he suggests this to his King.

If Vaudreuil was successful, what might be the consequences for the peace established by the treaty?

BREAKING THE TREATY OF PORTSMOUTH

Why did the British and the French keep building farther into First Nations territory?

Shortly after signing the Treaty of Portsmouth, the British stationed soldiers and built settlements inside Wabanaki territory. This broke the terms of the treaty. Borders between the French and the British were also in dispute. The French and the British were, once again, pushing farther into First Nations territory.

BRITISH, FRENCH, AND WABANAKI RELATIONS

The British began to displace and to enslave Wabanaki nations again. In response to the British actions, the Wabanaki attacked a newly built British fishing station in Acadia. For the next 10 years, the Wabanaki continued to raid British settlements on the eastern coast, as well as farther south in New England, a region in northeastern North America.

How did the Treaty of Utrecht create distrust between the British and the French?

The British knew the French had good relations with the Wabanaki and suspected the French were involved in the attacks. The French claimed that the Wabanaki were acting on their own. The British urged their government to take action. Britain responded by reinforcing the border area and Acadia. Since the British believed Acadians were helping the Wabanaki, they started chasing some Acadians away from Nova Scotia. The British also started to plan how they would bring New Englanders to settle Nova Scotia in order to outnumber the French and the First Nations.

FATHER RALE'S MISSION

The French government denied that the French were involved in the Wabanaki attacks against the British. In the 1720s, however, government letters were found that suggested something else. Read the excerpt in **Figure 1.31**. It is part of a letter written by Michel Bégon, an administrative official of New France. It was written to Father Sébastien Rale (also known as Father Sebastian Rale), a French Jesuit priest. The letter suggests that the French government had promised to give the Wabanaki guns and supplies to use against the British.

> "If they [the British] attack Them [First Nations] ill-advisedly ... we could help them only by The Munitions [weapons] that we would Give Them."
>
> — *Michel Bégon, administrative official of New France*

FIGURE 1.31 This excerpt is from a letter Bégon wrote to Father Rale in 1721.
Analyze: What was the significance of this letter for British and French relations?

Father Rale lived and worked with the Abenaki people for many years during the late 1600s and into the 1720s. He learned the eastern Algonquian language and began writing an Abenaki–French dictionary. Father Rale taught the Abenaki Catholicism and they attended Mass and evening prayer every day. He accompanied the Wabanaki Confederacy and other First Nations peoples on many raids of British settlements.

Read the account by Father Rale in **Figure 1.32**. He describes an incident between the Wabanaki Confederacy and the British after the Treaty of Portsmouth had been made. How would this incident between the British and the Wabanaki Confederacy benefit the French?

"About this time a score of Savages entered into one of the English houses, to trade or to rest ... they saw the house suddenly surrounded by a troop of nearly two hundred armed [British] men ... [The English] assuring them that they had come only to invite some of them to go to Boston, to confer there with the Governor, on the means of keeping peace and good understanding. The Savages, a little too credulous [trusting], [sent] four of their fellow-countrymen to Boston; but when they arrived there, they were diverted, [ending] in retaining them prisoners."

— *Father Rale*

FIGURE 1.32 This excerpt is taken from a letter written in 1721 by Father Rale. The letter was found after his death in 1724. **Analyze:** How do you think the Wabanaki would have described the same event?

Between 1722 and 1725, a series of battles occurred between the British and the Wabanaki Confederacy. This period was known as Father Rale's War. Father Rale was captured and killed by the British in 1724. **Figure 1.33** shows a depiction of the day Father Rale was killed.

FIGURE 1.33 This painting, entitled *Death of Father Sebastian Rale of the Society of Jesus*, was commissioned in 1856. **Analyze:** Do you think the events of the day Father Rale died are accurately represented in this painting?

CHECK-IN

1. **HISTORICAL SIGNIFICANCE** Vaudreuil said that the French treated Wabanaki First Nations "as allies ... not as subjects." Why was this significant for relationships between the French and the Wabanaki, and between the French and the British?

2. **COMMUNICATE** Write a newspaper article or blog post about the Treaty of Portsmouth and its consequences from the point of view of the British, the French, or the Wabanaki.

3. **INTERPRET AND ANALYZE** How did the Treaty of Utrecht lead to changes in the relationships among the French, the British, and First Nations?

HOW DID THE TREATY OF UTRECHT LEAD TO CHANGES IN NORTH AMERICA?

LEARNING GOALS

As you worked through this chapter, you had opportunities to
- identify the people who were living in North America in 1713 and why the land was important for different groups
- formulate questions about life in North America and examine the time period using continuity and change

- explain how the land was divided by the Treaty of Utrecht and how this division affected people's relationships and led to uncertainty in North America
- analyze maps to understand the changes in borders and the movement of people after 1713

In this chapter, you learned about the 1713 Treaty of Utrecht and how it changed North America. You read about French, British, and First Nations land claims in North America and considered why the 1713 Treaty of Utrecht led to a division of the land. You learned that the French had to hand over North American land to the British and that the treaty did not include First Nations' claims to the land. As well, you discovered that the treaty had major effects on First Nations.

Summarize Your Learning

Now that you have completed Chapter 1, you are ready to answer the Chapter Big Question:

How did the Treaty of Utrecht lead to changes in North America? Select one of the following tasks to summarize your learning:
- Create a plaque dedicated to the Treaty of Utrecht. Your plaque can be four to five sentences long. It should include the relevant information about the treaty and discuss the importance of the Treaty of Utrecht to Canadian history. Remember that plaques can have a visual.
- Create and present a plan for celebrating the anniversary of the Treaty of Utrecht in North America. Your proposal should include details on why this is an event worth recognizing, who should be involved in the planning, and how the event will be celebrated.

APPLY YOUR LEARNING

1. **GATHER AND ORGANIZE** Find different primary sources, such as letters, pictures, quotes, or artifacts, about life in New France that may give you the most clues about the beliefs, attitudes, and values of the time period. Explain why you selected each of your sources.

2. **CONTINUITY AND CHANGE** Create a chart to compare the changes that affected different groups before and after 1713, and things that may have stayed the same. For example, you may compare the experiences of the Ojibwe living around Lake Superior to those of the Wabanaki living on the East Coast.

3. **HISTORICAL PERSPECTIVE** Find evidence from the chapter to infer how Acadians felt and thought since the British took control of Acadia. Write a letter from the perspective of an Acadian. Tell the reader about what your life has been like since the British took over. What hopes and fears might you have?

4. **EVALUATE AND DRAW CONCLUSIONS** Using a chart, list all the changes to the lives of any three groups of people discussed in this chapter. Rank and order the most important improvements for each of the three groups. Then conclude whose life improved the most during the beginning of the 1700s.

5. **INTERPRET AND ANALYZE** Use the knowledge you have gained about the Treaty of Utrecht to answer the following questions:
   a) What is a treaty, and how is it a kind of legal contract?
   b) How could the Treaty of Utrecht have been negotiated and written differently in order to create stronger relationships among the different groups in North America?

6. **FORMULATE QUESTIONS** The Chapter Big Question is: How did the Treaty of Utrecht lead to changes in North America? Read the information on pages 26 and 27. Use this information to formulate research questions that would help you answer the question.

UNIT 1 CHALLENGE CHECK-IN

1. Review the Unit 1 Challenge on pages 18 to 19. Then create a log book for your work on your Heritage Fair presentation. A log book is a notebook (print or digital) where you record information and evidence you gather and details about the sources of your information and evidence, as well as your own thinking about your inquiry question. You can also include images and graphics, such as drawings, maps, graphic organizers, and a timeline. Number the pages and leave space on each page for adding future information or reflections. Record your responses to questions 2 to 4 in your log book.

2. Review the Focus On: Formulate Questions feature on pages 26 to 27. Develop and record questions you have about the Treaty of Utrecht and its impact on various groups, using the criteria provided in the feature.

3. Review the Focus On: Continuity and Change feature on pages 32 to 33. Using the criteria provided, consider the impact of the Treaty of Utrecht. What changed in North America? What remained the same? Which group of people was affected the most?

4. What were the consequences of the Treaty of Utrecht for different groups of people in North America? Use a concept map or another graphic organizer to show your thinking in your log book.

NEL

RISING TENSIONS
IN NORTH AMERICA:
1713–1755

HOW DID RELATIONSHIPS AMONG FIRST NATIONS, THE BRITISH, AND THE FRENCH LEAD TO CHANGE?

LEARNING GOALS

As you work through this chapter, you will

- gather and organize information about the daily lives of different groups in North America between 1713 and 1755
- analyze the importance of the fur trade
- describe the consequences of the French and British rivalry on First Nations and Acadian people
- closely read primary source texts

The lives of First Nations, British, and French people in North America were intertwined in the early 1700s. They depended on each other for certain things, so a level of peace was necessary.

The image on this page was painted by Lewis Parker in 1978. He called it *Scene of Daily Life at Fort Beauséjour, around 1753*. The French started building Fort Beauséjour in 1751. It is located on the border between present-day New Brunswick and Nova Scotia, at the head of the Bay of Fundy. The scene inside the fort shows workers moving supplies, French soldiers escorting away an English soldier, and a missionary with two members of the Abenaki First Nation speaking with a French officer. What else do you see? What do all these details on the painting tell you about interactions in the fort?

The British, the French, and First Nations were all involved in the historical events shaping North America in the 1700s. First Nations were highly motivated to protect their lands and needed to expand their trading networks to include Europeans. As you read through this chapter, examine the ways that First Nations, the French, and the British affected one another and how their relationships led to change.

WHAT SHAPED CANADIEN CULTURE?

Have you ever wondered how different cultures develop? Why do people speak different languages, eat certain foods, or have different beliefs? Some parts of a culture remain the same over time, and some parts change.

ORIGINS OF CANADIEN CULTURE

When the first permanent settlers travelled from France to North America in 1608, they probably never imagined they would change over time to become a distinct people. In some ways, the French settlers never let go of the traditions and culture of their past. In other ways, however, they adapted to their new land. For example, the settlers in New France still spoke French, but they developed a new dialect called *canadien-français*. This dialect of French has its own distinct expressions and words. For example, *poudrerie* (drifting snow) reflected the environment of New France. Words such as *toboggan*, *moose*, and *squash* were learned from First Nations peoples. The settlers began to call themselves *Canadiens* to differentiate themselves from the French who lived in France and other French-speaking people in North America, such as the Acadians.

> Does referring to themselves as "Canadiens" indicate a turning point in the development of French Canadian identity? Why, or why not?

HABITANTS

Most of the Canadien settlers who lived along the St. Lawrence River were farmers, called **habitants**. The settlements of the habitants were part of the seigneurial system that you learned about in Chapter 1. **Figure 2.1** shows a habitant farm. In 1713, the average amount of cleared land that each habitant had to farm was about the size of a football field. This was not big enough to support the needs of a large family. In response, habitants learned to fish, hunt, harvest timber, and trap animals.

habitant French settler who farmed a small plot of land in what is now Québec

FIGURE 2.1 Cornelius Krieghoff painted *The Habitant Farm* in 1856. Habitants built their homes with steep roofs so that the heavy snows would slide off. **Analyze:** What other adaptations to the environment can you spot in this painting?

THE CANADIENS AND THE FUR TRADE

Many Canadiens took part in the fur trade. They travelled far from home for long periods of time to find furs.

COUREURS DE BOIS

Many Canadien fur traders were known as *coureurs de bois*, which translates directly as "wood runners" but was used by the Canadiens to mean fur traders. The coureurs de bois met with First Nations trappers and purchased furs in exchange for goods such as wire, cloth, reading glasses, and guns. The coureurs de bois took on some of the habits, clothing, and practices of the First Nations with whom they interacted. Learning from the First Nations helped them survive. It was a working partnership that benefited both parties.

coureur de bois an independent French Canadian fur trader who travelled deep into the forests of New France

The coureurs de bois encountered many challenges on their journeys. In 1749, Pehr Kalm, a Swedish scientist, came to North America to collect seeds and plants. Examine **Figure 2.2**. What are Kalm's thoughts about the life of the coureurs de bois?

> "It is inconceivable what hardships the [coureurs de bois] must undergo on their hunting journeys. Sometimes, they must carry their goods a great way by land ... They often suffer hunger, thirst, heat, and cold, and ... dangerous animals and insects."
>
> — *Pehr Kalm, Swedish scientist*

FIGURE 2.2 An excerpt from Kalm's journal written during a visit to North America in 1749. **Analyze:** What image of the coureurs de bois does Kalm want to convey to his readers?

VOYAGEURS

As the fur trade expanded in the early 1700s, fur trading developed into small businesses. Some Canadiens became *voyageurs*. Voyageurs were canoeists who worked for fur trading firms. Unlike the coureurs de bois, the voyageurs could not trade or sell furs. Instead, they travelled by canoe to transport furs and goods for the fur trade. **Figure 2.3** depicts their travels. What does the painting tell you about the life of a voyageur?

voyageur a professional canoeist who transported furs

FIGURE 2.3 This 1879 painting by Frances Anne Hopkins entitled *Shooting the Rapids* shows a scene in the workday of a voyageur. **Analyze:** What can you see in this painting that may have been influenced by First Nations peoples?

GATHER AND ORGANIZE

To investigate the past, you must start gathering evidence or information, keeping your inquiry question in mind. Then you need to organize the information in a way that will help you understand and analyze it.

When you collect your evidence,
- keep your inquiry question in mind
- organize and record your evidence in a way that will help you understand it
- make sure that you use reliable sources
- investigate different sources and perspectives
- make a list of all the sources you have chosen to use

CASE STUDY: THE LIVES OF THE VOYAGEURS

As the fur trade industry developed in New France, it sparked increased demand for labourers. Canadien voyageurs were the main labour force for the fur trade in New France. Fur trade companies needed voyageurs to transport their goods, such as furs and supplies, to trading posts by canoe.

Consider this inquiry question to help you dig deeper into the lives of the voyageurs: How did the lives and experiences of the voyageurs differ from those of other settlers? Organize the evidence presented in this case study so that it is meaningful to you.

Many of the trading posts were located in First Nations territories, so the voyageurs were in frequent contact with First Nations people. Examine **Figure 2.4**, which is a secondary source from historian Carolyn Podruchny. Podruchny lists the ways that First Nations influenced the voyageurs. How could you organize the content about the influence of First Nations on the voyageurs presented in **Figure 2.4**?

"[Voyageurs] travelled great distances and met speakers of Iroquoian, Algonquin, Athapaskan, Siouan, Salishan, and Wakashan languages, and even Inuit. Voyageurs adopted Aboriginal technologies to survive harsh conditions of living in the [wilderness]. They ate Aboriginal food, dressed in Aboriginal clothing, and used Aboriginal tools along with their own ... coming into close contact with Aboriginal people offered voyageurs a new kind of life unknown to the habitants ..."

— *Carolyn Podruchny, historian*

FIGURE 2.4 In this excerpt from her 2006 book, *Making the Voyageur World: Travelers and Traders in the North American Fur Trade*, Podruchny comments on the interactions between the voyageurs and different First Nations peoples. **Analyze:** How would encountering these First Nations have changed the lives of the voyageurs?

FIGURE 2.5 This 1871 painting, entitled *Voyageurs at Dawn* by Frances Anne Hopkins, shows a typical voyageur camp. **Analyze:** What unique skills do you think voyageurs might have learned that other habitant settlers might not have learned?

Voyageurs were often fond of the freedom and independence that their jobs gave them. In exchange, they had to endure tough, dangerous working conditions. The voyageurs worked 16- to 18-hour days, beginning in the middle of the night. Sometimes the waterways they were travelling on turned into fierce rapids. This meant that the voyageurs would have to unload all of their goods from the canoe, haul everything overland, and then reload in calmer waters. Every 6 or 8 km, voyageurs would stop to smoke their pipes. Voyageurs began measuring each route using the number of "pipes" it took to complete.

Along with their pipes, the voyageurs had very distinctive accessories and clothing. Voyageurs often dressed in a blue capote, or long coat with a hood, deer skin leggings, a bright red sash that had a beaded pipe bag tied to it, and beaded moccasins. Examine **Figure 2.5**, which shows voyageurs setting up camp along the water. What other kinds of sources could help you understand what voyageur life was like?

TRY IT

1. Use a graphic organizer to organize the information on pages 50 to 51 so that you can respond to the inquiry question. Find a partner and compare how you organized the information. Explain why you think your organizing tool is appropriate.

2. Use the criteria from page 50 to identify any areas where you need more information. For example, ask yourself these questions: Are multiple perspectives represented? Whose viewpoint is missing? Are both primary and secondary sources included? Add any relevant information to your organizer.

FIGURE 2.6 This was painted by an unknown painter around 1710. It shows nuns caring for the sick in an abbey. **Analyze:** What does this painting tell you about healthcare in the early 1700s?

RELIGION

By 1713, French settlers had been living in New France for more than two or three generations. Most had never lived in France or visited Europe. However, they still held the same religious beliefs as those living in France, which was a Catholic country.

The French King Louis XIV had permitted only Catholics to settle in New France, so nearly all the people living in New France at this time were Catholic. But because there was a lack of priests in New France, the majority of Canadiens were only able to attend church services a few times each year. Despite this, the Catholic Church played a central role in people's lives.

The parish priests served as local leaders and set up important institutions, such as schools and hospitals, that the Canadiens needed. The Catholic Church was the only provider of healthcare in New France during this time. Hospitals were often run by nuns. The first hospital in New France, called Hôtel-Dieu, was built in Québec City in 1639. It was run by a group of nursing nuns called the Hospitaller Sisters and is still open today. Examine **Figure 2.6**, which shows nuns caring for the sick in the early 1700s. What connections can you make between New France's charitable hospitals and Canada's healthcare system today?

The Canadiens demonstrated their Catholic beliefs in traditional ways. For example, they painted votive paintings, which are paintings by ordinary people that express thanks to Catholic saints for miracles. These kinds of paintings were common in France. Settlers in New France continued to create votive paintings for centuries.

CANADIEN WOMEN

Earlier in this section, in **Figure 2.2**, you read Kalm's description of the life of the coureurs de bois. Read **Figure 2.7** to learn his thoughts about Canadien women.

Several factors shifted Canadien culture toward greater independence for women. Because of their circumstances, Canadien women had to be versatile and self-reliant. They learned how to cook with the foods that were available in North America, such as venison (deer meat), corn, and maple syrup. Without easy access to stores or ready-made clothing, they sewed their family's clothes and made meals from scratch. Women whose husbands left for weeks or months at a time to trade furs maintained the family farm on their own. As a result, women in New France enjoyed a level of independence that was not available to women in the British colonies or in France.

EDUCATION AND BUSINESS OPPORTUNITIES

Greater access to education was another way Canadien women could become more independent. Some girls were able to receive an education from Catholic nuns. Canadien women used the literacy skills they learned to work in commercial businesses. Some even ran their own businesses, such as mills, factories, and tanneries. This was possible because of a law passed in 1690 in New France. Eager to spark the colony's economy, officials in New France allowed nobles, including women, to engage in business. Nobles were wealthy people with high social status. **Figure 2.8** shows Marie-Charlotte Denys de la Ronde, a Canadien woman who ran a sawmill. This was very different from the situation in France and the British colonies. Women there were not encouraged to work or own their own businesses.

"[Unlike men in Europe, Canadien men did not undertake] matters of importance without their women's advice and approval."

— *Pehr Kalm, Swedish scientist*

FIGURE 2.7 Kalm wrote this observation during a 1749 visit to New France. **Analyze:** What does Kalm's observation say about the role of women in New France?

FIGURE 2.8 This reproduction of a portrait of Marie-Charlotte Denys de la Ronde was painted by Saint-Marc Moutillet in the 1950s. **Analyze:** Judging by the details in the painting, was Denys de la Ronde a habitant or a noble?

CHECK-**IN**

1. **GATHER AND ORGANIZE** Create a chart listing changes that influenced New France to develop a distinct Canadien culture. Identify the source of each change. Which changes resulted from interactions with another group of people?

2. **HISTORICAL PERSPECTIVE** Use evidence from this section to write a journal entry from the perspective of a young coureur de bois or Canadien businesswoman. Include aspects of daily life.

WHY WAS THE
FUR TRADE SIGNIFICANT?

Can an industry be historically significant? Consider four of Canada's current industries: forestry, mining, oil and gas, and manufacturing. Each of these has a positive impact. For example, people can earn an income that enables them to live more comfortably and the economy can prosper. Each of these industries also has a negative impact. For example, an industry can harm the environment, destroying animal habitats and ecosystems.

To determine historical significance, we look for evidence that the industry had a long-lasting impact on the lives of many people. Just as our current industries affect our lives today, the fur trade affected many people's lives 300 years ago. After 1713, expansion of the fur trade led to changes throughout North America.

> How can understanding the fur trade in the 1700s help us deal with economic issues today?

MOTIVATIONS IN THE FUR TRADE

In the early 1700s, both Britain and France were extending their power in Europe by developing colonies in North America. This strategy of taking over as many countries as possible was known as **imperialism**. The British colonies grew steadily along the eastern coast of North America. The settlers were mostly farmers, and the colonies supported themselves. New France did not grow as fast as the British colonies. The Canadiens needed more ways to sustain themselves, so they entered the fur trade. The French government helped to sponsor expeditions to find more First Nations fur trading partners because the fur trade was a large source of income for New France. Without a thriving colony, France's imperialist goal of ruling North America would fail.

imperialism the policy of extending a country's power and influence by creating colonies or conquering other countries

Gaining wealth was a motivation for fur traders and explorers. French explorer Pierre Gaultier de Varennes et de La Vérendrye prospered from the fur trade during his expeditions in North America. Though the King of France did not profit much from the fur trade itself, he financed La Vérendrye's explorations. Examine **Figure 2.9**, an excerpt from a letter La Vérendrye wrote to the governor of New France. In it, he mentions that he is close to finding the Western Sea, known today as the Pacific Ocean. Why would finding a route to the Pacific Ocean benefit the King?

> "The colony will receive a new benefit independently of the discovery of the Western Sea through the quantity of furs that will be produced."
>
> — *Pierre Gaultier de Varennes et de La Vérendrye, French explorer*

FIGURE 2.9 This excerpt is from a letter that La Vérendrye wrote to the governor of New France, Charles de Beauharnois de La Boische, in 1730. **Analyze:** Which two benefits does La Vérendrye identify?

PARTNERING WITH FIRST NATIONS

For more than 200 years, the French and First Nations developed relationships that were useful to both groups. Realizing that First Nations had a much larger population, the French decided they could benefit from developing good business relationships with First Nations peoples. For example, they took part in gift-giving ceremonies during negotiations to demonstrate their respect. In **Figure 2.10**, Chief Luther Standing Bear identifies principles that many First Nations peoples live by. If the French were also able to demonstrate these principles, how might it have helped them build their relationships with First Nations and their fur trading business?

The French depended on First Nations to supply the furs that they sold in Europe. First Nations depended on Europeans to supply European-made goods. Many of these goods were tools, such as rifles, metal traps, sewing needles, and cooking pots.

How does the artist who painted the scene in **Figure 2.11** depict a fur trading session between the French and First Nations representatives? The friendly relationships developed through the fur trade also helped the French in times of war. Their First Nations trading partners became their **military allies**. As well, Catholic missionaries tried hard to convince First Nations peoples to embrace Catholicism. When they were successful, the French–First Nations relationships were further strengthened.

FIGURE 2.10 Chief Luther Standing Bear explains principles that guide many First Nations peoples in their everyday life. **Analyze:** How does the quotation help to explain why First Nations peoples regarded gift giving as an important part of negotiations?

> "Out of the Indian approach to life there came a great freedom, an intense and absorbing respect for life ... and principles of truth, honesty, generosity, equity, and brotherhood as a guide to mundane relations."
>
> — *Chief Luther Standing Bear, Oglala Sioux First Nation*

military allies two or more parties that agree to support one another in case of war

FIGURE 2.11 This 1916 painting by Ontario artist George Reid is called *Traders at Montreal*.
Analyze: How does the artist portray the relationship between the French and First Nations?

READING
TEXT SOURCES

Historians are like detectives: they look at sources for evidence that can help them answer questions about the past and create an argument or a narrative.

Historians often look at text sources for evidence. Text sources are written records that can be descriptions of events. They can also be transcriptions of speeches, remarks, or conversations. Text sources can be found as primary sources or secondary sources.

To begin a historical investigation, historians first read secondary sources to gain background knowledge of the event or time period they have a question about. Next, they select primary sources that they think may be helpful. Then, historians do a **close reading** of each source. They examine the source carefully, asking questions about the source and making observations about any patterns or trends. **Figure 2.12** below lists some of the questions that historians ask themselves when they are closely reading a text source.

Question Category	Sample Questions
Source	• What type of document is it (a letter, diary, report, etc.)? • When and where was it created? Who wrote it? Who for? What for? • Is the author describing his or her own experiences, or those of others? • Was the information recorded when the events occurred, or later?
Content	• What claims does the author make? • What evidence does the author give to support these claims? • What is the author's perspective on the topic? How can I tell? • What information or perspective does the author leave out?
Writing style	• What words or phrases does the author use to persuade the reader? • What else does the writer's choice of words or details tell me? • What feelings does the writer express, or hope to inspire in the reader?
Audience response	• What effect did this text likely have on its readers? • How might a different audience have responded to it?

FIGURE 2.12 When doing a close reading of a text, it is important to ask questions about the source and its content.

In this activity, you will do a close reading of the text in **Figure 2.13** to look for evidence that can help you answer the following inquiry question: What caused tensions in North America to rise from 1713 to 1755?

"For the future we will sell no Lands [to you, unless] we know beforehand the Quantity of Goods we are to receive. Besides, we are not well used with respect to the Lands still unsold by us. Your People daily settle on these Lands, and spoil our Hunting. We must insist on your Removing them, as you know they have no Right to settle to the Northward of *Kittochtinny-Hills*. In particular, we renew our Complaints against some People who are settled at *Juniata*, a Branch of *Sasquahannah*, and all along the Banks of that River, as far as *Mahaniay*; and desire they may be forthwith made to go off the Land; for they do great Damage to our Cousins the *Delawares*.... your Horses and Cows have eat the Grass our Deer used to feed on. This has made them scarce ... we are really poor ..."

— *Chief Canasatego, Onondaga Iroquois First Nation*

FIGURE 2.13 Chief Canasatego from the Onondaga First Nation acted as a spokesperson for the Onondaga Iroquois First Nation. He spoke these words to the British during negotiations concerning Onondaga land in 1742. His words were recorded by a Pennsylvanian colonist in the minutes of the meeting.

HOW TO CLOSELY READ A TEXT SOURCE

STEP 1

Consider **Figure 2.13**. Write down everything you know about the creation of the source.

- What type of source is it?
- When and where was it created?
- Is the author recording his or her own words or Chief Canasatego's words?
- Was the speech recorded during the meeting or later?

STEP 2

Read the text carefully to understand what it says.

- What is Chief Canasatego's main argument?
- Why is British settlement spoiling the Onondaga's hunting?
- Locate the Susquehanna and Juniata rivers on a map.
- Who were the Delaware people? Why would Chief Canasatego refer to them as "cousins"?

STEP 3

Read the text again. How is Chief Canasatego's message communicated?

- What words does he use to show his people's displeasure?
- What words does he use to try to inspire sympathy in his listeners?
- What impact do you think this speech may have had on the British audience? Why?

STEP 4

What inferences can you make? For example, what can you infer from the first sentence about the quantity of goods given by the British to the Onondaga in exchange for their land?

STEP 5

What does this text suggest are some possible reasons why tensions in North America rose during this period?

EXPANSION OF THE FUR TRADE

In the early 1700s, the French received almost all furs in Montréal. Their First Nations trading partners brought furs to Montréal from what the Canadiens called *le pays d'en haut* ("the upper country"), a vast area north and west of the Great Lakes. In 1713, however, the Treaty of Utrecht gave a big piece of this area to the British, effectively cutting off the French from their source of furs. First Nations in the upper country paddled along the rivers to reach the British Hudson's Bay Company trading posts. Examine **Figure 2.14** to see where French trading posts were established by La Vérendrye to recapture trade from the British.

COMPETING TO TRADE WITH FIRST NATIONS

Competition in the fur trade was fierce. In some ways, the British and the French transferred their rivalry on the battlefield to the fur trade. Near the Ohio River and around the Great Lakes, the British tried hard to take the business of the Huron (Wyandot), Delaware, and Shawnee First Nations away from the French. In turn, the French worked to capture the business of the Cree First Nations in what is now Manitoba and Saskatchewan. This competition put First Nations trappers in a good bargaining position. Some trading posts were so close together that First Nations trappers could check who was offering the best prices or the finest goods before selling their furs. Read **Figure 2.15** to see how a Hudson's Bay Company employee described the reaction of First Nations trading partners to the goods the company was offering.

The competition for furs led to some harmful consequences. Over time, over-trapping brought the beaver to the brink of extinction. Another consequence was the spread of disease. Fur traders spread smallpox, which killed tens of thousands of First Nations people.

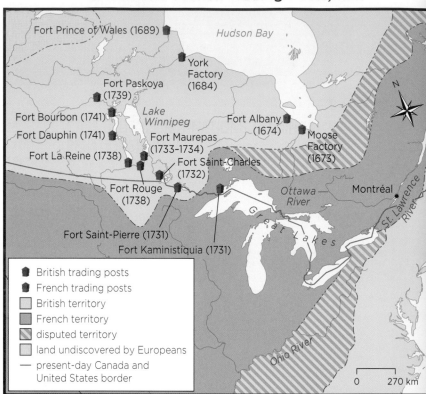

British and French Trading Posts, 1741

Fort Prince of Wales (1689)
Hudson Bay
York Factory (1684)
Fort Paskoya (1739)
Fort Bourbon (1741)
Lake Winnipeg
Fort Albany (1674)
Fort Dauphin (1741)
Fort Maurepas (1733-1734)
Moose Factory (1673)
Fort La Reine (1738)
Fort Saint-Charles (1732)
Fort Rouge (1738)
Ottawa River
Montréal
Fort Saint-Pierre (1731)
Great Lakes
Fort Kaministiquia (1731)
St. Lawrence River
Ohio River

- British trading posts
- French trading posts
- British territory
- French territory
- disputed territory
- land undiscovered by Europeans
- present-day Canada and United States border

0   270 km

FIGURE 2.14 This map shows the established British trading posts and the French trading posts that were built by 1741 to compete with the British. **Analyze:** What do the years the forts were built tell you about French and British actions after 1713?

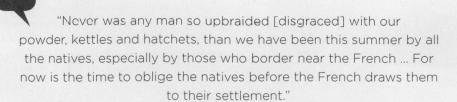

"Never was any man so upbraided [disgraced] with our powder, kettles and hatchets, than we have been this summer by all the natives, especially by those who border near the French ... For now is the time to oblige the natives before the French draws them to their settlement."

— *Thomas McCleish, Hudson's Bay Company employee*

FIGURE 2.15 This is an excerpt from a 1728 letter McCleish wrote to his employer in Britain. **Analyze:** Why was McCleish worried about First Nations establishing trading relationships with the French?

THANADELTHUR: AMBASSADOR OF PEACE

The fur trade depended heavily on First Nations women. They prepared the furs, which involved skinning, cleaning, and tanning the hides. Skillful preparation always increased the value of fur. After learning English or French, some women acted as interpreters, advisors, and guides. Some of them played a role in making deals between different peoples.

In 1713, a young Dene woman named Thanadelthur was captured by the Cree Nation. Escaping the following year, Thanadelthur headed to a Hudson's Bay Company outpost in York Factory. There she met James Knight, who was in charge of the post. Thanadelthur decided to help Knight establish trade in the region. In a year-long effort, she brought together the warring Dene and Cree First Nations and helped them make peace. Her efforts paved the way for years of peaceful trading with Hudson's Bay Company.

In 1952, Hudson's Bay Company commissioned a painting of Thanadelthur, who had lived more than two centuries earlier. Look at the painting in **Figure 2.16**. What does it tell you about why Hudson's Bay Company felt that Thanadelthur was historically significant?

> Why is it important to learn about the contributions made by women?

FIGURE 2.16 This painting shows Thanadelthur (centre) in the early 1700s, promoting peace through trade. Hudson's Bay Company commissioned Franklin Arbuckle to create this painting in 1952. He called it *Ambassadress of Peace*. **Analyze:** How does the artist depict the importance of Thanadelthur?

CHECK-IN

1. **CONTINUITY AND CHANGE** What were the motivations behind the fur trade? Do you think similar motivations exist for trade in Canada today? Explain your reasoning.

2. **INTERPRET AND ANALYZE** Compare **Figures 2.13** and **2.15**. What does this comparison reveal about British and First Nations' perspectives on the fur trade?

3. **EVALUATE AND DRAW CONCLUSIONS** Look at the quote from La Vérendrye in **Figure 2.9** and the map in **Figure 2.14**. What was the French strategy to expand the fur trade?

4. **HISTORICAL SIGNIFICANCE** What makes the fur trade historically significant? Consider how it affected the level of exploration, people's lives, and the relationships among the French, the British, and First Nations.

WHAT CAUSED TENSIONS TO RISE?

New France tripled its population between 1713 and 1754, reaching 55 000. However, the British colonies along the eastern coast grew even faster. By 1750, one million people were living there—20 times as many as in New France. The British government actively encouraged settlement in the colonies. In addition, people in all the colonies were having large families, which helped the total population grow quickly. The increasing need for settlers to have land led to increased conflicts among the settlers, the French, and First Nations.

> How might competition for land in the same place lead to rising tensions?

SEEKING FARMLAND AND FURS

As the population in the British colonies continued to grow, so did the settlers' demand for more farmland. However, all the best farmland in the British colonies had already been taken. In their search for farmland, British colonists moved westward, starting farms on First Nations territories near the Ohio River. The French were already present in that area, but they were there seeking fur. What potential for conflict do you see?

RACING TO BUILD FORTS

To expand the fur trade and maintain contact with their First Nations allies, the French built more and more fur trading posts throughout New France. Every time they built a post, they had a better chance of attracting First Nations business away from the British traders. Many of these posts were protected by the French military. Essentially, they were forts.

Examine the bar graph in **Figure 2.17**. Some of these forts were located on lands claimed by both France and Britain. At the same time, British colonists were settling on these same disputed lands. How did the French shift their fort-building efforts after 1710?

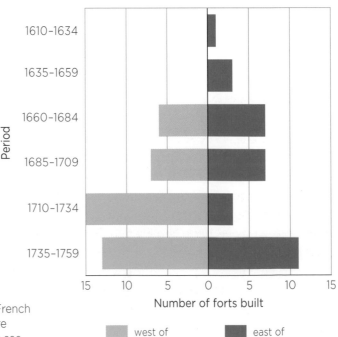

French Forts 1610–1759

FIGURE 2.17 This bar graph shows the expansion in the number of French forts from 1610 to 1759. The two colours show where the French were building forts over six periods of time. **Analyze:** What trends do you see that might have seemed threatening to British colonists?

west of Niagara Falls · east of Niagara Falls

FIGURE 2.18 This photo shows the reconstructed French Fortress Louisbourg. **Analyze:** What would be some advantages of building a fort alongside water?

FORTRESS LOUISBOURG

In 1713, the French decided to build a fortress. They wanted it to be massive and intimidating. It would be a centre for the French fisheries, a major trading port, and the largest military base in North America. The French chose a location on present-day Cape Breton Island, Nova Scotia, as the site for Fortress Louisbourg. Look at **Figure 2.18**. How do you think the presence of such a fortress might have affected the tensions in North America?

By 1740, 2000 people lived behind the huge fortifications at Fortress Louisbourg. The French viewed it as a safe place for French ships to dock. The British saw it as a protector of pirates who attacked British fishing and transport ships, and a major threat to their safety.

In 1744, another war broke out between France and Britain in North America. The British captured Louisbourg in 1745. In 1748, the peace treaty that ended the war restored Louisbourg to France. The British then built their own military base about 400 km southwest, in what is known today as Halifax.

THE IMPACT OF FORTS ON FIRST NATIONS

Earlier in this chapter, you read that European forts gave First Nations more options for buying and trading goods. However, most of those forts were built in territories that First Nations considered to be their own. Imagine the difficult position First Nations were in, with two strong European powers taking over their land. First Nations were more willing to have the French on their land because the French just traded furs. The French did not settle on the land and build farms. The British, however, built farms. Sometimes, they started farming without asking permission. Other times, they tried to buy the land. Read **Figure 2.19** to learn how Chief Canasatego of the Onondaga Iroquois First Nation responded to attempts by white people to buy Onondaga land. The term *white* refers to people of European descent. Why does he think that selling the land is an unreasonable option?

"We know our Lands are now become more valuable. The White People think we do not know their Value; but we are sensible that the Land is everlasting, and the few Goods we receive for it are soon worn out and gone ... Your people daily settle on these Lands and spoil our Hunting."

— *Chief Canasatego, Onondaga Iroquois First Nation*

FIGURE 2.19 Chief Canasatego spoke these words in 1742, during negotiations with the lieutenant-governor of Pennsylvania. **Analyze:** According to Chief Canasatego, how did settlement threaten First Nations in ways that the fur trade did not?

CHAPTER 2: *Rising Tensions in North America: 1713-1755*

ECONOMIC TENSIONS

In the 1740s, the conflict between the British and the French focused on hurting one another economically, rather than militarily. By hurting New France's economy, Britain hoped to weaken France's military strength. The 1745 attack on Louisbourg is an example of this. All the French goods that were destined for trading with First Nations passed through this port. By capturing Louisbourg, the British cut off the supply of French goods. This was a devastating blow to the French. In desperation, some First Nations peoples attacked French forts for whatever goods might be left. Although the French regained Louisbourg in 1748, British attempts to disrupt French trade continued.

COMPETING FOR LAND IN THE OHIO RIVER VALLEY

Tensions continued to rise as the British and the French clashed in the Ohio River Valley, an area surrounding the Ohio River, shown in **Figure 2.20**. This river had long been used by First Nations as a transportation route, because it joins the Mississippi River, which flows thousands of kilometres to the Gulf of Mexico. The British and the French both wanted control of this transportation route.

The key to gaining control of the river was to control the Ohio River Valley. The French had already established forts in the area, but the British wanted to occupy the land and establish settlements. The Ohio Company was formed by people in the British colony of Virginia to create these settlements. The company began planning to establish farms and move people from Virginia to the Ohio River Valley. This brought the conflict between the French and the British to a boiling point.

In 1753, George Washington, an investor in the Ohio Company, was sent with seven soldiers to deliver a message to the French. Washington's travels are depicted in the image in **Figure 2.21**. Read an excerpt from the letter Washington delivered on behalf of Governor of Virginia Robert Dinwiddie to French Commander Legardeur de St. Pierre in **Figure 2.22**. Then read the excerpt of the French commander's response in **Figure 2.23**. What did the British want the French to do and how did the French respond?

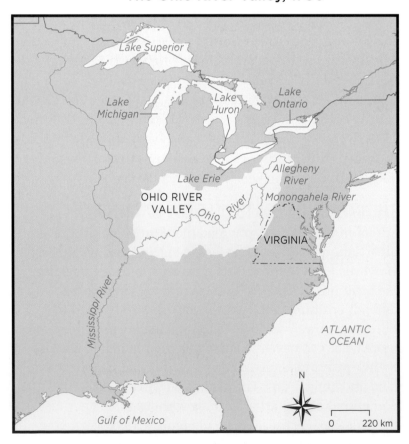

The Ohio River Valley, 1750

FIGURE 2.20 Map of the Ohio River Valley in 1750. **Analyze:** What makes the Ohio River an important transportation route?

FIGURE 2.21 This is a hand-coloured reproduction of Alonzo Chappel's original 1857 painting. It depicts George Washington on his mission to the Ohio River Valley on behalf of the British. **Analyze:** What does the artist show you about the mission?

FIGURE 2.22 This is an excerpt from a 1753 letter sent by Dinwiddie to Legardeur de St. Pierre. **Analyze:** What words and phrases reveal the British perspective about the territory of Ohio?

"The Lands upon the River Ohio, in the Western Parts of the Colony of Virginia, are so notoriously known to be the Property of the Crown of Great-Britain that it is a Matter of equal Concern and Surprise to me, to hear that a Body of French Forces are erecting Fortresses, and making Settlements upon that River.... The many and repeated Complaints I have received of these Acts of Hostility, lay me under the Necessity, of sending George Washington ... to complain to you of the ... Injuries done to the Subjects of Great-Britain.... Sir, in Obedience to my Instructions, it becomes my Duty to require your peaceable Departure."

— *Robert Dinwiddie, governor of Virginia*

FIGURE 2.23 This is an excerpt from Legardeur de St. Pierre's response to Dinwiddie's letter. **Analyze:** What words and phrases reveal the French perspective about the territory of Ohio?

"I should have been glad [had you sent Washington] to Canada, to see our General, to whom it better belongs than to me to set forth the Evidence and Reality of the Rights of the [French] King, my Master, upon the Lands situated along the River Ohio, and to contest the Pretensions [claim] of the King of Great-Britain."

— *Legardeur de St. Pierre, French commander*

CHECK-**IN**

1. [**CAUSE AND CONSEQUENCE**] How did each of the following increase tensions in North America? Which was the most important cause of increased tensions? Justify your position.
   - overlapping land claims
   - the construction of Fortress Louisbourg
   - competition for the Ohio River Valley

2. [**HISTORICAL PERSPECTIVE**] Take the historical perspectives of a British leader, a French leader, and a First Nations leader. Use evidence from the chapter to help you describe how each leader feels about the others. Why might it have been difficult for each leader to understand the others' perspectives at the time?

CHAPTER 2: *Rising Tensions in North America: 1713–1755*

WERE THE BRITISH JUSTIFIED IN EXPELLING THE ACADIANS?

Imagine that you are forced to leave your community. Your home is being destroyed, and all the people you know are going to be scattered far and wide. Oceans will separate you from your family and friends. Finding them again would be very difficult, if not impossible. This is what happened during the **Acadian Expulsion**. Between 1755 and 1763, thousands of Acadians were violently removed from their homes, had their property destroyed, and were forced onto ships headed to unfamiliar lands. Today, historians continue to debate the British actions—was the Expulsion a necessary action for the British to gain control of the land, or was it unnecessary and cruel?

Acadian Expulsion the historical event in which thousands of Acadians were forced from their homeland in Acadia by the British

ACADIA UNDER BRITISH RULE

The Acadians were the French-speaking people of Acadia. As you learned in Chapter 1, Acadia had been a French colony. In 1713, the Treaty of Utrecht sliced off part of Acadia (mainland Nova Scotia) and gave it to the British. The treaty allowed Acadians to relocate to other lands in New France. The Acadians, however, did not want to leave their established farms, like the one shown in **Figure 2.24**. What were some of the reasons the land was so important to the Acadians? The British did not want to increase the French population in the surrounding colonies. This would have made the British more vulnerable to future attacks.

FIGURE 2.24 *Early Acadia* was painted by Claude Picard in 1986 to show Acadian farming. **Analyze:** How does Picard show that Acadians valued their land?

AN UNEASY PEACE

In 1730, the British and the Acadians finally came to an agreement. The British allowed the Acadians to practise Catholicism, and the Acadians signed an oath declaring their loyalty to the British King, George II. As part of the agreement, the British agreed that the Acadians would not have to fight with the British against France. Thereafter, they became known as "the neutral French." The peace, however, was an uneasy one.

FIGURE 2.25 Parks Canada hired artist Lewis Parker to paint *The Expulsion of the Acadians* in 2011. Parks Canada provided him with historical information to help get the details accurate. **Analyze:** Based on the details in this painting, do you think the Acadians had any other choice but to leave? Why, or why not?

How might different groups have reacted to the Expulsion?

THE EXPULSION

As time went on, tensions grew between the Acadians and the British, just as they had grown between the French and the British in the rest of North America. France and Britain were on the verge of war. In 1755, Governor Charles Lawrence demanded that the Acadians sign an oath of allegiance. This meant that if Britain and France went to war, the Acadians would have to fight the French. The Acadians refused. In 1755, Britain ordered the expulsion of the Acadians.

Examine **Figure 2.25**, which depicts a scene from the Expulsion. What does this painting tell you about the experience of the Acadians? During the Expulsion, the Acadians were rounded up and deported. As many as 10 000 people were forced onto ships and sent to Europe or to distant British colonies in what is known as present-day United States.

Some Acadians managed to escape into the forest and find refuge with French or First Nations communities in the area. Others died of exposure or starvation while hiding. Nearly one-third of the people who were forced onto ships died before they reached their destination. In the terror and confusion, families were separated, and some never found each other again. After the Acadians were forcibly removed from their communities, the British burned down their homes and destroyed their farms so that the Acadians would have no reason to return. The Expulsion lasted for eight years, ending in 1763. What other factors might have led the British to decide to expel the Acadians from their homeland?

THE NEED FOR MORE LAND

The British population in North America was growing quickly in the 1700s. British settlers needed land—lots of land—so they could spread out and build more farms. The Ohio River Valley was inviting, but conflicts with the French and First Nations made it dangerous. Where else could British settlers go? The British hoped that Acadia offered a solution.

As it turned out, few British settlers wanted to accept Britain's offer to settle in Acadia. One reason was that the Acadians were already living on the best farmland. The photo in **Figure 2.26** shows an area of Acadia called Grand Pré, which is now a World Heritage site. Why might a site like this be a World Heritage site? Some historians have argued that the Acadian Expulsion was a way for the British to claim Acadian farmland. By developing a very effective system of dikes to drain the saltwater marshes, the Acadians had created some of the most fertile and desirable farmland in North America.

Read **Figure 2.27**, which is a letter written by British Chief Surveyor Charles Morris to his superiors. In his letter, Morris hints at another reason why the British might have wanted to expel the Acadians. At the time, Catholics and Protestants did not get along. The British in North America were mostly Protestants. Sharing Acadia with French-speaking Catholics would not have been an attractive option for British settlers.

FIGURE 2.26 In 2012, the United Nations declared the area of Grand Pré in Acadia to be Canada's 16th World Heritage site. **Analyze:** What does the photo tell you about why the British might have wanted to settle on this land?

FIGURE 2.27 In 1753, Morris wrote this letter to his superiors about the difficulty of attracting British settlers to Acadia. **Analyze:** How might his prejudice have influenced the decision to expel the Acadians?

"Without their removal, I am sure it would be impossible any large number of Protestants can ever be settled in the Country.... [The Catholic Acadians need to] be rooted out, and the most effectual way is to destroy all these [Acadian] settlements by burning down all their houses, cutting the dikes, and destroying all the grain now growing."

— *Charles Morris, British chief surveyor*

THREATS TO BRITISH SECURITY

In the years leading up to the Expulsion, the British felt threatened by First Nations who were fighting to defend their lands against British settlement. They also felt threatened by the Acadians and the French, whom they did not trust.

FIRST NATIONS RESISTANCE

As you learned in Chapter 1, the Treaty of Utrecht gave land that was occupied by First Nations peoples to the British. The British viewed the land as belonging to them. The Mi'kmaq and Maliseet peoples (who were part of the Wabanaki Confederacy) were allies of the French, and they opposed British settlement on their land. They viewed the British occupation of Acadia as illegal.

In 1749, the British increased their presence in the region by building the fortress at Halifax and bringing in 2500 British settlers to begin farming. Since the Mi'kmaq and the Maliseet viewed the land as their own, how might they have reacted to such a scene? Read the quote in **Figure 2.28** by Mi'kmaq First Nations to Edward Cornwallis, the British governor of Nova Scotia and founder of Halifax. How might this letter have affected the relationship between the British and the Mi'kmaq?

The British tried to negotiate with the Mi'kmaq and Maliseet, but these First Nations just wanted the British to leave. The British and First Nations started to attack one another, hoping to drive each other away. During these attacks, the Mi'kmaq abducted more than a thousand British settlers, many of them children. To protect the settlers, British soldiers needed to increase their presence. Look at **Figure 2.29**, which shows British settlers building a community in Halifax while guarded by British soldiers. Cornwallis offered a reward to British settlers and soldiers for killing Mi'kmaq people—men, women, or children.

> "My king [the King of France] and your king together distribute these lands [amongst themselves]; it is because of that they are now at peace, but for me, I can make neither alliance or peace with you."
>
> — *Mi'kmaq First Nations*

FIGURE 2.28 This excerpt is from a letter written in 1749 by the Mi'kmaq to Governor Cornwallis. It was originally translated into French by Father Maillard so that Cornwallis could read it. **Analyze:** What does this excerpt tell you about the perspective of the Mi'kmaq on British settlement?

FIGURE 2.29 In this 1934 painting, *The Founding of Halifax, 1749,* C.W. Jefferys shows the initial settlement at Halifax. **Analyze:** Why would British soldiers have to guard settlers as they built their homes?

ACADIAN RESISTANCE

In the 1700s, the Acadians were viewed differently by different people. This is emphasized in **Figure 2.30**, in which a historian describes three different perspectives of the Acadians in 1748. What does the quote tell you about the Acadians' position in the mid-1700s?

The Acadians and the Mi'kmaq had close ties. There was much intermarriage and much cooperation between them. Even before the Expulsion, some Acadians resented the British presence just as much as their First Nations neighbours did, so they joined the First Nations in raids on British settlements.

Joseph Broussard (**Figure 2.31**) was one of the most active leaders of the Acadian resistance. Broussard's legendary acts earned the secret admiration of many Acadians. In 1751, Broussard led 60 Mi'kmaq and Acadian militia to attack the town of Dartmouth before dawn, when everyone was asleep. Broussard's forces killed 20 British villagers and burned down 36 homes. The attack became known as the Dartmouth Massacre. How would the British have viewed Broussard after this surprise attack? Broussard also helped lead a group of First Nations warriors and Acadian and French soldiers to defend Fort Beauséjour. **Figure 2.32** shows the historic remains of the fort today. The French built this fort in 1751 on land that both the French and the British had claimed. Do the actions of the Acadians at Fort Beauséjour support or challenge the French and British perspectives in **Figure 2.30**?

> "In 1748, the Acadians considered themselves Acadian, the French considered them unreliable allies, and the English, unsatisfactory citizens."
>
> — *Naomi Griffiths, historian*

FIGURE 2.30 Griffiths wrote this comment in 1973 about the Acadians in 1748. **Analyze:** Why might the French have perceived the Acadians as "unreliable"?

FIGURE 2.31 Herb Roe created this oil painting of Joseph Broussard in 2009. **Analyze:** Based on what you read about Broussard, from whose perspective did the artist create this painting: the Acadians, the British, or First Nations?

FIGURE 2.32 Fort Beauséjour National Historic Site of Canada is located in present-day New Brunswick. **Analyze:** Why do you think the remains of this fort are considered historically significant?

THE FRENCH THREAT

Competition from the fur trade and the increasing number of French forts in the West made the British concerned about what the French would do in the East. They also suspected that France was actively encouraging Mi'kmaq and Acadian resistance to the British presence in Acadia. Read **Figure 2.33**, which is a letter written in secret by Jean-Louis Le Loutre, a French missionary in Acadia, to the French military in France. According to this letter, was the British suspicion justified?

The British grew concerned about the number and location of the forts France was building on nearby French territories and in the disputed territory near Nova Scotia. The British thought that the Treaty of Utrecht gave Britain all the disputed territory shown on the map in **Figure 2.34**. The French disagreed. They built forts throughout these lands. Some of their forts were very close to Acadia.

"As we cannot openly oppose the English ventures, I think that we cannot do better than to incite the Indians to continue warring on the English; my plan is to persuade the Indians to send word to the English that they will not permit new [British] settlements to be made in Acadia.... I shall do my best to make it look to the English as if this plan comes from the Indians and that I have no part in it."

— *Jean-Louis Le Loutre, French missionary*

FIGURE 2.33 Le Loutre wrote this letter to the French military headquarters in Paris, France, in 1749. **Analyze:** Why might the French want to encourage resistance but hide their own involvement?

FIGURE 2.34 This map shows the forts in Nova Scotia (Acadia) and surrounding area in 1751. **Analyze:** How does the number of British forts compare with the number of French forts?

Forts in Nova Scotia (Acadia) and Surrounding Area, 1751

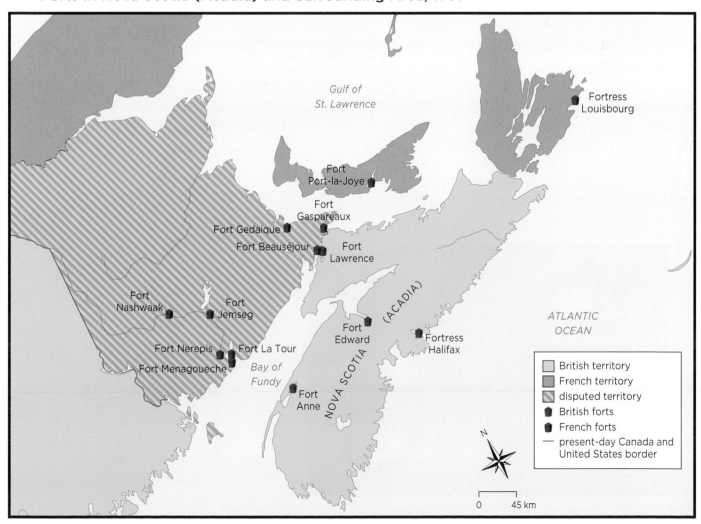

THE ACADIAN GRAND YOUTH RALLY

After the Acadian Expulsion, the Acadian culture seemed doomed to disappear. However, the Acadian culture did survive through the efforts of Acadians who were dedicated to saving it.

The Youth Acadian Commission (YAC) is the youth arm of Société Nationale de l'Acadie (SNA), the organization that represents Acadian people on the global stage. The YAC is made up of young Acadians from all over Canada. They work together to build an interactive, global community of Acadian youth (**Figure 2.35**). By promoting the Acadian culture and French language among Acadian youth, they hope to strengthen the Acadian community.

Once every five years, the YAC holds a large gathering called the Grand Youth Rally so that Acadian youth can connect in person. The 2014 Grand Youth Rally was held in the town of Pohénégamook, Québec. About 300 Acadian and French youth from around the world travelled to the five-day event.

> "[THE GRAND YOUTH RALLY ALLOWS ACADIAN YOUTH TO] DEVELOP STRONG TIES BETWEEN THEMSELVES … THAT WILL ALLOW THEM TO TAKE THEIR PLACE IN TODAY'S ACADIA."

They came from Atlantic Canada, Québec, Maine, and Louisiana, as well as France and Belgium. By taking part in a variety of artistic, cultural, and political activities—mostly in French—the youth were encouraged to think about the importance of the French language and to think about their futures. Talking about their shared past and speaking their shared language helped the participants develop the bonds of community.

On social media, Céleste Godin calls herself a *Patriote Acadienne*. She is the youth advisor and interim vice-president of the SNA. She says that the Grand Youth Rally offers participants "a profound and unforgettable experience … [so that] they can develop strong ties between themselves … that will allow them to take their place in today's Acadia."

FIGURE 2.35 The Grand Youth Rally is meant to inspire youth like these to embrace their Acadian and French heritage.

A CALL TO **ACTION**

1. Why would the expulsion of the Acadians be historically significant to Acadian youth? Is it historically significant to all Canadians? Should it be? Explain why, or why not.

2. What are some ways you could connect to a cultural community?

THE AFTERMATH OF THE EXPULSION

The Acadians who were deported had difficulty settling in the British colonies where they were sent. The most successful settlement was in New Orleans, Louisiana. The people who lived there were French-speaking Catholics. By 1785, nearly 2600 of the Acadians who had been deported from Acadia ended up in New Orleans. There, the locals began referring to them as Cajuns. In 1764, the British allowed the Acadians to return to Acadia. Nearly 3000 Acadians returned to their homeland. By then, however, their land had been given to British settlers. Many of the returnees settled in what is now known as New Brunswick. Why would so many Acadians return to a place where they had been treated so badly and where many British settlers still lived?

> Does the Expulsion mark a turning point toward progress or decline?

THE STORY OF EVANGELINE

The story of the Expulsion was told and retold over generations. It has become part of the Acadian identity. In 1847, American Henry Wadsworth Longfellow wrote the epic poem *Evangeline: A Tale of Acadie*. The poem tells the tale of a fictional Acadian who spends her life searching for her lost love, Gabriel. The poem became very popular. Since then, the fictional Evangeline has been brought to life in countless paintings, statues, plays, and movies. What do these representations, like the statue of Evangeline in **Figure 2.36**, tell us about the popularity and importance of the story of Evangeline to the Acadians?

FIGURE 2.36 This statue of Evangeline was erected in Grand-Pré in 1920, in front of the Memorial Church that was built to memorialize the Expulsion. **Analyze:** Why do you think Evangeline is depicted in this way and in front of a Catholic church?

CHECK-IN

1. **HISTORICAL SIGNIFICANCE** Why was the expulsion of the Acadians a historically significant event? To justify your answer, explain who it affected and if they were affected in a deep and lasting way.

2. **CAUSE AND CONSEQUENCE** List the causes of the Acadian Expulsion. Include conflicts, tensions, circumstances, and actions that influenced the course of events. What do you think was the trigger cause? Use evidence to help you explain your choice.

3. **CONTINUITY AND CHANGE** The British made drastic changes to create the colony that they wanted in Acadia. What might have been the benefits to the British, the French, First Nations, Acadians, and Canada today if the British had allowed the Acadians to continue living in Acadia?

4. **EVALUATE AND DRAW CONCLUSIONS** Consider the question on page 64: Were the British justified in expelling the Acadians? Work with a partner to determine an answer to this question, using evidence presented in the chapter.

HOW DID RELATIONSHIPS AMONG FIRST NATIONS, THE BRITISH, AND THE FRENCH LEAD TO CHANGE?

LEARNING GOALS

As you worked through this chapter, you had opportunities to

- gather and organize information about the daily lives of different groups in North America between 1713 and 1755

- analyze the importance of the fur trade
- describe the consequences of the French and British rivalry on First Nations and Acadian people
- closely read primary source texts

In this chapter, you learned how people can change in response to their environment or interactions with others. You also learned how the French, the British, and First Nations competed over trade and territories. Finally, you saw how tensions built up, ultimately leading to the death and displacement of thousands of people.

Summarize Your Learning

Now that you have completed Chapter 2, you are ready to answer the Chapter Big Question: How did relationships among First Nations, the British, and the French lead to change? Select one of the following tasks to summarize your learning:

- Ask yourself a "What if ..." question to imagine how events might have played out differently in the early 1700s in North America. For example, "What if First Nations and the Acadians had successfully driven the British out of Acadia?" or "What if fur had suddenly gone out of fashion in Europe?" Set up two flow charts to compare "How Things Happened" with "How Things Might Have Happened If ..."

- Identify an interaction in this chapter that was either friendly and mutually beneficial or tense and harmful. With a partner, write a dialogue that demonstrates how the interaction was shaped. When you present your dialogue, pause so that each character can explain his or her thoughts, feelings, and motivations.

APPLY **YOUR LEARNING**

1. **CAUSE AND CONSEQUENCE** Create a fishbone diagram that lists the causes and consequences of a significant event from this chapter. Are there any positive consequences? Are there any negative consequences?

2. **HISTORICAL SIGNIFICANCE** How could studying the relationships in the fur trade help Canada today?

3. **CONTINUITY AND CHANGE** Create a four-square chart to compare the similarities and differences in how First Nations shopped for trade goods and how you shop today.

4. **COMMUNICATE** Imagine you are documenting the Acadian Expulsion on social media. Create a few 140-character messages that list the causes of the Expulsion. Include the main conflicts, tensions, and actions that influenced the course of events.

5. **CAUSE AND CONSEQUENCE** List all the causes of the tensions between the French and the British in North America. Rank these causes in order of importance.

6. **HISTORICAL SIGNIFICANCE** Why does the expulsion of the Acadians still draw interest today, centuries after it occurred?

7. **GATHER AND ORGANIZE** People in North America in the early and mid-1700s faced challenges such as competition for trade, disputed land, a harsh climate, making a living, getting along with others, and achieving safety and security. Create a graphic organizer to show how people responded. What types of developments permit us to respond to these challenges in different ways today?

8. **CONTINUITY AND CHANGE** How was 1713 the beginning of the end for the French inhabitants of Acadia? How was the same time period just a continuation of old relationships?

9. **FORMULATE QUESTIONS** Create a strong inquiry question about the relationships between two of the following groups during this time period: the British, the French, the Acadians, and First Nations.

UNIT 1 CHALLENGE CHECK-IN

Record your responses to these questions in your log book.

1. Review the Focus On: Gather and Organize feature on pages 50 to 51. Based on the criteria provided, what sources in Chapter 2 provide evidence that can help you answer the inquiry question? Do these sources reveal the values and perspectives of people from the past?

2. What were the key changes during this time period? Which were the most significant, and for whom? Design a graphic organizer to help you communicate your analysis.

3. This chapter explores the relationships among First Nations, the British, and the French in the early to mid-1700s. How did these groups interact? Use a comparison chart, visual organizer, or diagram to illustrate examples of cooperation and conflict between the groups. What were the consequences of these interactions?

4. Review the description of the Unit 1 Challenge on pages 18 to 19 and the notes you made in your log book for Chapter 1. How are the events discussed in Chapters 1 and 2 connected? Has your thinking about the causes and consequences of these events changed? Add your reflections to your log book.

CHAPTER 3

THE **SEVEN YEARS'** WAR
AND THE CONQUEST OF
NEW FRANCE: 1754–1774

WHAT WAS THE IMPACT OF THE SEVEN YEARS' WAR ON NORTH AMERICA?

LEARNING GOALS

As you work through this chapter, you will
- analyze the causes of conflict among the French, the British, and First Nations in North America during the Seven Years' War
- consider the significance of different key people and events throughout the war
- understand the consequences of the war and the conquest on different groups of people
- create and analyze maps related to the Seven Years' War

The conflict that took place in North America in the mid-1700s has many different names: the Seven Years' War, the War of Conquest, the French and Indian War. This war has also been called the first true world war. Conflicts between the French and British in North America heightened in 1754. By 1756, the war had spread to Europe, India, the African coast, Central America, and the Philippines.

Britain and France were competing for control of trade and commerce around the world. Each wanted control of North America's vast resources. This led to fighting over forts. Troops from one side would attack and capture their opponent's fort, only to lose control of a fort somewhere else.

The engraving seen here, *A View of the Taking of Québec, Sept 13, 1759*, by John Bowles, is based on a sketch by Hervey Smyth. Smyth was British General James Wolfe's military aid during the siege of Québec City. The painting illustrates the battle of the Plains of Abraham, one of the most important battles of the Seven Years' War. Looking at this engraving, who do you think won this battle and how?

As you explore this chapter, consider how the Seven Years' War helped to shape the Canada you live in today.

WHAT WERE THE CAUSES OF THE SEVEN YEARS' WAR?

What causes wars to break out? Wars are like large-scale arguments. They have short- and long-term causes. Short-term causes are an immediate response to an event. Long-term causes can result from tensions that build over time between competing groups trying to gain power. In this section, you will examine some of the causes of the Seven Years' War and determine why the fighting broke out when it did.

> Why do you think some conflicts lead to war while others get resolved?

GROWING TENSIONS IN NORTH AMERICA

By 1754, tensions among the French, the British, and First Nations living in North America had been building for more than a decade. As you learned in Chapter 2, French and British settlers came into frequent conflict. The French and the British wanted control over North America's resources for trade purposes. To achieve control, they needed people to lay claim to the land and defend it. Conflicts also grew between groups of settlers and First Nations. The Reverend Jonathan Mayhew, a religious and political figure living in the British colony of Massachusetts, commented on these tensions. The quote in **Figure 3.1** is from his 1754 sermon. What does this quote reveal about the relationships between the French and the British in North America in 1754? Compare **Figure 3.1** to the quote in **Figure 3.2** from Christian Frederick Post, a missionary and representative of the British government.

> "We are peaceably extending our settlements upon our own territories. They [the French] are extending theirs beyond their own, by force of arms. We must meet at length, which cannot be without a violent concussion, and the time seems not to be far off.... The continent is not wide enough for us both."
>
> — Reverend Jonathan Mayhew

FIGURE 3.1 Reverend Mayhew highlights the growing conflict between the French and the British in this excerpt from a sermon he delivered on May 29, 1754, in Boston, Massachusetts. **Analyze:** What does this quote reveal about the British perspective on French claims to land in North America?

> "Brothers, this is the last time we shall come among you; for the French and the English intend to kill all the Indians, and then divide the land among themselves."
>
> — Christian Frederick Post, missionary and British diplomat (quoting a speech by Delaware Chief Shingas, King Beaver, Delaware George, and Pisquetumen)

FIGURE 3.2 This 1758 speech, recorded by Post, points to concerns about French and British intentions. **Analyze:** What does this statement tell you about the perspective of some First Nations on British and French settlement?

In 1754, Benjamin Franklin, one of the future founders of what would become known as the United States, published the cartoon shown in **Figure 3.3** in his newspaper, the *Pennsylvania Gazette*. This early political cartoon shows segments of a snake labelled with initials that represent some of the British colonies. What do you think Benjamin Franklin was trying to accomplish by publishing this cartoon?

FIGURE 3.3 This cartoon was published in the *Pennsylvania Gazette* on May 9, 1754. **Analyze:** What does this cartoon say about the relationship among British colonies in North America at the time?

COMPETITION FOR THE OHIO VALLEY

Around the time when the "Join, or Die" cartoon was published, conflict in the Ohio Valley was heating up. The British were planning to establish settlements in the area and were trying to drive out the French. The French reacted by attacking British colonists across the frontier and setting fire to their homes. Many colonists were injured or killed in these attacks, or were scared into fleeing the area. The French built more forts in the Ohio Valley to keep the British back. Examine the map in **Figure 3.4**. What information about the importance of the Ohio Valley can you gather? Look back at **Figure 1.6** from Chapter 1 to see where First Nations territories were located.

FIGURE 3.4 This map shows French and British land claims and the Ohio Valley, which was of great interest to both groups in 1754. **Analyze:** Why do you think the disputed territories are located where they are?

Ohio Valley and Surrounding Territory, 1754

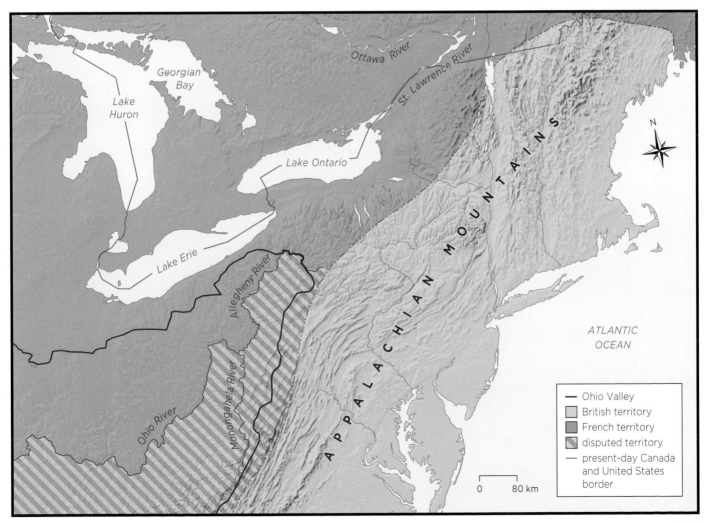

CHAPTER 3: *The Seven Years' War and the Conquest of New France: 1754–1774*

BATTLES FOR FORTRESS LOUISBOURG

As you learned in Chapter 2, in 1748, the British returned Louisbourg, which they had captured from the French in 1745. However, a few years later, in 1758, another military showdown resulted in the British capturing the fortress again. Their rivalry created further conflicts between the French and British settlers. What does the quote in **Figure 3.5**, recorded by Post, tell you about the impact on First Nations of the fighting between the French and the British?

BATTLE FOR FORT DUQUESNE

In 1754, the governor of New France, Marquis Duquesne, sent a French military team to build Fort Duquesne. It was built near present-day Pittsburgh, Pennsylvania, where the Monongahela and Allegheny rivers meet and form the Ohio River. **Figure 3.6** shows a sketch of Fort Duquesne. Because the fort was in a strategic location, the British wanted to control it. The governor of Virginia, Robert Dinwiddie, responded by sending his own troops, led by militia leader (and future American president) George Washington, to drive out the French. The French, along with warriors from the Shawnee, Delaware, and Seneca nations, responded with overwhelming force. Many historians point to the battle for Fort Duquesne as the start of the Seven Years' War. The British were forced to leave the area, but they returned multiple times to try to capture the fort from the French. The British finally succeeded in 1758, when the war began to turn in their favour.

FIGURE 3.5 Post recorded interactions with different First Nations groups in his journal as he travelled around the Ohio Valley delivering messages for the British government in 1758. **Analyze:** Why would the British government ask missionaries such as Post to communicate with First Nations peoples during the war?

> "It is plain that you white people are the cause of this war. Why do not you and the French fight in the old country, and on the sea? Why do you come to fight on our land?"
>
> — *Christian Frederick Post, missionary and British diplomat (quoting a speech by Delaware Chief Shingas, King Beaver, Delaware George, and Pisquetumen)*

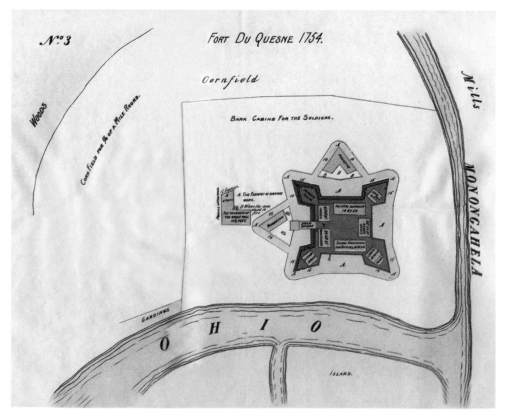

FIGURE 3.6 This 1754 diagram shows the design of Fort Duquesne. Other French forts, such as Fort Frontenac in Kingston, Ontario, were built in a similar style. **Analyze:** What do you think are the advantages of the location and design of Fort Duquesne?

ECONOMIC INTERESTS

In the 1700s, in Europe, the economy was based on a system called **mercantilism**. In this system, countries compete by trying to sell their goods to other countries for a profit, while limiting what they buy from other countries. Exploring other parts of the world was key to finding new markets in which to sell their products. Tea and spices from India and sugar from the West Indies were sold to colonists in North America. The more colonies a nation had around the world, the more goods that nation could sell. European nations aimed to source gold and silver from their colonies. But the French and British also valued resources such as fish, furs, grain, timber, and tobacco. They used the timber to build warships and used the grain for food. They sold the tobacco and furs in Europe.

In 1754, the British sent troops to North America and attacked French forts. The British also began seizing hundreds of French merchant ships (ships filled with goods for trade). **Figure 3.7** depicts an encounter between the British and the French off the coast of the island of Newfoundland on June 8, 1755. The British were chasing French ships carrying 3000 troops and supplies. Why would the British want to destroy French ships?

> **mercantilism** an economic system that increases wealth by increasing exports and by limiting imports through taxes

> What were some of the intended and unintended consequences of mercantilism?

FIGURE 3.7 This painting by an unknown artist, entitled *The Capture of the "Alcide" and "Lys," 8 June 1755*, shows three British ships (left) engaging in action against two French ships bound for New France. **Analyze:** What message do you think the artist is trying to deliver with this painting?

CHECK-IN

1. **CAUSE AND CONSEQUENCE** Identify and explain the causes of the Seven Years' War. Label each cause as a short-term cause or a long-term cause.

2. **HISTORICAL PERSPECTIVE** Form three groups to represent First Nations, the French, and the British. Debate what each might have said was the cause of the Seven Years' War in North America.

3. **FORMULATE QUESTIONS** Identify main ideas that were clear to you in this section and main ideas that were unclear. For each unclear idea, write a question that would help you to clarify the issue.

4. **CONTINUITY AND CHANGE** Create a Venn diagram to show which aspects of the Seven Years' War are similar to and different from wars today.

WAS THE BRITISH VICTORY INEVITABLE?

Knowing what we do about Canada today, it is tempting to conclude that the British victory was inevitable, or certain. However, when war breaks out, the outcome is never certain. Britain was determined to conquer North America, sending more and more troops and supplies to gain an advantage. The French and First Nations were equally determined to protect their interests in the area. Through their First Nations alliances, the French had learned about the land and how to survive, even through the harsh winters. Read the quote in **Figure 3.8** by William Clarke, a British colonist. How do you think the smaller population of French people could possibly defeat the British?

> "For my own part, I cannot help thinking that unless there be a united and vigorous opposition of the English Colonies to them, the French are laying a solid Foundation for being, some time or other, sole Masters of this Continent, notwithstanding our present Superiority to them in point of Numbers."
>
> — *William Clarke, British colonist*

FIGURE 3.8 Clarke wrote this comment in a letter to Benjamin Franklin on May 6, 1754. **Analyze:** What is Clarke recommending that the British colonies do?

COMPARING MILITARY STRATEGIES

Britain and France had different strategies when fighting the Seven Years' War. France focused its attention on fighting in Europe. This limited the number of troops it sent to defend its economic interests in North America. Protecting the sugar trade was a higher priority to France. By contrast, the British believed that success in North America would help them defeat the French in Europe. During the Seven Years' War, Britain sent 20 000 additional soldiers to North America. The French, for the most part, let their colonists fight for themselves.

The British and the French had different styles of fighting in North America. The British fought in the way that they had always fought on the open fields of Britain and Europe. **Figure 3.9A** shows British soldiers in traditional line formation. They believed this was an honourable way to fight: to face your opponent head-on. **Figure 3.9B** shows **guerilla warfare**, which is surprise attacks carried out by small groups of people. This strategy was often used by the French and their First Nations allies during the Seven Years' War. Which strategy do you think was more effective in North America at the time of the Seven Years' War?

guerilla warfare a type of fighting using small groups of soldiers to carry out surprise attacks against an opponent

FIGURE 3.9 (A) This painting by Robert Griffing (2002) is entitled *A Charming Field for an Encounter*. It depicts British soldiers in traditional line formation before the July 1754 battle at Fort Necessity. (B) *One Mile to Bushy Run Station*, also painted by Robert Griffing (1997), shows a clash between First Nations warriors and British soldiers during a 1763 battle. **Analyze:** What are the advantages and disadvantages of the types of fighting seen in both paintings?

CHAPTER 3: *The Seven Years' War and the Conquest of New France: 1754–1774*

FIRST NATIONS ALLIANCES

The key to French military strategy in North America was alliances with First Nations, such as the Ojibwe. Similarly, the Ojibwe sought alliances with the French to help protect their interests and ensure their survival in North America. Not only were the French outnumbered by British settlers, but also by the thousands of British troops that began to arrive. Read a quote from colonial fur trader Edmond Aitken in **Figure 3.10**. Why were alliances with First Nations important for the French?

> "The importance of Indians is now generally known and understood. A Doubt remains not that the prosperity of our Colonies will stand or fall with our Interest and favour among them. When they are our Friends, they are the Cheapest and strongest Barrier for the Protection of our Settlements; when Enemies, they are capable of ravaging in their methods of War."
>
> — *Edmond Aitken, colonial fur trader*

FIGURE 3.10 Aitken included this comment in a 1755 report to the British Board of Trade. **Analyze:** What is Aitken saying about the importance of First Nations alliances to winning the war?

The trade alliance that the Ojibwe had with the French helped them obtain European goods. As well, the tributes, or gifts (such as weapons, tools, and clothing), that the French gave were seen by the Ojibwe as important symbols of respect and partnership. The Ojibwe honoured their alliance with the French by fighting alongside them against the British. The British, the French, and their First Nations allies all benefited from taking material goods from fallen enemies.

How do you think the Ojibwe felt about their French trading partners and the new British settlers?

In southern Ontario, more than 1000 Ojibwe warriors supported the French. This support led to many victories in the war. In **Figure 3.11**, George Washington, who had become commander in chief of the British forces, gives a first-hand account of an attack he faced. The British were defeated in this battle, despite outnumbering their enemies. Why would First Nations choose to join the war?

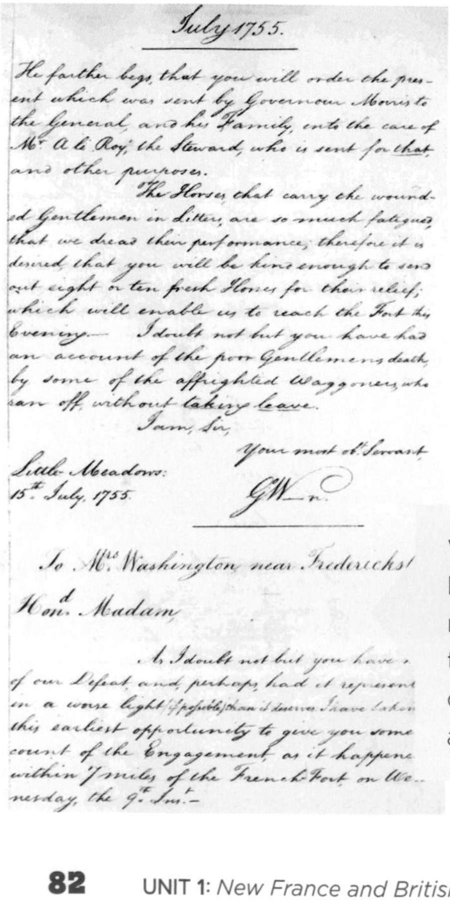
July 1755.

He farther begs, that you will order the present which was sent by Governour Morris to the General and his Family, into the care of Mr. A. le Roy, the Steward, who is sent for that and other purposes.

The Horses that carry the wounded Gentlemen in Litters, are so much fatigued that we dread their performance; therefore it is desired that you will be kind enough to send out eight or ten fresh Horses for their relief; which will enable us to reach the Fort this evening. I doubt not but you have had an account of the poor Gentlemens death by some of the affrighted Waggoners, who ran off without taking leave.

I am, Sir,

Your most obt. Servant

Little Meadows: 15th July, 1755.

G.W——n.

To Mrs. Washington near Fredericksb

Hond. Madam

As I doubt not but you have ... of our Defeat, and perhaps had it represented in a worse light (if possible) than it deserves; I have taken this earliest opportunity to give you some account of the Engagement, as it happened within 7 miles of the French Fort on Wednesday, the 9th Inst.—

> When we came there, we were attacked by a party of French and Indians, whose number, I am persuaded, did not exceed three hundred men; while ours consisted of about one thousand three hundred well-armed troops ...

FIGURE 3.11 George Washington, commander in chief of the British forces, recounts an attack by First Nations warriors and the French in a letter to his mother in July 1755. **Analyze:** Why do you think Washington documented this account?

Not all First Nations allied with the French. Most of the Haudenosaunee nations, including the Mohawk, allied with the British during the fighting. These nations were hostile to the French due to French support of their enemy nations, such as the Huron (Wyandot), in the early 1600s. The Seneca tended to remain neutral. The Ojibwe maintained their French alliance until the French started to lose the war. As the war went on, many Ojibwe were killed. The survivors either retreated or joined the British side.

CHANGING MILITARY TACTICS

The Seven Years' War consisted of many battles that took place over a number of years. Forts changed hands, often more than once. As the war went on, both Britain and France began to send more and more troops to North America to fight. The side that controlled a fort controlled the trade, so neither side would give up control of a fort without a fight.

CHANGE IN COMMAND

The first few years of the war went badly for the British. This began to change in 1757. Focused on winning the war in North America, Britain developed a new strategy to take over New France completely.

stronghold a fortified place, or fortress, that is difficult to attack

Britain started sending a lot more money and troops to North America. Britain began to capture key French forts one by one, including Fortress Louisbourg, Fort Frontenac, and Fort Duquesne. The British worked their way toward Québec City. Québec City was the geographic and strategic centre of New France. It was a central point in the fur trade, a shipping centre, and a stopping point for soldiers, traders, and settlers moving west. Geographically, it was a **stronghold**, hard to attack, because of its location high on a cliff overlooking the St. Lawrence River.

As the British gained the upper hand, the French faced more problems. Lieutenant-General Louis-Joseph de Montcalm arrived from France in 1756 to lead the French army. Montcalm was an experienced military commander, but he was familiar only with European-style tactics. The guerilla fighting style used by the French and their First Nations allies horrified him.

Examine the painting in **Figure 3.12**. What changes in French fighting tactics does it show?

FIGURE 3.12 This 1908 painting entitled *Montcalm Leading His Troops at the Plains of Abraham* is by Canadian historical artist C.W. Jefferys. **Analyze:** What can you infer about the artist's perspective of Montcalm from this portrayal?

CHAPTER 3: *The Seven Years' War and the Conquest of New France: 1754–1774*

CREATING AND ANALYZING
A THEMATIC MAP

A map, like a written document, is a communication tool. The features of a map tell a story and give information, just like paragraphs and words do. Maps connect the "what" to the "where." We can use maps in history to tell stories about groups of people or places, and to show patterns and relationships.

A series of battles marked the Seven Years' War. Forts were captured, lost, and recaptured. For example, the French Fortress Louisbourg was captured by the British in 1745, but was returned to the French with the signing of a peace treaty in 1748. Following another battle, it was recaptured by the British in 1758. Look at the data provided in **Figure 3.13**. The chart lists the locations of major battles over forts during the Seven Years' War, as well as who was in possession of each fort before and after each battle.

In this activity, you will create a map that captures the information in **Figure 3.13**. You will then use your map as a secondary source to help you decide whether the British victory was inevitable.

Location of Battle	Date	Outcome of Battle
Fort Necessity (Farmington, PA)	July 3, 1754	French victory
Fort Beauséjour (Aulac, NB)	June 16, 1755	British victory
Fort Duquesne (Pittsburgh, PA)	July 9, 1755	French victory
Fort Bull (Rome, NY)	March 27, 1756	French victory
Fort William Henry (Lake George, NY)	August 9, 1757	French victory
Fort Carillon (Ticonderoga, NY)	July 8, 1758	French victory
Fortress Louisbourg (Louisbourgh, NS)	July 26, 1758	British victory
Fort Frontenac (Kingston, ON)	August 28, 1758	British victory
Fort Duquesne (Pittsburgh, PA)	November 23, 1758	British victory

FIGURE 3.13 This chart includes the major battles over forts during the Seven Years' War. **Red** indicates British possession and **blue** indicates French possession.

HOW TO CREATE A THEMATIC MAP

STEP 1
Choose a base map that includes the location of all the battles listed in **Figure 3.13**. You will need a base map that shows eastern North America. Ensure that your base map has space for a title, legend, scale, and north arrow.

STEP 2
Create a legend for the information you show on your map. You need a symbol to identify the location of a fort and a colour to represent British or French possession. For example, you could use a square to represent the location of a fort. You could use red to represent British possession and blue to represent French possession. A British fort that was captured by the French could be half red and half blue.

STEP 3
Use an atlas or the Internet to determine the location of the forts. (Modern-day locations are given in **Figure 3.13** below each fort.) Place the fort symbol at each location, and neatly write the name of the fort beside the symbol. Also, write the date of each battle beside the fort symbol.

STEP 4
Add a title, a north arrow, and a scale to your map. What information can you gather from your map about the progression of the war? In what year do you see a turning point?

BATTLE FOR THE HEART OF NEW FRANCE

After the expulsion of the Acadians and the capture of Louisbourg, the British closed in on New France. In the summer of 1759, British forces attacked Québec City, but they were not able to destroy the walled town. British General James Wolfe needed a new battle plan. His action plan is illustrated in the engraving in the chapter opener on pages 74 to 75. It shows the three stages of the Battle of the Plains of Abraham (or Battle of Québec): British ships coming down the river at night; British soldiers climbing the cliff to reach the plains; and the actual battle between the British and the French on the plains.

In the early morning hours of September 13, 1759, about 4500 British troops sailed down the St. Lawrence River, fooling the few French guards by speaking French. **Figure 3.14** contains an account by Rear-Admiral Charles Holmes, General Wolfe's naval commander, of some of the other challenges the British faced.

The painting in **Figure 3.15** depicts the second stage of the battle plan. Just before dawn, the British landed in a cove called L'Anse au Foulon, which lay west of Québec City. Led by Wolfe, the troops climbed the 65 m cliff, grabbing roots and vines to pull themselves up. After reaching the top, the British arranged themselves in two lines on the Plains of Abraham. This forced Montcalm and his French troops to come into open space and fight the British head-on. The battle would prove to be the beginning of the end of New France.

Québec City fell to the British in less than one hour. This was an important win for the British, since the French were not able to recover from the loss.

> "The Care of landing the Troops & sustaining them by the Ships, fell to my share—The most hazardous & difficult Task I was ever engaged in—For the distance of the landing place; the impetuosity of the Tide; the darkness of the Night; & the great Chance of exactly hitting the very spot intended, without discovery or alarm, made the whole extremely difficult ..."
>
> — *Rear-Admiral Charles Holmes*

FIGURE 3.14 Excerpt from a letter written on September 18, 1759, by Holmes, General Wolfe's naval commander. **Analyze:** What do you think Holmes might have said to Wolfe when he presented this plan?

FIGURE 3.15 This painting, entitled *Soldiers Climbing the Heights of Abraham* by Peter Jackson (1965), shows the British making the challenging and quiet climb up the cliff to make a surprise attack on the French. **Analyze:** How does the artist depict the challenges the British faced getting to the Plains of Abraham?

FIGURE 3.16 *The Death of General Wolfe* was painted in 1770 by Benjamin West. **Analyze:** Who do you think is surrounding Wolfe in this scene?

LUCK VERSUS GOOD DECISION-MAKING

Despite his victory, Wolfe was killed on the battlefield in the Battle of the Plains of Abraham, along with French General Montcalm. The painting in **Figure 3.16** shows Wolfe's death. This painting is considered famous today. Why do you think Wolfe's death is portrayed in this way?

Sometimes a war is won for reasons that have more to do with luck than good decisions. Read the quote in **Figure 3.17** by historian E.R. Adair. Adair is criticizing General Wolfe's military strategy. If Wolfe's strategy won the war, why would Adair criticize Wolfe?

FRENCH SURRENDER

After Britain's victory on the Plains of Abraham, the war in North America continued for another year. The British moved on from Québec City to take Montréal in 1760. The French had put up a strong fight over the winter, holding off the British troops. Both sides were waiting for more reinforcements (additional supplies and people) to come from Europe by ship. The first ship to come down the St. Lawrence River in the spring belonged to the British. The French surrendered. With the French surrender, the British had gained control of New France. In 1763, the Treaty of Paris was signed to officially end the Seven Years' War between Britain and France and all their respective allies. France had to give up all its main territory claims in North America to the British. If the first ship to come down the St. Lawrence River in the spring of 1760 had belonged to the French instead of the British, do you think New France could have survived?

"[Wolfe's strategy was] Unsound on the basis of any recognized military tactics."

— E.R. Adair, historian

FIGURE 3.17 In a 1936 lecture to the Canadian Historical Society, Adair assesses Wolfe's decision making during the Plains of Abraham campaign. **Analyze:** What do you think Adair means by "unsound"?

CARTOONIST

Kate Beaton (**Figure 3.18A**) has always been interested in history and art. These two passions became the basis for her job as a cartoonist. She earned a history degree from Mount Allison University in New Brunswick and went on to work at a museum in Victoria, British Columbia. She then decided to pursue a career in art through her web comics project *Hark! A Vagrant*. Her work became very popular because of its humorous and clever portrayals of historical figures and events, such as the Battle of the Plains of Abraham (**Figure 3.18B**) and the War of 1812.

Beaton eventually began to create comics for major publications and has now published several books.

Beaton's process involves reading, researching, and keeping a notebook with names of potential cartoon subjects. Selecting who and what to feature in her comics is something that Beaton takes seriously. She likes to draw lesser-known historical figures because "they're always known to somebody." To Beaton, historical topics are particularly great for storytelling. She remains committed to bettering her skills and continuing to educate and entertain people about history through her cartoons.

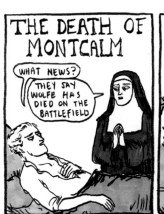

FIGURE 3.18 (A) Cartoonist Kate Beaton. (B) Beaton's comic gives a humorous take on General Montcalm's reaction to General Wolfe's death in the Battle of the Plains of Abraham.

MAKING CONNECTIONS

1. Beaton uses her artistic skills to draw historical cartoons. Name one skill or interest that you have. Brainstorm ways you could use that skill or interest to pursue a history-related career.

2. What challenges do you think a historical cartoonist might face?

CHECK-IN

1. **CAUSE AND CONSEQUENCE** Identify several reasons for the British victory in North America. Rank the reasons in order from greatest to least impact. Justify your ranking.

2. **HISTORICAL SIGNIFICANCE** The Battle of the Plains of Abraham continues to be one of the most significant battles in Canadian history. Why do you think it is seen to be so significant?

3. **EVALUATE AND DRAW CONCLUSIONS** Think of what you have read about the series of events that took place throughout the war. What do you think could have been done differently to change the outcome for the French?

HOW DID THE SEVEN YEARS' WAR
IMPACT FIRST NATIONS?

The British had defeated the French. What did that mean for the First Nations who had fought alongside the French and the British to protect their own interests and ensure their survival? The end of the Seven Years' War led to a series of short- and long-term consequences for First Nations in North America after 1763. Consider the viewpoint of Ojibwe Chief Minavavana in **Figure 3.19**. How widespread do you think this viewpoint was among First Nations after the Seven Years' War?

BROKEN ALLIANCES

Trade between First Nations and the French came to an end after the war. The British limited First Nations' access to European goods, such as weapons, tools, and clothing. They also stopped paying established prices for First Nations goods.

Governor General Jeffery Amherst, who represented the British monarch, did not see the need to pursue goodwill relationships with First Nations, against the advice of many of his officials. While First Nations viewed gift giving as symbolic of peace and friendship, Amherst felt the practice amounted to bribery.

NEW CONFLICTS

First Nations viewed the movement of more and more British officials, soldiers, and settlers into their territories as a threat to their way of life. Their resistance to any takeover became increasingly problematic for the British. **Figure 3.20** is an excerpt from just one of several letters exchanged between Amherst and his officials in 1763, discussing ways to deal with the resistance.

"Englishman! Although you have conquered the French, you have not yet conquered us! We are not your slaves. These lakes, these woods and mountains were left to us by our ancestors. They are our inheritance; and we will part with them to none ...

Englishman, our father, the King of France, employed our young men to make war upon your nation. In this warfare many of them have been killed, and it is our custom to retaliate until such time as the spirits of the slain are satisfied."

— *Ojibwe Chief Minavavana*

FIGURE 3.19 Chief Minavavana spoke these words to British fur trader Alexander Henry in 1761. **Analyze:** Why do you think Chief Minavavana uses the word *father* to refer to the King of France?

"You will Do well to try to Innoculate the Indians, by means of Blankets, as well as to Try Every other Method, that can Serve to Extirpate [destroy] this Execrable [very bad] Race. – I should be very glad your Scheme for Hunting them down by Dogs could take Effect; but England is at too great a Distance to think that at present."

— *Governor General Jeffery Amherst*

FIGURE 3.20 Postscript of a letter from Amherst to Colonel Henry Bouquet, July 1763. European blankets given in trade were thought to be one way First Nations caught the deadly smallpox virus. **Analyze:** Do you think Amherst was a good choice for British leadership in North America after the war?

CHIEF PONTIAC'S REBELLION

After the war, Chief Pontiac led the Odawa Nation. In 1762, a secret council meeting of the Odawa, Ojibwe, Huron (Wyandot), and Potawatomi was held on Chief Pontiac's territory. At this meeting, the nations discussed planning an attack on the British. By 1763, the Senecas had begun sending secret war messages, in the form of wampum war belts, to neighbouring Delaware, Shawnee, and Huron (Wyandot) nations. **Wampum** are beads made of shells, which are used as currency, or money, among some First Nations. Sometimes wampum are beaded together on string to record messages. On May 5, 1763, the Odawa, Potawatomi, and Huron (Wyandot) nations met in council and made a decision to continue to fight against the British. Look at **Figure 3.21**. What do you think Chief Pontiac is telling the others? Read the quote in **Figure 3.22**. What similarities can you identify between Chief Pontiac's speech and Amherst's words in **Figure 3.20**?

PONTIAC TAKING UP THE HATCHET.

FIGURE 3.21 This colour engraving by an unnamed artist from the 1800s shows Chief Pontiac leading a war council in 1763. **Analyze:** What is Chief Pontiac's body language and what could he be holding in his hand?

wampum beads made of shells, used as currency or as a method of recording messages

FIGURE 3.22 Chief Pontiac issued this call to action (translated into English), May 5, 1763. **Analyze:** What reasons does Chief Pontiac give for rising up against the British?

"It is important for us, my brothers, that we exterminate from our lands this nation which seeks only to destroy us. You see as well as I that we can no longer supply our needs, as we have done, from our brothers, the French. The English sell us goods twice as dear as the French do, and their goods do not last ...

When I go to see the English commander and say to him that some of our comrades are dead, instead of bewailing their death, as our French brothers do, he laughs at me and at you. If I ask anything for our sick, he refuses with the reply that he has no use for us. From all this you can well see that they are seeking our ruin. Therefore, my brothers, we must all swear their destruction and wait no longer."

— *Odawa Chief Pontiac*

ATTACK ON FORT MICHILIMACKINAC

In May and June 1763, the allied First Nations led successful attacks on eight British-held posts around Lake Erie and Lake Huron. These attacks, such as the one on Fort Michilimackinac (on the shores of Lake Michigan), often took the British by surprise. At Fort Michilimackinac, hundreds of Odawa, Ojibwe, and their allied nations gathered outside the fort for a game of *bag'gat'iway* (similar to lacrosse). The British understood the cultural significance of this game to First Nations. The game was often played to resolve conflicts and strengthen alliances. It also helped keep warriors in good physical condition for hunting and fighting. Colonists became used to seeing this ball-and-stick game played over large areas with hundreds of participants.

Figure 3.23 contains a first-person account of the attack on the fort. It was recorded by Alexander Henry, a British fur trader. He explains how the First Nations launched a surprise attack on the British and won. **Figure 3.24** shows that a meeting of First Nations took place prior to the attack.

Although Chief Pontiac was successful in convincing many allies to join forces with him, the French refused to join the resistance. They had already suffered many losses to the British and had accepted the terms of surrender. As the violent raids and ambushes went on, many of Chief Pontiac's allies began to abandon him. Chief Pontiac was losing the upper hand. However, the British realized that they must find a way to make peace with the Odawa, Ojibwe, and Potawatomi (Three Fires Confederacy) to prevent further violence. Jeffery Amherst was sent back to Britain and replaced by James Murray, whom the British thought would work more effectively with First Nations.

> "The morning was sultry. A Chipeway came to tell me that his nation was going to play at bag'gat'iway, with the Sacs or Saäkies, another Indian nation, for a high wager. He invited me to witness the sport.... I went to the commandant ... representing that the Indians might possibly have some sinister end in view; but, the commandant only smiled at my suspicions ...
>
> I did not go myself to see the match which was now to be played without the fort.... I heard an Indian war-cry, and a noise of general confusion.
>
> Going instantly to my window, I saw a crowd of Indians, within the fort ...
>
> Amid the slaughter which was raging, I observed many of the Canadian inhabitants of the fort, calmly looking on, neither opposing the Indians, nor suffering injury; and, from this circumstance, I conceived a hope of finding security in their houses ..."
>
> — *Alexander Henry, British fur trader*

FIGURE 3.23 This excerpt is from Henry's account of the First Nations attack on Fort Michilimackinac in 1763. **Analyze:** How was the game of bag'gat'iway an effective cover for the attack?

FIGURE 3.24 This 2003 painting by Robert Griffing is entitled *The Conspiracy—Fort Michilimackinac.* **Analyze:** What do you think this group is discussing?

CHAPTER 3: *The Seven Years' War and the Conquest of New France: 1754–1774*

CREATION OF A ROYAL PROCLAMATION

proclamation an official announcement, statement, or declaration

The British delivered a Royal Proclamation in 1763, outlining new rules for all the people who were living in North America. This **proclamation**, or official statement, announced that the British were taking over the government of Québec. It also clearly reserved land for First Nations and promised hunting and fishing rights. As you read the excerpts from the document in **Figure 3.25**, consider why the British would think that this document would establish peace with First Nations.

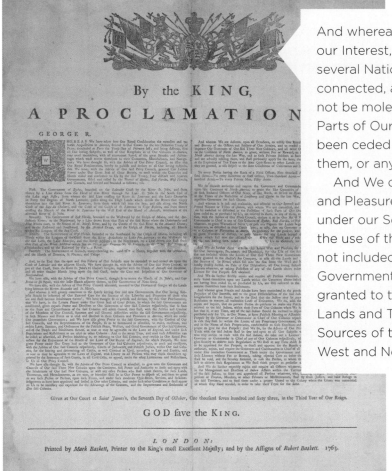

And whereas it is just and reasonable, and essential to our Interest, and the Security of our Colonies, that the several Nations or Tribes of Indians with whom We are connected, and who live under our Protection, should not be molested or disturbed in the Possession of such Parts of Our Dominions and Territories as, not having been ceded to or purchased by Us, are reserved to them, or any of them, as their Hunting Grounds....

And We do further declare it to be Our Royal Will and Pleasure, for the present as aforesaid, to reserve under our Sovereignty, Protection, and Dominion, for the use of the said Indians, all the Lands and Territories not included within the Limits of Our said Three new Governments, or within the Limits of the Territory granted to the Hudson's Bay Company, as also all the Lands and Territories lying to the Westward of the Sources of the Rivers which fall into the Sea from the West and North West as aforesaid.

FIGURE 3.25 This is an image of the Royal Proclamation, 1763. Excerpts from the document are included above. **Analyze:** How might the wording have been different if First Nations had drafted the proclamation?

The Royal Proclamation called for all land deals to be made in public and formalized by a treaty. In the 50 years following the Royal Proclamation, the British government and various First Nations entered into a number of treaties to maintain peace as more and more British settlers moved onto the land. Chief Wabbicommicot of the Mississauga First Nation had a good relationship with the British, who paid tribute to him with gifts. Chief Wabbicommicot encouraged other First Nations in the western Great Lakes region to make peace with the British as well.

TREATY OF NIAGARA

In July 1764, more than 2000 people representing 24 First Nations and members of the British monarchy met to sign the Treaty of Niagara. Under the terms of the Treaty of Niagara, the British promised to keep settlers out of the Ohio Valley. The promises made were symbolized and preserved in the wampum belt shown in **Figure 3.26**. The signing of the Treaty of Niagara became known as The Great Peace of 1764.

FIGURE 3.26 The 1764 Treaty of Niagara wampum belt preserves Britain's promise to give annual gifts, in keeping with First Nations tradition, "for as long as the sun shone, and the grass grew, and the British wore red coats." **Analyze:** How would you interpret the symbols in the belt?

A NEW LEGAL FOUNDATION

The principles of the Royal Proclamation and the agreements woven into the Treaty of Niagara wampum belt are central to negotiations between First Nations and the Government of Canada today. Many consider these artifacts to be among Canada's first constitutional documents to guarantee Aboriginal rights. Protests like the one shown in **Figure 3.27** were held across Canada starting in November 2012 to remind Canadians of agreements made hundreds of years ago.

FIGURE 3.27 On December 19, 2012, protesters in London, Ontario, marched in support of the Canada-wide Idle No More movement. **Analyze:** What is the main message of this photo?

CHECK-**IN**

1. **CAUSE AND CONSEQUENCE** Why did the British need to address First Nations issues after winning the Seven Years' War?

2. **HISTORICAL SIGNIFICANCE** What is the significance of the 1764 Treaty of Niagara for First Nations? What is its significance for Canada today?

3. **INTERPRET AND ANALYZE** What was Chief Pontiac's role in redefining relationships between Europeans and First Nations in North America?

HOW DID THE SEVEN YEARS' WAR
IMPACT THE FRENCH?

The Seven Years' War still stirs strong emotions in Québec, even 250 years later. In the chapter opener, "the War of Conquest" was listed as another name for the Seven Years' War. That is because, in Québec, the Seven Years' War is seen as a hostile takeover of the French by a foreign power. **Figure 3.28** shows a cannonball, believed to be from 1759, stuck in a tree on Rue St. Louis in Québec City. Imagine living in New France at the time of the British takeover. How might you have felt?

TERMS OF FRENCH SURRENDER

The French proposed specific conditions of their surrender in a document called Articles of Capitulation, which they presented to the British. These conditions were intended to protect the future of all residents of New France, including the Canadiens, Acadians, and First Nations. **Figure 3.29** shows the occupation of Québec by British soldiers. What do you think would be important to the French as they negotiated their surrender?

FIGURE 3.28 This 1759 cannonball remains stuck in a tree in Québec City. **Analyze:** What might the cannonball symbolize for the people who live in Québec today?

FIGURE 3.29 This painting, entitled *View of the Cathedral, Jesuits College, and Recollect Friars Church, Quebec City, 1761*, is by British naval officer Richard Short and believed to have been painted in 1761 while he was stationed in Québec. **Analyze:** What does this image tell you about the presence of the British in Québec?

LIFE UNDER BRITISH RULE

The British agreed to the terms outlined in the Articles of Capitulation. The conditions were related to the treatment of French soldiers and citizens, property rights, and religion. The British put General James Murray in charge of making sure that his soldiers obeyed this document as they went about the business of rebuilding Québec City and ruling the French.

In the years immediately following the war, the British had to decide how to govern a colony where most of the people were French-speaking and Roman Catholic. The British had several options, which are listed in **Figure 3.30**.

Which aspects of French daily life may have changed after the war?

Option	Explanation
expulsion	Force the French to leave.
preservation	Allow the French to keep their laws, language, and religion; allow First Nations to stay on lands reserved for them.
isolation	Create separate areas for French, British, and First Nations to live, where they could have their own governments, religions, and languages.
assimilation	Force the French and First Nations to become British subjects and enforce British laws, language, customs, and religion.
biculturalism	Allow both British and French cultures to co-exist.

FIGURE 3.30 British options for dealing with the French and First Nations are listed here. **Analyze:** Which option would have been the best for the peace of all involved?

With the Royal Proclamation of 1763, the British government began to assert its power over the French by creating new rules for them to live by. This meant that the Catholic Church lost a lot of its power to govern the people and that new British laws replaced French laws. French-speaking Catholics were not allowed to hold positions of power within the government. The British planned to move a great number of British settlers into the area to outnumber the French and make them fit into, or **assimilate** to, the British way of life. Many of the wealthy and educated French people decided to leave for other areas, which left openings for the British to take over businesses, industries, and the fur trade.

assimilate to bring into conformity or adapt to the customs and attitudes of a group

OATH OF ALLEGIANCE

To keep control, the British wanted the French to swear an oath of allegiance to the King of England. This oath was a public declaration of loyalty to the British King. By swearing the oath, the French were promising to be good and loyal citizens and follow the new British rules.

As part of their oath of allegiance, anyone who wanted to hold a position of power within the government had to swear an oath accepting the Protestant faith. This was part of the 1678 *Test Act* in Britain, which was created to ban Catholics from the government. Catholics would have to deny key aspects of their faith in order to hold office. French Catholics in North America were unwilling to do this and so they were barred from important positions of power.

CAUSE AND CONSEQUENCE

All events, both past and present, have causes and consequences. For example, imagine that you did not do a homework assignment. The cause may have been that you decided to hang out at a friend's place after school instead, or perhaps you simply forgot. The consequence may be that your teacher will not accept a late assignment. A further consequence will be that your class grade falls.

Which of these consequences were intended (planned)? Which were unintended (unplanned)? You may have *planned* on meeting your friend after school. But your class grade falling because you failed to hand in one assignment was *unplanned*. Consequences can also be short term or long term. Not all consequences are equally important over time. If missing handing in one assignment was a one-time event, it likely has only short-term consequences.

When you think about the causes and consequences of a historical event, you can ask the following questions:
- What were the causes of the event?
- Who were the people who influenced the event?
- What were the social, political, or economic conditions that influenced the event?
- What were the ideas and beliefs that influenced the event?
- What were the consequences of the event?
- What were the intended and unintended consequences of the event?

CASE STUDY: THE CONQUEST

Following their victory in the Battle of the Plains of Abraham in 1759, British soldiers took control of Québec City and the rest of New France. By 1763, 70 000 Canadiens were living under British rule.

Examine some of the consequences of what many people living in Québec today refer to as "the Conquest."

Consequence: By 1760, many homes in Québec City had been burned down and all the public buildings needed repair. Examine the evidence shown in **Figures 3.31** and **3.32**. What would it be like to live in the aftermath of a war?

Consequence: The British were English-speaking Protestants, which set them apart from the French-speaking Catholics of New France. The two groups had different laws and customs. The British tried to force the French to assimilate to the British way of life and swear an oath of allegiance to the King of England.

> "During one night, upwards of fifty of the best houses in the Lower Town were destroyed. The vaults containing merchandise and many precious articles, did not escape the effects of the artillery."
>
> — *Nun (unnamed)*

FIGURE 3.32 An unnamed nun from the General Hospital of Québec described the aftermath of the war. The exact date is unknown. **Analyze:** What is she saying about the conditions in Québec City?

> "In Quebec's popular lore, the Battle of the Plains of Abraham is considered the end of francophone autonomy [independence] in North America and the start of British dominance [power]. Canada's heritage minister said he's disappointed the re-enactment was cancelled due to threats from inside the separatist movement. 'That people threatened violence and it resulted in an event of this magnitude being cancelled I think is a real disappointment.'"
>
> — Toronto Star

FIGURE 3.33 This excerpt is from the *Toronto Star* newspaper (online), February 17, 2009. **Analyze:** Why was the re-enactment cancelled?

FIGURE 3.31 *A View of the Bishop's House with the Ruins* was painted in 1761 by British naval officer Richard Short. **Analyze:** What does the painting tell you about conditions in Québec City in 1761?

Consequence: In 2009, the National Battlefields Commission planned a 250th anniversary commemoration of the Battle of the Plains of Abraham. The plan called for 2000 people in period clothing and uniforms to re-enact the events. However, threats from separatists (people who want Québec to be a country separate from Canada) and opposition from francophone historians led to the cancellation of the event. What does **Figure 3.33** tell you about the long-term consequences of the Conquest?

TRY IT

1. What were the intended and unintended consequences of the Conquest? What were the short- and long-term consequences?
2. The Conquest led to Canada becoming a bilingual country. What might British leadership in the 1760s have thought about this unintended consequence?

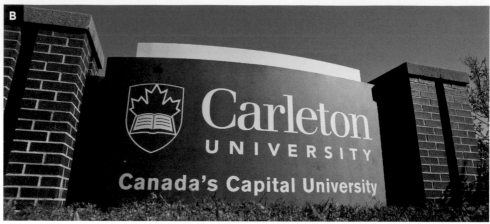

FIGURE 3.34 (A) A portrait of Sir Guy Carleton painted in 1923 is shown here. (B) Carleton University in Ottawa, Ontario, is named after him. **Analyze:** Why was the university named in honour of Sir Guy Carleton?

A NEW ORDER

By 1770, the French people understood that their religion, language, and way of life were still under attack as the British continued their attempts at assimilation.

Sir Guy Carleton (**Figure 3.34A**) replaced James Murray and became Governor of Québec in 1768. Since the French were unhappy with British institutions, Carleton was afraid that they might fight with the enemy if Britain was dragged into another war, which seemed likely. Some settlers in the British colonies were becoming even more unhappy with British rule than the French. Some of the British colonies concluded that it would be better to be an independent country than to continue as part of the British Empire. This made it essential for Carleton to secure the loyalty of the French.

Carleton decided to appoint some Canadiens to government positions and to support the Catholic Church, which played such a central role in their social and religious life. He also believed that many of the French laws relating to civilian life should be restored. In 1770, Carleton travelled to London, England, where he spent four years trying to convince the British government to reform the laws to preserve harmony in the colony. Ontario's Carleton University (**Figure 3.34B**), founded in 1942, is named after Sir Guy Carleton.

QUÉBEC ACT, 1774

Carleton's efforts paid off. The British government passed the *Québec Act, 1774,* which returned to the French many of the rights they had lost with the Royal Proclamation. These rights included the following:

- guarantee of religious freedom, which meant that Catholics would be allowed to practise their religion even under a Protestant government

- allowance for Catholics to hold political positions without giving up their religion

- restoration of the French civil law system (relating to the private rights of individuals), while maintaining British criminal law

- restoration of the seigneurial system of land ownership and use

- expansion of French territory, but into lands that were established for First Nations use in the Royal Proclamation of 1763

> Which of these rights do you think would be the most significant to the Canadiens?

The *Québec Act, 1774* still met with opposition. Many Canadiens wanted the government to consist of elected rather than appointed officials. However, the governor and his council continued to rule. Examine the maps in **Figure 3.35**. Describe how the *Québec Act, 1774* changed the boundaries.

Boundaries of the Royal Proclamation, 1763

Québec Act, 1774

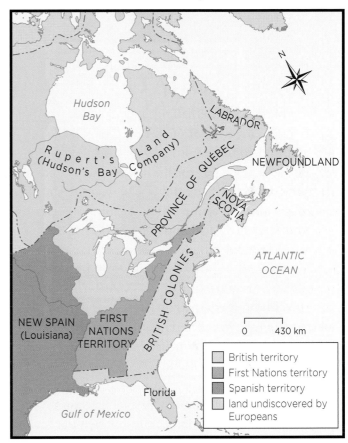

FIGURE 3.35 The map on the left shows how the British divided the land as a result of the Royal Proclamation of 1763. The map on the right shows the new boundaries that the British created with the *Québec Act, 1774*. **Analyze:** For which groups were the land changes most significant?

CHECK-**IN**

1. **CAUSE AND CONSEQUENCE** What were the economic, political, and cultural consequences of the Seven Years' War for the French? Which were intended consequences, and which were unintended?

2. **INTERPRET AND ANALYZE** Review the primary source evidence that was included in this section. What types of artifacts left from the war can help us understand life at the time of the conflict? Give examples. How do these artifacts affect the way that historians learn about this time period?

3. **HISTORICAL PERSPECTIVE** When important decisions were being made about North America, whose voices were heard? Whose voices were not heard? How does this affect what is discussed during decision making?

4. **COMMUNICATE** Create a series of short postings for a media website in the role of one of the missing voices you identified in question 3. Work with a partner to develop an appropriate word or phrase to identify your postings.

CHAPTER 3: *The Seven Years' War and the Conquest of New France: 1754–1774*

WHAT WAS THE IMPACT OF THE SEVEN YEARS' WAR ON NORTH AMERICA?

LEARNING GOALS

As you worked through this chapter, you had opportunities to

- analyze the causes of conflict among the French, the British, and First Nations in North America during the Seven Years' War
- consider the significance of different key people and events throughout the war
- understand the consequences of the war and the conquest on different groups of people
- create and analyze maps related to the Seven Years' War

In this chapter, you learned how the British took control of North America as a result of the Seven Years' War. You also read about some of the people involved in the war and the events that contributed to the British victory. The conquest took years of hard battles, unfolding between 1756 and 1763 and resulting in the deaths of thousands of British, French, and First Nations. Based on what you have read, how would you answer the following question: What was the impact of the Seven Years' War on North America?

Summarize Your Learning

Now that you have completed Chapter 3, you are ready to answer the Chapter Big Question:

What was the impact of the Seven Years' War on North America? Select one of the following tasks to summarize your learning:

- Outline some of the reasons the conquest of North America was challenging for the British. What led to their victory? Create a graphic timeline or flow chart to highlight your main ideas.
- Jot down ideas for a discussion about the following statement: The roots of multiculturalism in Canada today can be traced back to compromises made during and after the Seven Years' War. Think about how you can use the primary source evidence included in this chapter to support your opinion.

APPLY **YOUR LEARNING**

1. `HISTORICAL PERSPECTIVE` Whose perspectives were represented in this chapter? Whose perspectives were not represented or under-represented? Why do you think there were differences in representation? Write a short speech or rant from the perspective of someone who would have liked his or her experiences during the Seven Years' War to be included in this chapter.

2. `FORMULATE QUESTIONS` What questions do you still have about the Seven Years' War? Of the people mentioned throughout this chapter, who would you want to interview to obtain answers to your questions?

3. `CAUSE AND CONSEQUENCE` Fighting back against the British led to both positive and negative consequences for the French and First Nations. Create a t-chart to compare these consequences.

4. `EVALUATE AND DRAW CONCLUSIONS` Refer to the t-chart you completed for question 3. Do you think fighting back was worthwhile for the French or First Nations? Create a political cartoon, poster, brochure, radio commercial, or social media campaign that would convince people to fight against the British during the Seven Years' War.

5. `INTERPRET AND ANALYZE` Choose one of the topics covered in this chapter. Research other sources that have information about this topic. How does the research add to your understanding of the Seven Years' War?

6. `CONTINUITY AND CHANGE` It is sometimes easier to see all the things that changed as a result of war, rather than the things that stayed the same. What aspects of life in New France would have stayed the same for the people living there throughout and after the war?

7. `HISTORICAL SIGNIFICANCE` Which individuals stand out in this chapter as being historically significant? Why do you think we have chosen to remember them? What makes someone historically significant? Design a trading card for someone you think is most significant to this time period in Canadian history. Include a full profile of the person (important details, highlights from the person's career or life), and explain why this person is worth remembering.

8. `CONTINUITY AND CHANGE` What issues raised in the Seven Years' War continue to be important to people in Canada today? Why?

UNIT 1 CHALLENGE CHECK-IN

Record your responses to these questions in your log book.

1. Review the Focus On: Cause and Consequence feature on pages 96 to 97. Using the criteria provided, identify the short-term and long-term consequences of the Seven Years' War. What sources provide the best evidence of these consequences? What other types of sources would be useful?

2. A turning point can be an event or period in time when there is a significant change in how a situation is progressing. What was the turning point in the Seven Years' War? What sources in the chapter can you use to support your answer?

3. What groups or individuals were significant during this time period? Why? Which groups benefited, and which groups did not?

4. Review the description of the Unit 1 Challenge on pages 18 to 19 and the notes you made in your log book for Chapters 1 and 2. Do you see any connections between your notes and what you have just learned in Chapter 3? Has your thinking changed? Add your reflections to your log book.

LOYALISTS
IN BRITISH NORTH AMERICA: 1775–1800

HOW DID THE LOYALIST MIGRATION AFFECT BRITISH NORTH AMERICA?

LEARNING GOALS

As you work through this chapter, you will
- examine the various causes of the Loyalist migration
- identify the various groups that made up the Loyalists and examine their experiences as immigrants
- determine whether the Loyalist migration created any significant political, social, or economic changes
- analyze and contextualize images

What is loyalty, and what happens when it is challenged? Loyalty is the ability to stay committed to someone or something. Starting in the 1770s, a group of people referred to as *Loyalists* began arriving in British North America in large numbers. Loyalists were settlers from the Thirteen Colonies, the colonies that formed the original United States of America after the 1775 American Revolution. Loyalists got their name because they stayed loyal to Britain during the American Revolution.

Some Loyalists were wealthy, but many were soldiers, farmers, shopkeepers, and tradespeople. They came from different backgrounds and places. Some had African, English, Irish, or Scottish backgrounds. They arrived in an unfamiliar land, often bringing only what they were able to carry with them. This painting is entitled *Maritime Landings 1783*. It was created by K. Darling in 1982 and depicts the arrival of Loyalists in New Brunswick around 1783. Do you think this is an accurate depiction of the migration? What details in the painting support your opinion?

As you explore this chapter, you will discover why the Loyalists left the Thirteen Colonies. You will also understand what challenges the Loyalists faced and how they affected the people living in what we today know as Canada.

WHAT CAUSED THE
MASS MIGRATION OF LOYALISTS?

Have you ever moved to a different city or country? It can be very challenging to start a new life somewhere. There are new places to get used to and new friends to make. There is often a feeling of sadness when leaving something behind. The settlers who came to what became Canada from the **Thirteen Colonies**, the 13 British colonies on North America's East Coast, experienced many of the same challenges.

In the early 1770s, the Thirteen Colonies were under British control. Some settlers living there wanted to separate from Britain, while others wanted to remain under British control. The **Loyalists** were settlers who were loyal to Britain and supported British rule. In 1775, the American Revolution broke out between the British and the colonists who opposed their rule. Many Loyalists chose or were forced to leave the Thirteen Colonies and settle elsewhere. This migration increased throughout the war and after the war ended. What might some aspects of the migration have looked like? Examine **Figure 4.1**, which depicts a Loyalist encampment, or campsite, and Loyalist settlers near Prescott, Ontario. Can you predict what challenges the Loyalists would have faced when they first arrived at this encampment?

Thirteen Colonies the 13 British colonies on the east coast of North America, south of Nova Scotia, which eventually joined together to form the United States of America

Loyalist a person living in the Thirteen Colonies who remained loyal to Britain during the American Revolution

FIGURE 4.1 This watercolour entitled *Encampment of the Loyalists in Johnstown, a new settlement on the banks of the River St. Lawrence in Canada West* was originally painted by James Peachey on June 6, 1784. This is a reproduction by J.R. Simpson in 1925. **Analyze:** How do you think these Loyalists felt arriving in this type of settlement?

Encampment of the Loyalists at Johnston, a New Settlement, on the Banks of the River St. Laurence in Canada, taken June 6th 1784.
taken from A marked in the Plan.

PRE-LOYALISTS: NEW ENGLAND PLANTERS

New England a region in present-day northeastern United States, made up of the states of Connecticut, Maine, Massachusetts, New Hampshire, Rhode Island, and Vermont

Planter a British settler (colonist) from New England who migrated to Atlantic Canada between 1759 and 1774

Even before the American Revolution, settlers loyal to Britain were migrating north to the land known today as Canada. After the fall of Louisbourg and the Acadian Expulsion, many farms and lands were available in Nova Scotia, which included present-day New Brunswick. In the late autumn of 1758, the British government began posting newspaper ads throughout **New England**, an area located today in the northeastern United States. These ads targeted **Planters**, New England colonists who had "planted" a new England on North America's Atlantic coast. Read the ad in **Figure 4.2**. Why do you think the British government was willing to offer land to the Planters instead of First Nations or Canadiens?

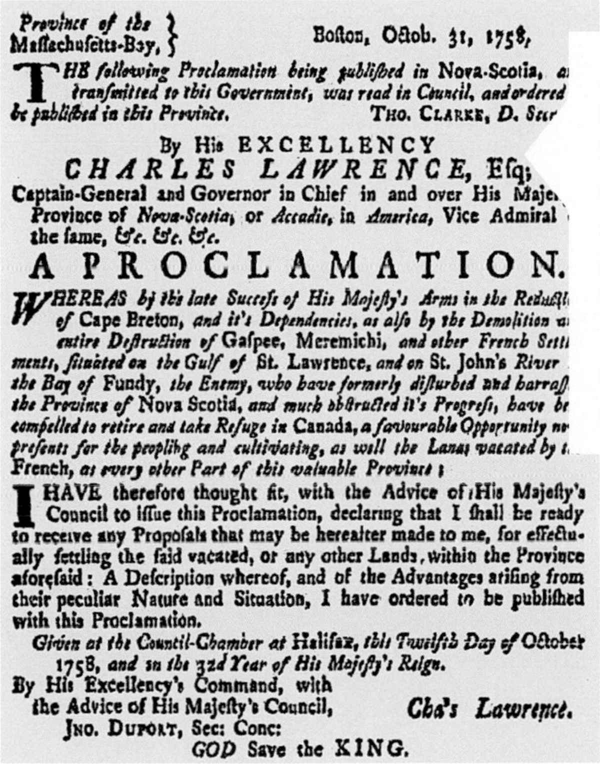

Province of the Maſſachuſetts-Bay, } Boſton, Octob. 31, 1758,

THE *following Proclamation being publiſhed in* Nova-Scotia, *a* *tranſmitted to this Government, was read in Council, and ordered be publiſhed in this Province.* Tho. Clarke, *D. Secr*

By His EXCELLENCY
CHARLES LAWRENCE, Eſq;
Captain-General and Governor in Chief in and over His Maje Province of *Nova-Scotia,* or *Accadie,* in *America,* Vice Admiral the ſame, &c. &c. &c.

A PROCLAMATION.

WHEREAS by the late Succeſs of His Majeſty's Arms in the Reducti of Cape Breton, *and it's Dependencies, as alſo by the Demolition a entire Deſtruction of* Gaſpee, Meremichi, *and other French Setti ments, ſituated on the Gulf of* St. Lawrence, *and on* St. John's *River the Bay of* Fundy, *the Enemy, who have formerly diſturbed and harraſ the Province of* Nova Scotia, *and much obſtructed it's Progreſs, have be compelled to retire and take Refuge in* Canada, *a favourable Opportunity no preſents for the peopling and cultivating, as well the Lands vacated by t* French, *as every other Part of this valuable Province;*

I HAVE therefore thought fit, with the Advice of His Majeſty's Council to iſſue this Proclamation, declaring that I ſhall be ready to receive any Propoſals that may be hereafter made to me, for effectually ſettling the ſaid vacated, or any other Lands, within the Province aforeſaid: A Deſcription whereof, and of the Advantages ariſing from their peculiar Nature and Situation, I have ordered to be publiſhed with this Proclamation.

Given at the Council-Chamber at Halifax, *this Twelfth Day of* October 1758, *and in the 32d Year of His Majeſty's Reign.*

By His Excellency's Command, with the Advice of His Majeſty's Council,
Jno. Duport, Sec: Conc: *Cha's Lawrence.*

GOD Save the KING.

... a favourable Opportunity now presents for the peopling and cultivating, as well the Lands vacated by the French, as every other Part of this valuable Province ... upwards of One Hundred Thousand Acres of Internal Plow Lands, producing Wheat, Rye, Barley, Oats, Hemp, Flax, &c. These have been cultivated for more than a Hundred Years past, and never fail of Crops, nor need manuring....

FIGURE 4.2 This proclamation was posted in the *Boston Evening Post* in October 1758, shortly after the fall of Louisbourg. **Analyze:** What skills would the Planters need to live successfully on these new lands?

PURSUING LAND OWNERSHIP

pull factor a social, political, economic, or environmental benefit that draws migrants to an area

push factor a social, political, economic, or environmental force that drives migrants out of an area

land grant an area of land given by the government in exchange for settling the land

The chance to own land was the main **pull factor**, or draw, for the Planters. Land ownership gave people more economic advantages in life. For example, they could pass down land to their children. What was the main **push factor**, or force that drives away, behind the Planter migration? New England had become crowded, and settlers were eager to acquire more land. To take advantage of the available **land grants**, land given to settlers by the government, the Planters had to endure a difficult journey. They also had to resist threats from the French and their First Nations allies. Between 1760 and 1768, approximately 8000 Planters accepted the government's offer of land in Nova Scotia and what would become New Brunswick. The British government was eager to have loyal Protestant settlers take over these lands in order to increase Britain's territory and wealth. The Planters were among the first English-speaking immigrants. They built communities, loyal to Britain, all over the Maritimes.

THE AMERICAN REVOLUTION

After the end of the Seven Years' War in 1763, tensions grew between some British colonists and the British government. To cover the high costs of supporting the colonies, the British government began to charge colonists taxes on goods from Britain, such as sugar and stamps. Many colonists protested having to pay more taxes.

Some colonists felt that the British government was making decisions that affected their lives without consulting them first. Many colonists refused to obey laws that were created without their input. They wanted their voices and rights to be represented in the British government—they wanted **representation**. Their motto became "no taxation without representation."

representation the act of speaking or acting on behalf of an individual or group

> How do you think the British government would have reacted to this event?

THE BOSTON TEA PARTY

On December 16, 1773, British ships carrying tea from the East India Company arrived in the Boston harbour. A group of protestors, some disguised as First Nations people, seized the ships and dumped all the tea into the water. This event has become known as the Boston Tea Party. Examine **Figure 4.3**. Why do you think the colonists are dumping the tea?

Earlier that year, on April 27, 1773, the British government introduced the Tea Act. The Tea Act allowed only the British tea company, the East India Company, to pay lower taxes on tea. This meant that the company could sell tea to the colonies at lower prices. Colonial tea merchants could not compete with these lower prices. When the British ships arrived in Boston in December, stocked with British tea, the colonists decided to protest. The Boston Tea Party triggered a series of events that led to the start of the American Revolution in 1775.

FIGURE 4.3 This is an 1846 lithograph by Nathaniel Currier entitled *The Destruction of Tea at Boston Harbor*. A lithograph is a print that is a copy of an original painting. **Analyze:** Why do you think the protestors disguised themselves as First Nations people?

LOYALISTS VERSUS PATRIOTS

Patriot a person living in the Thirteen Colonies who supported the rebellion against Britain during the American Revolution

treason the act of betraying one's country

The settlers in the Thirteen Colonies were deeply divided over their loyalty to Britain. Many were tired of paying taxes to the faraway British King and getting little in return. Some settlers wanted to break free from Britain and create their own country. They called themselves **Patriots**. The British government saw the Patriots as rebels, guilty of **treason**, or betrayal. On the other hand, Loyalists wanted to remain British citizens because they did not believe the Patriots could create a strong country. Some believed that the King was the true leader, while others wanted to keep their business and political ties with Britain. In addition, there were settlers who wanted to stay neutral so that they could avoid conflict. **Figure 4.4A** is a poster that was used to convince people to join the Patriots. **Figure 4.4B** is a poster that was used to recruit colonists for the Loyalists. What elements in each poster were used to catch people's attention?

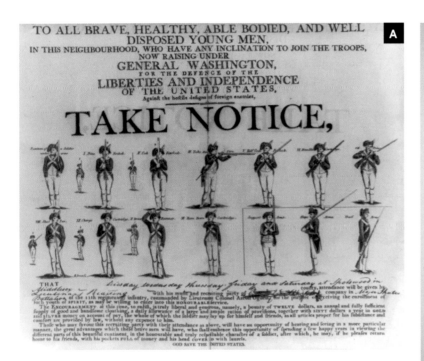

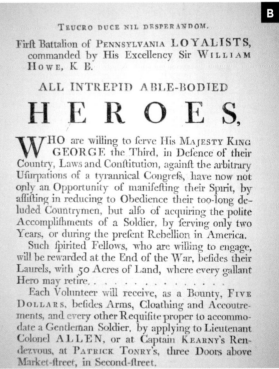

FIGURE 4.4 These posters were used to recruit soldiers for the Patriot cause (A) and the Loyalist cause (B) in 1775. **Analyze:** Which poster do you think is more convincing, and why?

British North America the remaining British colonies in North America, north of the United States in what is known as Canada today, after the American Revolution ended in 1783

The American Revolution began in 1775, when tensions between the Patriots and the Loyalists reached a tipping point. Battles raged throughout the Thirteen Colonies for six years, until the Patriots won a decisive victory at Yorktown, Virginia, in 1781. In 1783, the war officially ended with the Treaty of Paris, in which the British gave up their control of the Thirteen Colonies to the Patriot forces. This is how the United States of America became an independent country and the lands to the north of the United States became known as **British North America**.

LOYALISTS LIVING IN FEAR

The American Revolution divided the continent and pitted neighbour against neighbour. After Britain's defeat, life in the Thirteen Colonies became even more difficult for Loyalists. Their loyalty to Britain was challenged by the Patriot victors, who harassed and attacked them. The Loyalists also risked having their property taken away even before the war officially broke out. Loyalists who spoke publicly about their loyalty to the King risked public humiliation. A popular way of attacking Loyalists was tarring and feathering—pouring hot tar over them and then covering them in feathers. Examine **Figure 4.5**, which is a political cartoon published by a British newspaper. In the cartoon, a tax collector is being tarred and feathered by Bostonian Patriots, and also forced to drink tea, all under a copy of the *Stamp Act* (a tax on printed paper) tacked to a tree. Why do you think public humiliation was a popular way to harass Loyalists?

FIGURE 4.5 This political cartoon was published in a British newspaper in 1774. **Analyze:** What does this cartoon suggest Britain's opinion of the Patriots was at this time?

WOMEN LEFT BEHIND

How did John Munro's beliefs and values influence his decisions?

Despite living in such hostile conditions, Loyalists still had to provide for and protect their families. Consider the perspective of Loyalist women. Many were left behind when their Loyalist husbands fled the Thirteen Colonies during the war. One of these women was Mary Munro, who lived in Vermont. Her husband, John, had been recruiting for the Loyalists. The Patriots had sentenced him to death, so John had to flee Vermont. Mary and her eight children were left behind, vulnerable to violence and the risk of having their home seized by Patriots. Read **Figure 4.6**, which is an excerpt from a letter written by Mary to John. How was she feeling in this situation?

> "For heavens sake, my dear Mr. Munro, send me some relief by the first safe hand. Is there no possibility of your sending for us? If there is no method fallen upon we shall perish [die], for you can have no idea of our sufferings here; Let me once more intreat [beg] you to try every method to save your family; my heart is so full it is ready to break; adieu my Dearest John, may God Almighty bless preserve and protect you, that we may live to see each other is the constant prayer of your affectionate tho' afflicted [distressed] wife ..."
>
> — *Mary Munro, Loyalist*

FIGURE 4.6 This excerpt is from an undated letter written sometime between 1777 and 1778 by Munro to her husband John. **Analyze:** What does Mary say will happen to her and the children if they stay in Vermont?

Now read **Figure 4.7**, an excerpt from the diary of a Scottish woman named Janet Schaw who was visiting her brother in North Carolina during the same period. Compare this excerpt with **Figure 4.6**. What do these two excerpts suggest about how Loyalists were being treated? If you were a Loyalist at that time, would you have stayed in the Thirteen Colonies and become a Patriot? Or would you have left everything behind for the chance of a better life elsewhere?

> "At present the martial law stands thus: An officer or committeeman enters a plantation with his posse. The alternative is proposed. Agree to join us [Patriots] and your persons and properties are safe ... if you refuse, we are directly to cut up your corn, shoot your pigs, burn your houses, seize your Negroes and perhaps tar and feather yourself. Not to choose the first requires more courage than they are possessed of, and I believe this method has seldom failed with the lower sort."
>
> — *Janet Schaw, Scottish woman*

FIGURE 4.7 This is an entry from the diary of Schaw in June 1775. *Martial law* refers to when ordinary law is suspended and the military takes control of the government. The quote uses the term *Negroes*, which was common at that time. Today, some people find it offensive so a preferred and more commonly used term is *Black people*. **Analyze:** To whom do you think Schaw is referring when she says "the lower sort"?

REWARDING LOYALTY

Loyalists had many strong reasons for wanting to leave their land. British North America had many pull factors that attracted the Loyalists. Since the British government still had control over British North America, Loyalists were invited to find safety there. Most Loyalists, especially those who had fought for the British, were offered free land, tools, and seeds to grow crops. Britain even provided transportation for many Loyalists, evacuating large groups by ships out of places such as the New York harbour.

Of the over 70 000 Loyalists who fled the Thirteen Colonies, about 50 000 travelled north to British North America. More than half of these Loyalists went to Nova Scotia. Why do you think so many Loyalists fled to Nova Scotia? The decision to leave was often made very quickly, sometimes just ahead of Patriots arriving at their door. One such scene is depicted in **Figure 4.8**. Like many, these Loyalists left their home to find safety in British North America. The rest of the American Loyalists either fled south or returned to Britain.

BLACK LOYALISTS

During the American Revolution, the British promised freedom for enslaved Black people. They also promised them land and equal rights if they deserted their Patriot masters and joined the Loyalists. About 3000 Black Loyalists moved to Nova Scotia on the strength of this promise. Look at **Figure 4.9**, which shows a family of Black Loyalists travelling by wagon cart in Nova Scotia. What hopes and expectations might this family have had when they left the Thirteen Colonies for Nova Scotia? Later in this chapter, you will examine whether or not Black Loyalists were rewarded fairly for their loyalty.

FIGURE 4.8 This painting, entitled *Tory Refugees on Their Way to Canada* by Howard Pyle, was created in 1901, long after the actual event. Loyalists were often called "Tories" by the Patriots. **Analyze:** Look closely at the foreground and background. What story is told by the details in each?

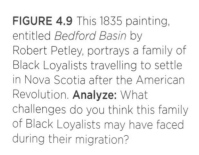

FIGURE 4.9 This 1835 painting, entitled *Bedford Basin* by Robert Petley, portrays a family of Black Loyalists travelling to settle in Nova Scotia after the American Revolution. **Analyze:** What challenges do you think this family of Black Loyalists may have faced during their migration?

FIGURE 4.10 This 1786 portrait by Gilbert Stuart depicts Thayendanegea, also known as Joseph Brant. **Analyze:** Based on this portrait, what characteristics do you think Thayendanegea had?

FIGURE 4.11 This excerpt is from the 1784 Haldimand Proclamation, which granted land to the Haudenosaunee refugees. **Analyze:** What do you think is the British government's perspective of the Haudenosaunee?

HAUDENOSAUNEE LOYALISTS

The Haudenosaunee Six Nations were divided by the war. Most of the Haudenosaunee were British allies, but some had sided with the Patriots. When the British government gave up all of its land in the Thirteen Colonies, this included the Haudenosaunee territory south of the Great Lakes. Mohawk leaders John Deseronto and Thayendanegea, also known as Joseph Brant, met with Governor-in-Chief Frederick Haldimand to discuss their territory losses. **Figure 4.10** shows a portrait of Thayendanegea.

Read the quote in **Figure 4.11** from Haldimand in 1784, addressing the issue of lost land. Based on Haldimand's words, what kind of relationship do you think he had with the Haudenosaunee? To reward the Haudenosaunee's loyalty, the British government purchased a tract, or a large area of land, from the Mississauga and Ojibwe peoples. Many First Nations families settled on this land, which is often called the Haldimand tract.

> "I have at the earnest desire of many of these His Majesty's faithful Allies purchased a tract of land from the Indians situated between the Lakes Ontario, Erie and Huron and I do hereby in His Majesty's name authorize and permit the said Mohawk Nation and such others of the Six Nation Indians as wish to settle in that quarter to take possession of and settle upon the Banks of the River commonly called Ours [Ouse] or Grand River, running into Lake Erie, allotting to them for that purpose six miles deep from each side of the river beginning at Lake Erie and extending in that proportion to the head of the said river, which them and their posterity are to enjoy for ever."
>
> — *Haldimand Proclamation*

CHECK-**IN**

1. **HISTORICAL PERSPECTIVE** The Loyalists were a diverse group of individuals from the Thirteen Colonies. Explain possible reasons why they remained loyal to Britain.

2. **INTERPRET AND ANALYZE** Examine the evidence for the push and pull factors that drove the Loyalists to British North America. Which factors do you think had a greater impact?

3. **EVALUATE AND DRAW CONCLUSIONS** Based on the evidence in this section, do you think the Loyalists who moved to British North America made the right decision? Explain why, or why not.

4. **COMMUNICATE** Design an advertisement to attract Loyalist settlers to British North America. What text and design elements will you use to appeal to Loyalists?

WHAT CHALLENGES DID THE LOYALISTS FACE IN THEIR NEW LAND?

The thousands of Loyalists who arrived in the Maritimes and Québec brought with them hopes for a good life in British North America. Many families left behind thriving farms and became refugees, on the promise of freedom and new land. They soon found out that rebuilding their lives in British North America would bring unexpected challenges.

AN UNTAMED NEW LAND

The journey to British North America was long and difficult for many of the Loyalist refugees. Loyalist Sarah Frost left New York by ship for Nova Scotia in the spring of 1783. She and her family lived on the crowded ship for more than 30 days before finally reaching the banks of present-day New Brunswick. Her diary tells of an uncomfortable trip on an overcrowded ship where many people were ill. Upon landing in British North America, Frost set eyes on a rough and unsettled land. Read an excerpt from her diary in **Figure 4.12**. What is Frost's first impression of her new home?

Land had to be divided up into lots before it could be given to the arriving Loyalists. The British government sent out surveyors to divide up the land. **Figure 4.13** shows surveyors at work near the old Fort Frontenac. What do you think Loyalist settlers had to do to make a home out of this land?

"It is now afternoon and I have been on shore. It is I think the roughest land I ever saw. It beats 'Shortrocks' [in Stamford]. I think that is nothing to this; but this is to be our city they say.... We are to have our land sixty miles further up the river. We are all ordered to land tomorrow, and not a shelter to go under."

— *Sarah Frost, Loyalist*

FIGURE 4.12 This diary entry was written in 1783 by Frost upon arriving in British North America. **Analyze:** How does Frost's experience compare with the way the Loyalist arrival was shown in **Figure 4.1**?

FIGURE 4.13 This painting entitled *A View of the Ruins of the Fort at Cataraqui* by James Peachey in 1783 shows British cartographer (map-maker) Samuel Holland and his team surveying land. Their job was to divide the land into settler plots on the site of ruins of the old French Fort Frontenac. **Analyze:** Who do you think was not invited to settle in the site of the old Fort Frontenac?

WAITING TO OWN LAND

Once Loyalists had arrived, they could begin the process of acquiring land. Individual Loyalists or groups of Loyalists could petition, or request, one or more lots. They would often divide the land they acquired among themselves by lottery. Examine the land lottery shown in **Figure 4.14**. Do you think this was a fair or effective way to give out land?

Along with land, Loyalists were given some free supplies, such as farm tools, food, and clothing. As well, they did not have to pay taxes for a number of years. In exchange for all of this, the Loyalists needed to complete certain tasks or else they had to give the land back. This usually meant that they had to clear and farm a set amount of their land within a certain time period. However, many Loyalists did not receive land right away. Read the quote in **Figure 4.15** from Loyalist Mary Barbara Fisher, which describes her and her family's harsh living conditions. What other supplies could the British government have provided to help Loyalist refugees when arriving in British North America?

FIGURE 4.14 This image is an undated pen and ink drawing by C.W. Jefferys called *Loyalists Drawing Lots For Their Lands, 1784*. Jefferys did not live in this time period. He drew this scene of the 1784 lottery system showing settlers drawing a lot of land from a hat. **Analyze:** Based on this depiction, how do you think the Loyalists felt while waiting to randomly choose a lot of land?

> "We pitched our tents in the shelter of the woods and tried to cover them with spruce boughs. We used stones for fireplaces. Our tents had no floors but the ground ... how we lived through that winter, I barely know ..."
>
> — *Mary Barbara Fisher, Loyalist*

FIGURE 4.15 Fisher recounts her family's arrival in October 1783. The account was found in a manuscript written by her granddaughter Georgianna in the 1880s or 1890s. **Analyze:** What does this tell you about the living conditions that many Loyalists had to endure as they waited for their land?

CLEARING LAND

Some of the land that you see around present-day Lake Ontario's north shore and the St. Lawrence River has been cleared for farmland, roads, and buildings. When the Loyalist settlers arrived in British North America, the land was very different. It was wild, with great forests often to the edge of the water. Look at **Figure 4.16**. The painting shows what part of the Thousand Islands looked like in 1796. The painter, Elizabeth Simcoe, was the wife of John Graves Simcoe, the first lieutenant-governor of what is southern Ontario today. How did she see her new land? Compare **Figure 4.16** with **Figure 4.17**, a present-day photo of part of the Thousand Islands. What has changed? What has stayed the same?

Once Loyalist settlers claimed their lots, trees needed to be cut down, tree roots removed, soil turned, and homes built. Doing these tasks with human strength alone was extremely difficult. There were no bulldozers or power tools to clear land and build homes quickly. It was crucial for settlers to have a warm shelter in order to survive their first winter. Some settlers did not survive the harsh conditions.

FIGURE 4.16 Elizabeth Simcoe's watercolour painting *Thousand Islands* dated July 1796 shows a rugged coastline, thick with trees. **Analyze:** Look at the people in the foreground of the painting. What could they be doing?

FIGURE 4.17 This is a present-day photo of part of the Thousand Islands. **Analyze:** Why do you think the coastline has not been completely cleared?

BROKEN PROMISES

For most of the Loyalist refugees who survived the first few years in British North America, their hard work eventually paid off. Many present-day towns across southern Ontario, Québec, Nova Scotia, New Brunswick, and Prince Edward Island can trace their roots back to the Loyalists. However, the promise of a better life did not come true for all the Loyalists who came to British North America.

> What could be some reasons why Loyalist families were able to survive their first few years in British North America?

LACK OF COMPENSATION

Whenever British subjects lost their property due to war, the British government would compensate, or pay back, a portion of their losses. Some of the Loyalists who left behind property in the Thirteen Colonies expected they would receive government money, in addition to free land, to help them start over. They petitioned the government for this compensation, but the money was slow to arrive. Some Loyalists, such as the Black Loyalists, never received any compensation. Read **Figure 4.18**, a quote from Sir Guy Carleton, the British commander-in-chief in British North America, whom you learned about in Chapter 3. Do you think that the British and American governments had a responsibility to pay back all the Loyalists for their losses?

> "Ten years have elapsed since many [Loyalists] have been deprived of their fortunes, their helpless families reduced from independent affluence [wealth] to poverty and want. Some are now languishing [suffering] in British jails, unable to pay their debtors. Provision should now be made for payment of those whose claims have been settled and reported. It will not only relieve them of their distress but give credit to others whose claims remain to be considered and enable them all to provide for their wretched [unhappy] families and become again useful members of society."
>
> — Sir Guy Carleton, British commander-in-chief

FIGURE 4.18 This excerpt, written by Carleton, was part of a 1786 submission to the British House of Commons that supported paying Loyalist compensation claims. **Analyze:** What are the arguments that Carleton makes for compensating the Loyalists?

Now read **Figure 4.19**, a quote from Carleton about the Loyalist refugees. How does **Figure 4.19** support his views in **Figure 4.18**?

> "Brave, unfortunate people, many of them of the very first families, reduced to a condition that makes one's heart bleed."
>
> — Sir Guy Carleton, British commander-in-chief

FIGURE 4.19 This undated quote by Carleton is in response to the state of Loyalist refugees. **Analyze:** Who do you think Carleton was referring to when he said "first families"?

INTERPRET AND ANALYZE

Having a strong inquiry question and researching reliable information are only the first steps in conducting a historical investigation. Once you have your inquiry question and information, you need to analyze, or make sense of, your findings. Ask yourself what your information means. Think about how different pieces of information fit together. How do you think people would have thought, or felt, based on your evidence?

When you interpret and analyze information, you need to
- think about your evidence in different ways using the historical thinking concepts
- try to uncover new details and perspectives
- look for ways that different pieces fit together
- try to find patterns
- put the evidence you have found into your own words

CASE STUDY: THE DAILY LIVES OF BLACK LOYALISTS IN NOVA SCOTIA

The majority of Black Loyalists settled in Nova Scotia and New Brunswick. However, many did not have the same support as white Loyalists. Along with the lack of compensation, the Black Loyalists received either poor quality land or no land at all. Consider this inquiry question as you interpret and analyze the information in this case study: Did Black Loyalists in Nova Scotia experience the better life they were promised by the British?

In 1773, a large group of Black Loyalists arrived in Nova Scotia. They settled in Birchtown, just outside Shelburne, Nova Scotia. With the arrival of so many Loyalists in the area, food and shelter quickly became scarce. The Black Loyalists were the last to get provisions, tools, and land, if they got them at all. Only one-third of the Black Loyalists ever received land. Those who did, found that the land was often unsuitable for farming. Often they were unable to wait for land and had to work as labourers or indentured servants.

Indentured service was a temporary form of slavery. People would sign away their freedom for a specific amount of time and receive a sum of money at the end of the term.

Racial tension between white and Black Loyalists increased as some white Loyalists arrived in British North America with enslaved people. Some free Black Loyalists were kidnapped and sold back into slavery. Black Loyalists also faced discrimination. They were not allowed to vote or allowed to have a jury trial. Their punishment for crimes was often whipping or being returned to slavery. There were even laws that prohibited them from dancing and having social gatherings.

Read Lieutenant William Dyott's description of the conditions in Birchtown in **Figure 4.20**.

" ... walked through the woods about two miles from the barracks to a negro town called Birch Town. At the evacuation of New York there were a great number of these poor devils given lands and settled here—The place is beyond description wretched, situated on the coast in the middle of barren rocks, and partly surrounded by a thick impenetrable wood—Their huts miserable to guard against ... a Nova Scotia winter, and their existence almost depending on what they could lay up in summer. I think I never saw wretchedness and poverty so strongly perceptible in the garb and the countenance of the human species as in these miserable outcasts."

— *Lieutenant William Dyott,*
British infantry officer

FIGURE 4.20 This excerpt is from Dyott's diary. It was written in October 1788. **Analyze:** What are the key points in this excerpt?

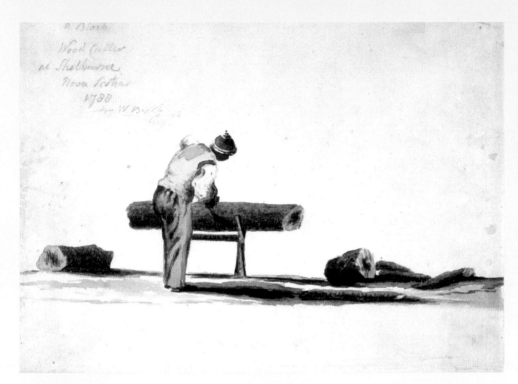

FIGURE 4.21 This watercolour of a Black woodcutter in Shelburne, Nova Scotia, was painted by Captain William Booth in 1788. It is one of the few images from the period showing Black Loyalists. **Analyze:** How would you interpret this watercolour with and without the other two sources?

"About this time the country was visited with a dreadful famine, which not only prevailed at Birchtown, but likewise at Chebucto, Annapolis, Digby, and other places. Many of the poor people were compelled to sell their best gowns for five pounds of flour, in order to support life. When they had parted with all their clothes, even to their blankets, several of them fell down dead in the streets, thro' hunger ... poverty and distress prevailed on every side; so that to my great grief I was obliged to leave Birchtown, because I could get no employment."

— *Boston King, Black Loyalist*

FIGURE 4.22 This description of conditions in Birchtown during a 1787 famine was written by a Black Loyalist named Boston King. **Analyze:** How is King's description similar to or different from Dyott's diary in **Figure 4.20**?

Despite the harsh conditions, Birchtown became the largest Black settlement in North America. Black Loyalists who were skilled workers were able to find jobs as shoemakers, teachers, ministers, or woodcutters, as pictured in **Figure 4.21**. Some enslaved people escaped and found refuge in the free Black communities. **Figure 4.22** is a description of life in Birchtown, written by a Black Loyalist named Boston King. When you examine **Figure 4.22**, what new understanding do you have about the lives of Black Loyalists?

TRY IT

1. Consider the sources in this feature. What patterns emerge?
2. Compare the sources here with other sources in the chapter. How did the experiences of white Loyalists differ? Are they similar in any way? Consider what perspective each source represents. How do the sources help you to answer the inquiry question?

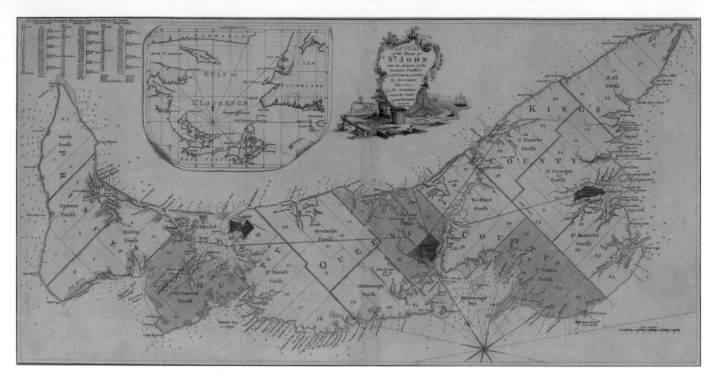

FIGURE 4.23 Samuel Holland created the first map of P.E.I. to help the British government divide the land into lots for settlement following the expulsion of the Acadians. **Analyze:** Where do you think the most desirable plots of land were?

> What might be the consequences of landowners living in Britain rather than in P.E.I.?

ABSENTEE LANDLORDS

In 1764, Samuel Holland began mapping out Île Saint Jean (*Île* means "island"), which we now call Prince Edward Island (P.E.I.). His purpose was to divide the island, which included former Acadian land after the Acadian Expulsion, into large lots for new settlements. You can see Holland's finished work in **Figure 4.23**. The government gave the plots of land to 17 friends of the British Crown, who were required to settle the island in exchange for land ownership. Many landowners lived in Britain, and a few were women who inherited the land from their families. One such landowner was Anne Saunders, Lady Melville. Saunders inherited two lots of land from her father since she did not have any brothers. She never visited P.E.I. while she owned land there. Instead, she used a land agent in P.E.I. to manage her lots for her.

Many of the overseas landowners managed their land badly, often leaving much of the land untouched throughout the 1770s. This created a legacy of "absentee landlords." Why do you think so much of this land belonging to absentee landlords stayed undeveloped for so long?

As the Loyalists' demand for land continued to increase, the landlords agreed, in 1783, to give up about 109 000 acres. This is about the size of present-day Kingston, Ontario. The Loyalists were told that they would be allowed to keep the land if they did the hard work of clearing it and building roads. Although Loyalist settlers did their part and worked the land, many landowners never intended to keep their promise to hand over ownership. The settlers in P.E.I. continued to fight the government over the land issue for more than 100 years, finally resolving it with a bill named *The Land Purchase Act, 1875.*

THE FALL OF SHELBURNE

Shelburne, Nova Scotia, was a small port settlement isolated from other parts of Nova Scotia. It was a quiet place with a small population. Everything changed when masses of Loyalist refugees began arriving on Shelburne's shores. By December 1784, Shelburne's population had increased drastically to more than 10 000 inhabitants. It became the largest city in the British colonies and the fourth largest in North America after New York, Philadelphia, and Boston. However, despite arriving in a location with a large supply of unsettled land, hundreds of Loyalist families still found themselves without land. The British government had claimed large tracts of land in Shelburne for the King, as well as for naval and military purposes. These kinds of restrictions caused a land shortage and slowed down the land grant process. Loyalists without land were left frustrated and homeless, with no way to support themselves. They were dependent on government aid in the form of food and shelter. In 1787, the British government stopped all aid to the Shelburne Loyalists.

People then began leaving for better opportunities elsewhere. By 1791, two-thirds of Shelburne's population had left. Despite this, Loyalists still left their mark on Shelburne. In present-day Shelburne, there are many heritage buildings in the town that date back to the Loyalist migration. **Figure 4.24** is an image of Cooper's Inn, built in 1784 and protected today as a heritage property. Why do you think Shelburne preserves buildings from the Loyalist era?

FIGURE 4.24 Cooper's Inn is one of several historic buildings in Shelburne that date back to the Loyalist migration. **Analyze:** Why is it important to protect historical buildings?

CHECK-IN

1. **GATHER AND ORGANIZE** What other types of evidence might help you understand more about the challenges that the Loyalists faced?

2. **FORMULATE QUESTIONS** Create an inquiry question that will help you investigate the similarities and differences between the various Loyalist groups. For example, you can compare different groups' reasons for staying loyal to Britain.

3. **CONTINUITY AND CHANGE** For which Loyalist immigrants did life get better, stay the same, or get worse after the American Revolution?

4. **COMMUNICATE** Imagine you are an Acadian farmer watching the British government claim your land on Île Saint Jean. Write a diary entry expressing your feelings and concerns about how your old home is being taken away from you.

HOW DID THE LOYALIST MIGRATION IMPACT BRITISH NORTH AMERICA'S POPULATION?

The end of the American Revolution brought tens of thousands of Loyalist refugees to the doorstep of First Nations, Canadiens, and existing Maritime settlers. How would their arrival affect these communities?

IMPACT ON FIRST NATIONS

Since first contact with European settlers, First Nations peoples in British North America were forced to partner with British or French colonizers. Although First Nations never surrendered their sovereignty, or independence, they had to make alliances with the colonizers to keep as much power and control over their lives as possible. Their decisions and the strength of their alliances would directly affect the survival of First Nations peoples.

As you learned in Chapter 2, First Nations benefited from the rivalry between the British and the French for many years. By creating military and trade alliances with both the British and the French, they maximized the number of gifts, goods, and agreements they received. However, after the French defeat on the Plains of Abraham, First Nations were concerned about the growing British presence and what an increase in British settlers would mean for their future.

ESTABLISHING TREATIES

Now that the British had control over the Maritimes, they wanted to establish more peaceful relationships with First Nations. In the Maritimes, Peace and Friendship treaties were signed between the British government and the Mi'kmaq, Maliseet, and Passamaquoddy (pa-zim-a-kwah-dee) First Nations. The largest First Nation in the Maritime region was the Mi'kmaq. **Figure 4.25** is an excerpt from the 1752 Articles of Peace and Friendship. How did the British want to establish peace with the Mi'kmaq? In exchange for land, First Nations were promised money, gifts, and smaller reserve lands to live on.

"That to Cherish a good Harmony & mutual [correspondence] between the said Indians & this Government ... the said Indians shall upon the first day of October Yearly, so long as they shall Continue in Friendship, Receive Presents of Blankets, Tobacco, and some Powder & Shot; and the said Indians promise once every Year, upon the first of October to come by themselves or their Delegates and Receive the said Presents and Renew their Friendship and Submissions."

— *Articles of Peace and Friendship Treaty (1752)*

FIGURE 4.25 This excerpt is from Section 6 of the 1752 Articles of Peace and Friendship Treaty between the British government and the Mi'kmaq. **Analyze:** What were First Nations required to do in order to receive their gifts?

Although the Mi'kmaq were British allies, the massive growth in the Loyalist population was overwhelming. The Loyalist migration to Nova Scotia alone added over 35 000 British inhabitants to the existing population of 12 000. The Loyalists wanted land to settle and clear for farms. Despite existing First Nations encampments, like the one shown in **Figure 4.26**, the Loyalists began to take over First Nations lands for themselves.

Between 1783 and 1812, a number of land surrender treaties affecting First Nations land were signed, officially turning over First Nations land to the British. These land surrender treaties went beyond the Maritimes. For example, one land surrender treaty, signed in 1790 between the British government and a group of First Nations, surrendered land that included a large part of present-day southwestern Ontario, north of Lake Erie. The First Nations involved in the treaty included the Odawa, Chippewa, Potawatomi, and Huron (Wyandot).

The land treaty process was often hurried and unfair. Sometimes, the British gave verbal promises to First Nations, instead of creating a written document. This was done to rush through the process so that First Nations land could be handed over quickly to waiting Loyalists. Often, these verbal promises were never kept. This pattern of treatment by the government carried on well after the Loyalist migration. Today, First Nations groups continue to campaign for their land rights.

FIRST NATIONS POPULATION DECLINE

The Loyalist migration was one of the causes of the Mi'kmaq population decline. In 1986, the Grand Council of the Mi'kmaq Nation submitted a report to the United Nations about Canada's treatment of the Mi'kmaq. What does the quote in **Figure 4.27** tell you about how the Loyalist expansion affected the Mi'kmaq?

"To strengthen their strategic position, and to accommodate the many loyalists who moved north from the thirteen colonies, the British intensified their colonization of [Mi'kmaq]. This activity disrupted our economies and began to severely restrict our people's access to the land and resources that were so essential to their survival. By the 1790s, many of our communities were starving ..."

— *Grand Council of the Mi'kmaq Nation*

FIGURE 4.27 This excerpt is from a 1986 report submitted by the Grand Council of the Mi'kmaq Nation, detailing their people's lack of political rights in British North America. **Analyze:** Why do you think people were discussing the impact of the Loyalist migration on the Mi'kmaq nearly 200 years after the event?

IMPACT ON CANADIENS

The 8000 Loyalists who landed along the St. Lawrence River in southern Québec were not happy in their new homes. Canadiens made up the majority of the population in Québec. Québec was still governed by the *Québec Act of 1774*. This meant Canadiens spoke mostly French, followed Catholicism, and lived under a system of French civil law. What would be the consequences of a growing Loyalist population in Québec?

As more Loyalists moved into the area, political tensions between the two groups increased. Loyalists did not like the seigneurial system of leasing land. They demanded to have access to land that they could own, like other Loyalist settlers. They began to build their own Protestant schools and churches. The Loyalists also did not want to obey French law and wanted a House of Assembly that followed British law. A British-style House of Assembly was a government made up of both elected and appointed members. Officials, like the governor general, were appointed. Read **Figure 4.28**, which is an excerpt from a letter written by Lord Sydney in 1787. What is Lord Sydney's opinion on how the growing Loyalist population could change the government?

> Was the *Québec Act of 1774* significant? Why, or why not?

"No plan of [a House of] Assembly has been suggested by any one ... but I foresee, as well as your Lordship, that in proportion as the number of British and Loyalists increases in the Province, the applications for one will grow more frequent and pressing."

— *Lord Sydney, British politician*

FIGURE 4.28 This excerpt is from a letter from Lord Sydney, written on September 20, 1787. **Analyze:** Why would having an English-controlled House of Assembly be important for Loyalists?

Instead of an English-controlled House of Assembly, the Canadiens petitioned for their own elected assembly. They wanted to keep the type of government they were used to, which included following French civil law. The Canadiens also wanted all officials to be elected, not appointed.

CHANGING BORDERS

To keep the peace, the British government established new Loyalist settlements beyond the Ottawa Valley, which freed the Loyalists from French seigneurial law. The creation of the Eastern Townships began the division of Québec. The British government then passed the *Constitutional Act, 1791* to formally split Québec into two colonies: **Upper Canada**, the area around the upper St. Lawrence River and the Great Lakes, and **Lower Canada**, the area around the lower St. Lawrence River and the Gulf of the St. Lawrence.

Upper Canada created by the *Constitutional Act, 1791*, a region of the upper St. Lawrence River and the Great Lakes (roughly the region of southern Ontario today) that was part of the former colony of the Province of Québec

Lower Canada created by the *Constitutional Act, 1791*, a region of the lower St. Lawrence River and the Gulf of the St. Lawrence (roughly the region of southern Québec today) that was part of the former colony of the Province of Québec

FIGURE 4.29 The first Legislative Assembly of Upper Canada met in 1792, in present-day Niagara-on-the-Lake. This painting was completed in 1955 by F.S. Challener. John Graves Simcoe, lieutenant-governor of Upper Canada, is the man addressing the crowd. **Analyze:** What clues does the artist give you about the mood in this scene?

Each colony would have its own elected assembly, but would be led by appointed officials from Britain. **Figure 4.29** shows the first elected House of Assembly of Upper Canada. The British majority in Upper Canada were able to have Protestant churches and schools, British law, and could own land. The Canadiens in Lower Canada were able to keep their language, religion, and seigneurial land-use practices. How did the Canadiens and English of British North America react to the split? **Figure 4.30** is a quote from Québec sculptor François Baillairgé. Compare this quote with **Figure 4.31**, an excerpt of a letter from John Graves Simcoe. Do the speakers have the same or different perspectives?

"1792 is the first year of freedom in this country."

— *François Baillairgé, Québec sculptor*

FIGURE 4.30 Baillairgé wrote these words in his personal diary on January 1, 1792. **Analyze:** What could have influenced Baillairgé's perspective on the division of Québec?

"The utmost attention should be paid that British Customs, Manners and Principles in the most trivial as well as serious matters should be promoted."

— *John Graves Simcoe, Upper Canada's first lieutenant-governor*

FIGURE 4.31 This is an excerpt from a letter Simcoe wrote to a British government official on June 30, 1791. Simcoe wanted to recreate Britain in Upper Canada. **Analyze:** Based on this quote, do you think Simcoe welcomed Loyalists and Canadiens to Upper Canada?

CHAPTER 4: *Loyalists in British North America: 1775–1800*

ANALYZING AND CONTEXTUALIZING
IMAGES

Doing a close reading of, or analyzing, an image (such as a painting, drawing, photograph, or cartoon) is very similar to doing a close reading of a document. However, you need to take some extra steps at the beginning.

In this activity, you will do a close reading of **Figure 4.26** on page 121. You will consider how the painting might help you answer the following question: How did the Loyalist migration impact the Mi'kmaq?

When you begin to analyze an image, you need to start by trying to see the image as the artist intended. This will help you understand its meaning and message. **Figure 4.32** provides you with key questions that you should ask when you begin your analysis.

FIGURE 4.32 These questions will help you to analyze different images.

Questions to Ask When Analyzing an Image

About	Examples
Creation of the image	• What type of image is it? For example, is it a painting, a photograph, or an illustration? • When and where was the image created? Who created it? Who for? What for? • Did the artist portray his or her own experiences, or those of others? • Was the image created at the time of the events portrayed, or later?
Content of the image	• What do I see? For example, do I see people, places, objects, activities, or events? • Who or what is the most important part of the image? Why do I think this? • What is the artist's perspective on the subject? How can I tell? • Who or what did the artist leave out?
Creative choices of the artist	• What did the artist want viewers to feel as they look at the image? • How do the decisions made by the artist create this feeling? • Why might the artist have chosen the medium and style used?
Audience's response	• What effect did the image have on its viewers? • How might a different audience have responded?

HOW TO ANALYZE AN IMAGE

STEP 1

Observe **Figure 4.26** closely for about a minute. List the things you see. Use only your eyes, not your historical knowledge. For example, look at the people stepping out of a canoe. Notice that one is a child, and one of the two adults has a gun. Several people are sitting together on the ground talking with each other, while other people are standing around the tents. What do you think the artist is trying to tell us about Mi'kmaq life through this scene?

STEP 2

Where in the painting did your eyes go first? How did your eyes move through the painting? What does this tell you about what the artist wanted you to notice?

STEP 3

Describe how you feel as you look at the painting. Can you work out what the artist has done to make you feel this way?

STEP 4

Use the questions in **Figure 4.32** to complete your close reading of the painting. Record your observations and inferences.

Understanding an image also involves exploring the relationship between the content of the image, its meaning, and the world in which it was created and viewed. You need to look for information about the historical **context** in reliable secondary sources, such as other images or written documents. You can also contextualize an image by asking questions like the following: What else was going on at the time? How was the world in which the image was created different from ours? These questions and others are listed in **Figure 4.33**.

Consider the context in which **Figure 4.26** was created. The painting shows one of the last surviving Mi'kmaq communities in the Halifax area. Mi'kmaq bands moved between winter settlements in the forests and summer camps on the shores. Shorelines were claimed first by Loyalists because the land was the most fertile. Think about how the events and tensions at the time might have affected the artist's choices and how people likely understood the painting at the time.

Questions to Ask When Contextualizing an Image

About	Examples
Events and conditions at the time	• What else was going on at the time when the image was created, in this community, region, or country, or in the world? • How might this context help me interpret the image?
Life at the time	• What was it like to be alive in that place, at that time? • What things were different then? What things were the same? • How might this context help me understand the image?
Position of artist in society	• How was the artist involved in events of the time? What was his or her position or role in society? • How might this context have influenced the artist's motivation? • How might it have shaped the artist's message?
Worldviews	• How did people's beliefs and customs at the time differ from ours today? • How might this context have affected the content of the image? • How might it have influenced how the audience responded to the image?

FIGURE 4.33 Asking contextual questions can help you understand the artist's intended message.

HOW TO CONTEXTUALIZE AN IMAGE

STEP 1

By 1791, colonists had pushed the Mi'kmaq off almost all their land. Why might the artist have painted the shores in **Figure 4.26** to look like they had not been settled?

STEP 2

By the time the painting was created, most of the Mi'kmaq had died from disease and starvation. Do the people in the painting look happy or sad? Do they look healthy? Why might the artist have painted them in this way?

STEP 3

The artist, Hibbert Newton Binney, was a member of a prominent Halifax family. Would he likely be more sympathetic to the Loyalist settlers or the Mi'kmaq?

STEP 4

What beliefs did European settlers at the time have about First Nations and ownership of North American land? How might these beliefs have affected the content of the painting?

IMPACT ON EXISTING MARITIME SETTLERS

The Loyalists' arrival also affected how geographic borders were drawn in the Maritime region. Many Loyalist refugees did not trust the existing settlers in Nova Scotia, since they had remained neutral during the American Revolution. The Maritime Loyalists demanded that the government create separate Loyalist settlements. This resulted in dividing Nova Scotia into three separate colonies: Nova Scotia, New Brunswick, and Cape Breton Island. The area's remaining 8500 Acadians were dispersed across these colonies, as well.

Unlike Nova Scotia and New Brunswick, Cape Breton Island had a very small Loyalist population. Only about 100 Loyalists moved to Cape Breton. As a result, this colony of Loyalists did not prosper. Cape Breton did not grow until the arrival of Scottish immigrants in the 1800s.

Do you think that separating the Maritimes and Québec into smaller colonies was the right decision? Examine the map in **Figure 4.34**. What other options might the government have considered, instead of splitting them? Think about the different groups of Loyalists who arrived in British North America. What consequences do you think these decisions might have?

> Were the geographic changes that resulted from the Loyalist migration significant? Why, or why not?

FIGURE 4.34 This map shows how the Loyalist migration created geographic change in Canada. **Analyze:** What would have been some negative and positive consequences of these geographic changes?

British North America, 1791–1792

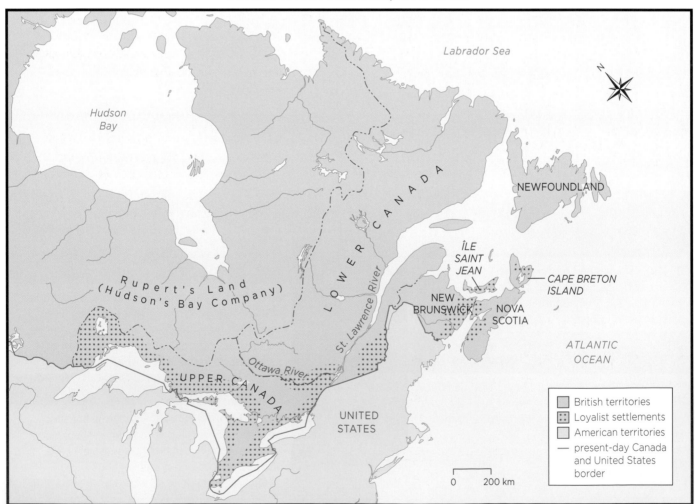

In 2002, Kathryn Lake Hogan began taking online courses with the National Institute for Genealogical Studies to learn about her family history. She soon realized that she could work professionally in the field of genealogical studies. She went on to complete a certificate in genealogical studies.

Today, Hogan is the Dominion Genealogist for the United Empire Loyalists' Association of Canada (UELAC), an organization that is dedicated to preserving Loyalist history and traditions. She has been a member of the UELAC since 2007.

FIGURE 4.35 Hogan speaking at the North American Black Historical Museum in November 2013

Most of Hogan's work with the UELAC involves helping people research their family's Loyalist history. Hogan herself is a descendant of Loyalist Johannes Ryckman of Barton Township in Ontario. She finds "researching in this early time period of Canada ... frustrating, challenging, and rewarding." Hogan believes that her interest in and knowledge of Canadian history is essential to her genealogical work: "Understanding how our country came into being, and knowing about the people who shaped our nation, can help us understand why and how our ancestors came to Canada, where they emigrated from, and where in Canada they immigrated, and migrated."

Hogan also participates in public appearances and outreach for the genealogy community. This work includes speaking at international, national, and local events, as you see in **Figure 4.35**. She also provides webinars and presentations for historians around the world. Hogan's career shows how understanding Canadian history can help us uncover fascinating personal stories.

MAKING CONNECTIONS

1. What skills do you think a genealogist needs to have? Create a list. Then, compare it with a classmate's list.
2. How could online tools benefit genealogists?

CHECK-**IN**

1. **CONTINUITY AND CHANGE** Do you think the arrival of Loyalists improved life for people already living in British North America at the time? Use evidence to support your answer.

2. **CAUSE AND CONSEQUENCE** What do you think were some positive and negative consequences of splitting Québec into Upper Canada and Lower Canada?

3. **HISTORICAL PERSPECTIVE** How do you think the First Nations, Canadiens, and existing settlers felt upon seeing so many Loyalists move into their communities? Use evidence to support your answer.

4. **INTERPRET AND ANALYZE** What were the key challenges for First Nations when the Loyalists arrived?

HOW DID THE LOYALIST MIGRATION AFFECT BRITISH NORTH AMERICA?

LEARNING GOALS

As you worked through this chapter, you had opportunities to
- examine the various causes of the Loyalist migration
- identify the various groups that made up the Loyalists and examine their experiences as immigrants
- determine whether the Loyalist migration created any significant political, social, or economic changes
- analyze and contextualize images

In this chapter, you learned about the causes and consequences of the Loyalist migration to British North America. This was a period of great change. The population boomed as 50 000 refugees, who were loyal to Britain, came over the border looking for land to settle. Their need for land created competition between different groups and them. As well, the dominant political power shifted from French to British, leading to changes in political, economic, religious, and social life for the settlers.

Summarize Your Learning

Now that you have completed Chapter 4, you are ready to answer the Chapter Big Question: How did the Loyalist migration affect British North America?

Select one of the following tasks to summarize your learning:
- Create an infographic that outlines the Loyalist migration. Your infographic should illustrate the reasons why the Loyalists moved, the challenges of moving and settling, and the impact of their settlement on others.
- Create a mini graphic novel or a series of diary entries that outlines the experience of one fictional Loyalist immigrant. Your work should outline a series of significant events from the time when the immigrant left the Thirteen Colonies to the time when she or he built a home in British North America.

APPLY **YOUR LEARNING**

1. **FORMULATE QUESTIONS** Consider the changes that were happening in communities across British North America at the time of the Loyalist migration. Create an inquiry question that addresses what happens following the migration.

2. **CAUSE AND CONSEQUENCE** Write a script for an argument between two members of a Loyalist family over the decision to stay or go. The script should outline all the causes of migration and identify the most important cause for the family.

3. **CONTINUITY AND CHANGE** Review the different experiences of Loyalists when they arrived in British North America. How were their experiences similar to the experiences of refugees arriving in Canada today? How were their experiences different?

4. **GATHER AND ORGANIZE** Create a list of all the reasons why the Loyalists remained faithful to the British government. Rank the reasons in order of importance. Share your rankings with a classmate, and explain your rationale for your rankings.

5. **HISTORICAL PERSPECTIVE** Write a letter of petition to the government of the time, asking for changes, from the perspective of a Black Loyalist, a white Loyalist, a Haudenosaunee, or a Canadien.

6. **GATHER AND ORGANIZE** Create a table that shows the pros and cons of Loyalist settlement for each of the following groups: white Loyalists, Black Loyalists, First Nations, and Canadiens.

7. **EVALUATE AND DRAW CONCLUSIONS** Using the information in your table from question 6, choose the one group that you think was most negatively impacted by Loyalist migration. Create a poster or public service announcement that warns people in this group against the dangers of migrating to British North America.

8. **HISTORICAL SIGNIFICANCE** Identify ways that life in Canada today has been affected by events related to the Loyalist migration.

UNIT1 CHALLENGE CHECK-IN

Record your responses to these questions in your log book.

1. What changes occurred because of the Loyalist migration? What stayed the same? How did the Loyalist migration affect the lives of different groups of people in British North America?

2. What challenges did the Loyalists face in British North America? How were the challenges different for the different groups of Loyalists? Which group faced the most significant challenges?

3. Was the Loyalist migration a significant event for British North America? Why, or why not? Use evidence from sources in the chapter to support your answer. Organize the evidence in a way that will help you understand it.

4. Review the Focus On: Interpret and Analyze feature on pages 116 to 117. Using the criteria provided, analyze and interpret the evidence you gathered for question 3. Record key points in your own words. Look for patterns and relationships in the evidence you gathered. What new understanding do you have after analyzing the evidence?

5. Review the description of the Unit 1 Challenge on pages 18 to 19 and the notes you made in your log book. What story is told when you put together your notes? Who is represented in your story? Are there other sources that might provide a broader or more accurate perspective? Has your thinking changed as you studied Chapter 4? What conclusions can you make by reviewing the information in your log book? Add your new information and reflections to your log book.

LOOKING BACK: UNIT 1

HOW DID KEY CHANGES DURING THIS PERIOD LEAD TO BRITISH NORTH AMERICA?

The Treaty of Portsmouth is signed between the British and the Wabanaki Confederacy.

The Treaty of Utrecht is signed.

The Seven Years' War begins.

The Battle of the Plains of Abraham takes place.

| 1713 | 1754 | 1755 | 1759 |

Thanadelthur is captured by Cree First Nation, and later goes on to bring peace and trading between Dene, Cree, and Hudson's Bay Company.

The expulsion of the Acadians begins.

Travel time from Québec to the East Coast by ship
15 DAYS

About **10 000** Acadians were expelled from their homeland between 1755–1764.

UNIT1 CHALLENGE

DESIGN A HERITAGE FAIR PRESENTATION

Throughout Unit 1, you have been gathering information and evidence about the key changes that led to British North America.

Choose an event, a series of events, a person, or a group that you feel made a significant contribution to the creation of British North America. This will be the focus of your Heritage Fair presentation. In your presentation, you will also reflect on the impact of the event(s), person, or group on Canadian society today.

Now it is time to design your presentation. Consider who your audience will be. Design your presentation to increase your audience's awareness of and interest in Canadian history. Select a format for your presentation: a project or display (a display board, model, or poster), a performance (a re-enactment or drama), or a multimedia presentation or web page. Go back to the description of the Unit 1 Challenge on pages 18 to 19, and review the features that should be included in your presentation.

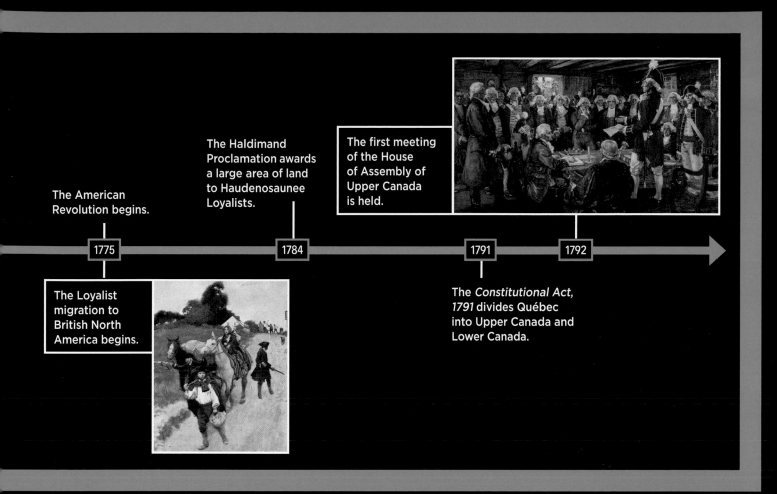

The American Revolution begins.

1775

The Loyalist migration to British North America begins.

The Haldimand Proclamation awards a large area of land to Haudenosaunee Loyalists.

1784

The first meeting of the House of Assembly of Upper Canada is held.

1791

The *Constitutional Act, 1791* divides Québec into Upper Canada and Lower Canada.

1792

Over **50 000**
Loyalists moved to Canada after the American Revolution began in 1775.

ESTIMATED POPULATION OF BRITISH NORTH AMERICA IN **1791** **395 000**

Self-Check List

Use the following to check that you have met all the criteria for your Heritage Fair presentation.

Knowledge and Understanding

☐ I identified events or people that contributed to the creation of British North America.

☐ I explained why these events or people were significant to the creation of British North America.

☐ I described the impact of the events or people I identified on various groups.

Thinking

☐ I selected and used a variety of appropriate sources as evidence.

☐ I included the perspectives of different groups.

☐ I used the inquiry process and historical thinking concepts to plan and design my Heritage Fair presentation.

Communication

☐ I selected an appropriate method of communication, keeping in mind my purpose and my audience.

Application

☐ I made connections between the events or people I identified and Canadian society today.

☐ I used the inquiry process and applied the historical thinking concepts to tell a story about a significant event or person that helped create British North America.

UN

CONFLICTS AND CHALLENGES IN CANADA: 1800–1850

DID CANADA PROGRESS AS A RESULT OF THE CONFLICTS AND CHALLENGES FROM 1800 TO 1850?

The 1800s were a period of great change for Canada. As the century started, people were building and growing communities. Canada soon found itself in the middle of conflict as the War of 1812 broke out between Britain and the United States. Following the war, more and more people moved to Canada, and the colonies quickly faced the challenges of a rapidly growing population. Social and political tensions began to rise, leading to conflicts in Upper and Lower Canada. During this time, many Canadians worked toward social and political change.

This photo shows *The Encampment*, rows of 200 tents set up at Fort York in Toronto as part of the 200th anniversary of the War of 1812. Each tent contains an exhibit that tells the story of the many civilians who were affected by the war. In this unit, you will explore how different people and groups responded to the many conflicts and challenges of the time. Did these conflicts and challenges make Canada a better place to live by the 1850s?

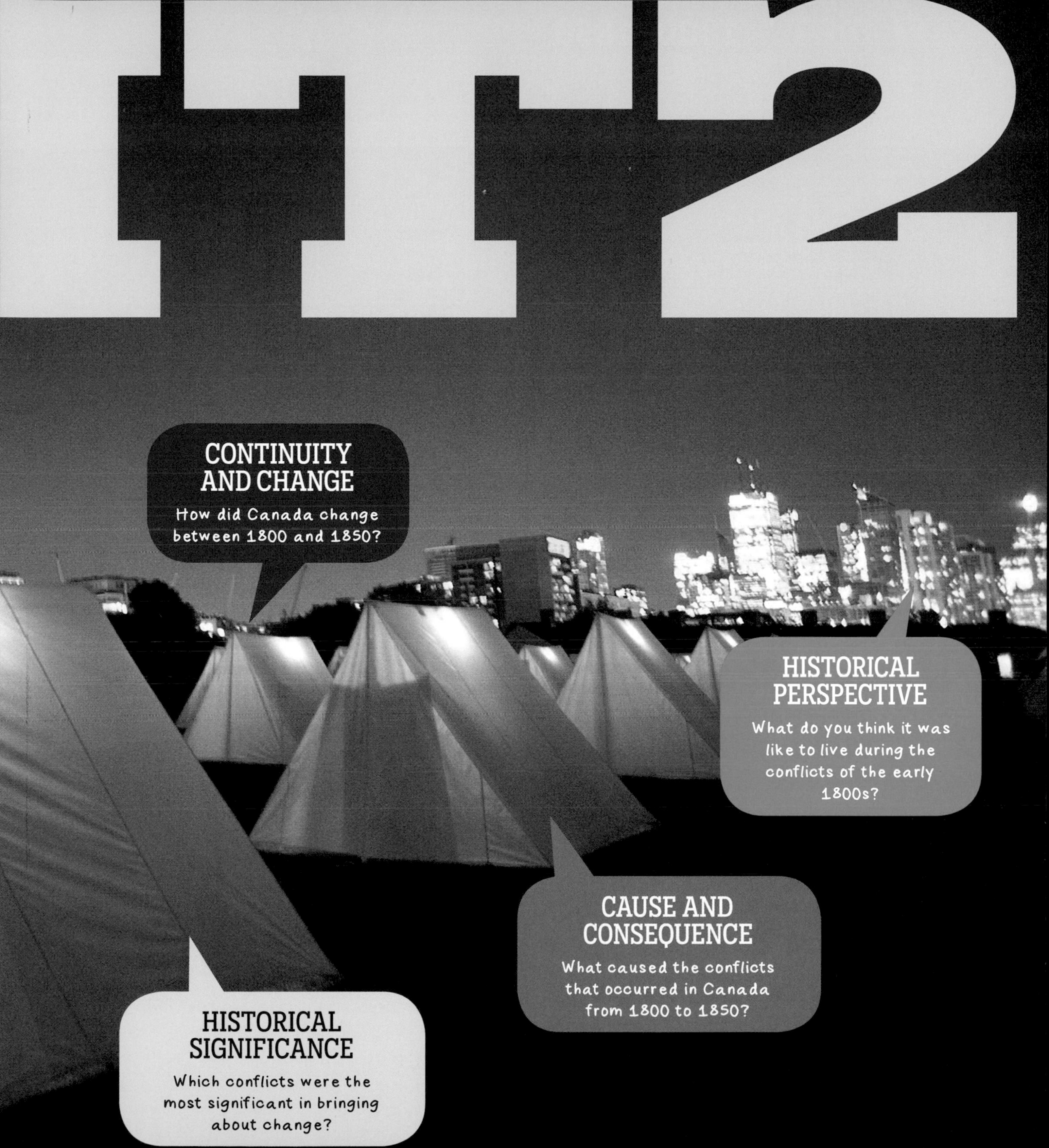

UT 2

CONTINUITY AND CHANGE

How did Canada change between 1800 and 1850?

HISTORICAL PERSPECTIVE

What do you think it was like to live during the conflicts of the early 1800s?

CAUSE AND CONSEQUENCE

What caused the conflicts that occurred in Canada from 1800 to 1850?

HISTORICAL SIGNIFICANCE

Which conflicts were the most significant in bringing about change?

UNIT 2: 1800–1850

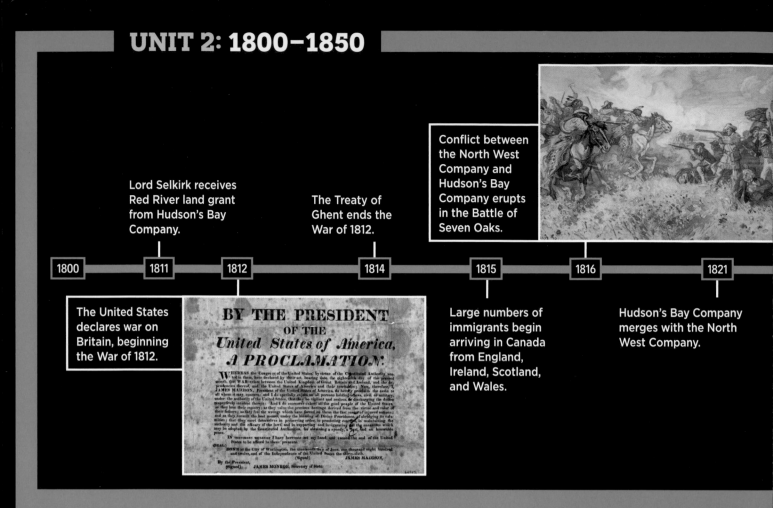

Lord Selkirk receives Red River land grant from Hudson's Bay Company.

The Treaty of Ghent ends the War of 1812.

Conflict between the North West Company and Hudson's Bay Company erupts in the Battle of Seven Oaks.

| 1800 | 1811 | 1812 | 1814 | 1815 | 1816 | 1821 |

The United States declares war on Britain, beginning the War of 1812.

BY THE PRESIDENT
OF THE
United States of America,
A PROCLAMATION.

Large numbers of immigrants begin arriving in Canada from England, Ireland, Scotland, and Wales.

Hudson's Bay Company merges with the North West Company.

ESTIMATED POPULATION IN **1806**

Upper Canada **70 718**
Lower Canada **250 000**

Estimated number of British immigrants to Canada **1815–1850**
650 000

CREATE A PROGRESS AND DECLINE TIMELINE

In Unit 2, you will focus on the following Big Question: *Did Canada progress as a result of the conflicts and challenges from 1800 to 1850?* You will consider progress and its opposite, decline, by looking at what changed and what stayed the same during the time period. Then you will decide whether Canada got better or worse as a result. Historians call this an investigation of continuity and change. You will also consider the impact on different groups. What may be a time of progress for one group may be a time of decline for another.

As you work through Unit 2, you will create a timeline of the significant events and developments that occurred from 1800 to 1850. On your timeline, you will show whether each event or development represented progress or decline. As well, you will include the contributions of key people or groups. At the end of the unit, you will decide if Canada was a better place to live by 1850.

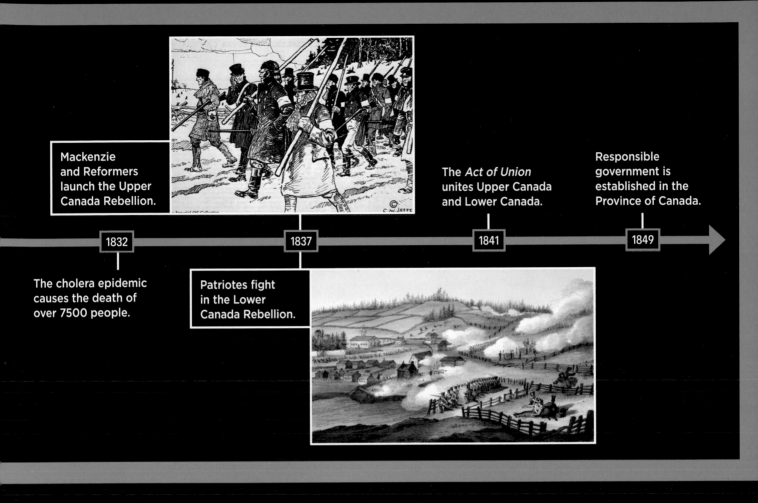

Mackenzie and Reformers launch the Upper Canada Rebellion.

The *Act of Union* unites Upper Canada and Lower Canada.

Responsible government is established in the Province of Canada.

1832

1837

1841

1849

The cholera epidemic causes the death of over 7500 people.

Patriotes fight in the Lower Canada Rebellion.

AVERAGE FAMILY SIZE IN

1851 **6.6** CHILDREN

2011 **1.6** CHILDREN

What to Consider

Your timeline will have a horizontal axis and a vertical axis. The dates of events and developments will be plotted on the horizontal axis. You will determine criteria to measure how strongly the events or developments represented progress or decline and then plot these values on the vertical axis. Positive changes will be plotted above the timeline and negative changes below the timeline.

Your timeline should include the following features:

- **Purpose:** How will you identify significant events and developments on your timeline? How will you identify each event or development as either progress or decline for Canada? How will you explain the criteria you use to do this?

- **Historical thinking:** Why are the events and developments historically significant? What caused each event or development, and what were the consequences?
- **Research:** Which sources will you use to gather information and evidence? How will you check the evidence you find?
- **Perspective:** From whose perspective did the event or development result in progress? From whose perspective did it lead to decline? What evidence will you use to support your judgments?
- **Conclusion:** What conclusion will you make about whether Canada was a better place to live by 1850? What evidence will you use to support your conclusion?

CHAPTER 5
LIFE IN CANADA:
EARLY 1800s

WHY DID PEOPLE EXPERIENCE DIFFERENT CHALLENGES IN EARLY CANADA?

LEARNING GOALS

As you work through this chapter, you will
- identify the factors that affected how a variety of people lived in the early 1800s and the challenges they faced
- examine the significance of people, events, and developments from the early 1800s
- explore historical perspectives on debtors' prison
- analyze and contextualize text sources

How does who you are and where you live affect your daily life? Like Canadians today, the people who lived in Canada in the 1800s all had different life experiences and faced different challenges. The people who lived in early Canada were mostly First Nations, French, and British. They were Catholic and Protestant, male and female, young and old, rich and poor. Some lived in towns, while others lived on farms they created from forested areas.

This watercolour painting, entitled *York, Upper Canada*, was painted by Elizabeth Hale in 1804. It shows the town of York, which became the city of Toronto in 1834. Look closely, and you will see four people: a First Nations couple with a baby and a seated British soldier. We do not know the details of these individuals' lives. We do know, however, that their experiences of life in this town were likely quite different.

As you explore this chapter, think about who was able to adapt to life in a new home and who was not, who benefited and who did not, and how people found ways to get along with others in their communities.

WHAT WAS LIFE LIKE IN
A TOWN?

Think about walking on a crowded city street. What sights, smells, and noises come to mind? Towns in the early 1800s had busy streets, too. The streets were muddier and people had to watch out for horses rather than cars. Those who lived in towns had many opportunities to create relationships because people lived close together and created strong communities.

TOWN LOCATIONS AND POPULATIONS

The larger, more established communities were located on the East Coast and in Lower Canada. Look at **Figure 5.1**, which is a map of communities in Canada in 1800. The towns varied greatly in population size. Québec City, founded in 1608, was Canada's largest community. What patterns can you see on the map in terms of population size and languages spoken? What do they tell you about life in Canada?

FIGURE 5.1 This map shows communities in Canada in 1800. **Analyze:** What other settlement patterns can you see?

Communities in Canada, 1800

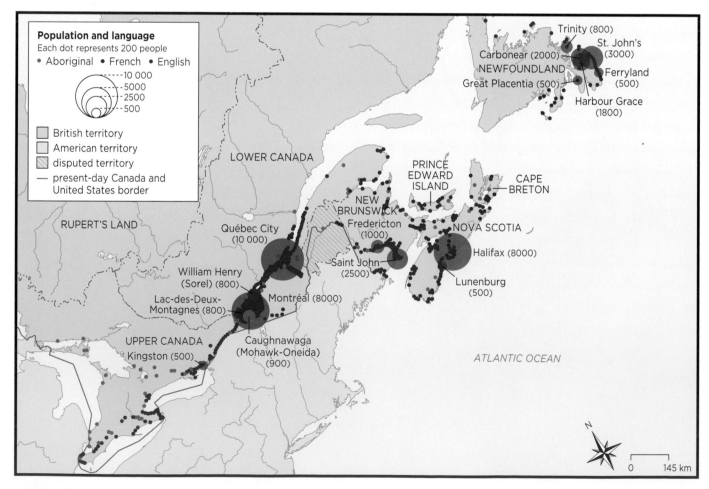

LIFE FOR THE UPPER CLASS

Societies can be organized using a class structure. **Class structure** is determined through social or economic status. The upper class consists of wealthy people with power. Most wealthy people in towns were from Britain. Many had inherited money from their families. These people included government officials, bankers, lawyers, and merchants who controlled the sales and exports of goods.

Elizabeth Simcoe was married to John Graves Simcoe, who was Upper Canada's first lieutenant-governor from 1791 to 1796. She travelled with her husband across Upper and Lower Canada and kept detailed diaries that included descriptions of the places she saw and the people she met. Read an excerpt from her diary in **Figure 5.2**. How might Simcoe's high status as the wife of a lieutenant-governor have affected her experience as a visitor to Montréal?

People who lived in Canadian towns had access to many services and goods. However, only wealthy townspeople could pay for these goods and services. They could afford to hire servants and send their children to school. Their money could buy food, clothing, and jewellery. They had time to socialize with family and friends, and attend parties. **Figure 5.3** shows a social dance with wealthy families. Social dances were common in England and France. This dance was held in Château St. Louis in Québec City. The château had been an official residence to many upper-class people, including the French governor of New France, the British governor of Québec, and the lieutenant-governor of Lower Canada. What details in the painting show wealth and status?

> **class structure** a system for ordering society based on social or economic status

> "We arrived in Montréal ... and I was delighted by the size and loftiness of the rooms, which are so much better than any I have been in at Québec ... The town of Montréal is large, and the spires of the churches, covered with tin, give a brilliancy to the scene and look like mosques. The country around is much cultivated, and orchards cover nearly all the top of the mountain."
>
> — *Elizabeth Simcoe, wife of Lieutenant-Governor Simcoe*

FIGURE 5.2 Simcoe wrote this entry in her diary in 1792. **Analyze:** What might someone with a different social status have written about instead?

FIGURE 5.3 This painting, entitled *Dance in the Château St. Louis*, was painted by George Heriot in 1801. **Analyze:** Do you think the workers, such as the musicians, are from wealthy families? Why, or why not?

FIGURE 5.4 James Pattison Cockburn painted *Cutting Ice for the Summer at Quebec City, Lower Canada* in 1830. **Analyze:** What reasons do you think the workers could have had for cutting ice?

LIFE FOR THE MIDDLE AND LOWER CLASSES

Most townspeople in the early 1800s in Canada belonged to the middle and lower classes. Compared to the upper class, which was mostly made up of wealthy British people, the middle class in Lower Canada was mainly made up of Canadiens. They worked as independent shopkeepers, bakers, blacksmiths, dressmakers, glassblowers, and grocers. Their standard of living varied. Some people just scraped by, while others managed well because their skills were in demand.

Some people had permanent positions as domestic servants, such as housekeepers and nannies. Many servants worked for wealthy families and had little time for themselves or their own families. Servant positions were filled quickly because jobs were hard to find.

The jobs that paid very little usually involved hard labour. Examine **Figure 5.4**, which shows workers cutting ice in Québec City. What would make this job difficult and dangerous?

SLAVERY IN EARLY CANADA

FIGURE 5.5 This advertisement appeared in the *Niagara Herald* from November 18, 1801, until January 9, 1802. "Good pay" does not refer to wages but to the selling price. **Analyze:** What does the publication of this ad tell you about Canadian society in the early 1800s?

Between 1671 and 1833, about 4200 people were enslaved in Canada. Two-thirds were First Nations people, and one-third were Black. Enslaved people were considered property. Owners could buy them, sell them, and even pass them down to their children in their wills. People placed advertisements in local newspapers to buy and sell people, and to offer rewards for the return of enslaved people who had run away.

The advertisement in **Figure 5.5** appeared in the *Niagara Herald* in 1801. How do you think it would have felt to be bought and sold through newspaper ads?

Most enslaved people in Canada worked as domestic servants in wealthy households in towns. This meant that they lived in the same house as their masters and were closely supervised. Peter Russell was a government official in Upper Canada in 1801. He lived with his sister Elizabeth in York (present-day Toronto). A woman named Peggy and her children were enslaved in Russell's household. Read **Figure 5.6**, an excerpt from a letter that Russell wrote to complain about Peggy's "troublesome" behaviour. Historians have described such behaviour as deliberate resistance to slavery. Are Russell's views more understandable in 1801 than they would be today?

> How does Peggy's story help us to better understand views of other enslaved people?

> "My slave Peggy ... is now at large, being not permitted by my sister to enter this house, and shows a disposition at times to be very troublesome, which may perhaps compel me to commit her again to prison. I shall be glad that you would either take her away immediately, or return to me the bill of sale I gave you to enable you to do so."
>
> — *Peter Russell, government official in Upper Canada*

FIGURE 5.6 This is an excerpt from a letter that Russell wrote in 1801 about an enslaved woman in his household named Peggy. **Analyze:** What might Peggy be trying to say through her actions?

Lieutenant-Governor Simcoe opposed slavery. He passed the 1793 *Act to Limit Slavery*, which made it illegal to import enslaved people into Upper Canada. It meant that everyone who came to Upper Canada would be free. The word spread, and many Black people from the United States made the long journey north.

Although Simcoe's law made slavery uncommon in Canada, it did not end it completely. That did not happen until Britain banned slavery in 1833.

HISTORICAL PERSPECTIVE

To understand people from the past, a historian needs to take a historical perspective. This means trying to see the world from their point of view. It does not mean agreeing with their thoughts, feelings, and motivations. It means working to *understand* their thoughts, feelings, and motivations. To do this, a historian must try to consider the historical context in which people lived.

When you attempt to understand the people of the past, you can ask the following questions:

- What were the beliefs, values, perspectives, and motivations of people who lived at that time?
- How do those beliefs and values differ from today's beliefs and values?
- Did the people make understandable decisions based on the information they had available to them?
- What beliefs, values, and ideas do I already have that affect how I think about this event, period, or person?
- What inferences can I make about the person's thoughts, feelings, and motivations from the evidence I have?

CASE STUDY: DEBTORS' PRISON

In the early 1800s, prisons in Canada housed not only criminals but also debtors: people who could not or would not pay back money that they owed to a lender. The laws of the day gave merchants and banks the power to bring a debtor to court. If the debtor could not pay back the loan, she or he would go to prison until the loan was paid. In some prisons, nearly half of the prisoners were debtors. Debtors were imprisoned alongside thieves, murderers, and other criminals.

In Canada today, a court might force a debtor to give up belongings or wages but does not send her or him to jail. Look at the jail cell in **Figure 5.7**. How might this photo help you understand the experience of debtors imprisoned in the 1800s?

FIGURE 5.7 This is a prison cell in the first Québec City Common Gaol (prison). The prison was in operation from 1813 to 1868. **Analyze:** How would you feel walking toward this cell because you were unable to pay back a loan?

Read **Figure 5.8**, an excerpt from a letter written by John Woolstencroft about life as a jailed debtor. What can you infer from this excerpt about his thoughts and feelings about his experience in jail?

"Our situation is in some respects more appalling than a Criminal imprisoned for murder, he is allowed a straw bed, blankets, bread and fuel, and knows the termination of his imprisonment, we poor wretches ... have not so much as a bench to sit on, a shelf or cupboard to place a loaf of bread upon, not even a straw bed to lay on, no blanket to cover us, no fire to warm us."

— *John Woolstencroft, jailed debtor*

FIGURE 5.8 Woolstencroft wrote this plea in 1831 for debtors' prison reform from his jail cell in York. **Analyze:** What reasons could there be that murderers were given more comfort in jail than debtors?

A person imprisoned for debt would have had a different perspective on debtors' prison than a merchant who was trying to get a loan repaid. Merchants often took large risks by loaning money to people who had no possessions to guarantee their loan. Prison represented security for these merchants because they knew that a debtor would be sent to jail if a loan was not repaid. Why might a merchant's perspective on debtors' prison be different from Woolstencroft's?

Mohawk leader Thayendanegea, also known as Joseph Brant, was a war hero from the American Revolution and a Loyalist. Read Thayendanegea's perspective on debtors' prison in **Figure 5.9**. He had a unique view of debtors' prisons because of his deep immersion in two cultures: the Haudenosaunee society in which he was born and raised, and the British colonial society that he later embraced. As well, Thayendanegea had converted to Christianity.

"Yet for what are many of your prisoners confined?—for debt!—astonishing! ... —here is no crime, nor even a fault; and yet your laws put it in the power of the [lender] to throw the debtor into prison and confine him there for life! A punishment infinitely worse than death to a brave man! ... Cease, then, to call yourselves Christians, lest you publish to the world your hypocrisy. Cease, too, to call other nations savage when you are tenfold more the children of cruelty than they."

— *Thayendanegea, Mohawk leader*

FIGURE 5.9 Thayendanegea spoke these words to his biographer before his death in 1807. Note that *hypocrisy* means to do things that you tell others not to. **Analyze:** What do you think were Thayendanegea's feelings about people who called First Nations "savages"?

TRY IT

1. Consider the sources presented here. What can you learn about attitudes during this time?
2. What beliefs, values, or ideas do you have that might help or hinder your research on debtors' prison in the early 1800s?
3. How might Thayendanegea's Haudenosaunee upbringing, his immersion in British colonial society, and his conversion to Christianity affect his perspective on debtors' prison?

OTHER CHALLENGES OF TOWN LIFE

In the early 1800s, towns were exciting, bustling places, but they were also dirty, crowded, and crime-ridden. Without sewage treatment or garbage collection, the air smelled bad. Without water filtration plants, the water carried diseases. Because of poor housing, fires spread quickly.

FIRES

Homes were not built like they are today in Canada. Many buildings were made of wood and burned quickly if a fire broke out. Examine **Figure 5.10**, which depicts soldiers trying to put out a fire in St. Andrews, New Brunswick. Although this is a country scene, how does it illustrate the challenge of trying to put out a raging fire with no water hoses, using only the firefighting equipment that was available in the early 1800s?

In towns, buildings were close to one another. If one building caught fire, others could go up in flames very quickly. Many towns and cities have stories of a "Great Fire" in their history. In St. John's, Newfoundland, there were three fires in 1816 and 1817, which drove one-quarter of the population from their homes. Québec City had two fires in 1845, which left over 15 000 people homeless. As towns grew, the need for firefighters, police officers, and other services also grew.

FIGURE 5.10 This 1854 watercolour painting by James Clark is entitled *Detachment of the 76th Regiment Putting out a Fire, St. Andrew's*. It shows soldiers fighting a fire. **Analyze:** What equipment and strategies are the soldiers using to fight the fire?

DISEASES

People living in towns were in constant danger of catching deadly contagious diseases, such as smallpox. In part, the problem was a lack of understanding about diseases. What does the excerpt in **Figure 5.11** by Father Pierre Frechette tell you about what he blamed for the spread of diseases?

The spread of disease had been a major challenge in Europe for hundreds of years. Because of this, diseases were often carried to Canada by European settlers. Various contagious diseases are spread through air, water, insects, and physical contact. If people live close together and do not wash their hands, diseases can spread quickly. For centuries in Europe and in early Canada, many people did not wash themselves often. Some historians link this behaviour to the plague. Starting in 1347, the plague killed more than one-third of the population of Europe. At the time, some people thought it was spread by contact with water, so they avoided bathing regularly. Today, we know that the plague was spread through fleas on rats.

"Last winter a sort of grippe [flu] and scarlet fever made the rounds.... Many people died, especially young people.... I put somewhat of a stop to the balls and dances last winter by representing to the people the above mentioned sickness as a punishment for their disorders and debaucherie [immoral, improper behaviour]."

— *Father Pierre Frechette*

FIGURE 5.11 This excerpt is from a letter written by Father Frechette to his superiors in 1786. **Analyze:** Why would Father Frechette believe that disease was punishment for behaviour he saw as improper?

THE CHURCH AND THE COMMUNITY

In the early 1800s, the government did not provide social services, such as healthcare, education, and care of seniors. Instead, people organized themselves to help one another. Churches provided social services, such as help for those in need and leadership in times of crisis. **Figure 5.12** shows Notre-Dame-des-Victoires, which is the oldest church in North America. It was built in 1688 and is still located in a square in Québec City's lower town.

The Catholic Church was a central part of community life for virtually all Canadiens. The priests provided spiritual guidance. The nuns provided essential services, such as nursing and education, and took care of orphans. Read **Figure 5.13**. How does Elizabeth Simcoe help us to understand the importance of nuns to the community?

> Do you think the role of the church has changed or stayed the same in present-day Canada?

FIGURE 5.12 This photo shows Notre-Dame-des-Victoires today. **Analyze:** What do the location of the church and the people outside suggest about the church's importance to the community?

> "The nuns [at the Convent des Ursulines] ... carry cleanliness and neatness to the greatest pitch of perfection in every part of the convent.... They educate children at this convent.... all the desserts in Québec are [made and sold] by the nuns.... Another convent is called the Hotel Dieu, for the reception of the sick, whether English or French."
>
> — *Elizabeth Simcoe, wife of Lieutenant-Governor Simcoe*

FIGURE 5.13 This is an excerpt from Simcoe's diary during her visit to Montréal in 1791. **Analyze:** What words does Simcoe use that show how the nuns did not exclude anyone?

CHECK-IN

1. **INTERPRET AND ANALYZE** Looking at the evidence in this chapter so far, what were some positive aspects about life in a town? What were some negative aspects?

2. **COMMUNICATE** Suppose that online media existed in the early 1800s. Create a series of postings for a website about town life in the early 1800s. Include different perspectives. Each posting can be only 140 characters long.

3. **HISTORICAL SIGNIFICANCE** Can studying the lives of people in towns in the early 1800s help us cope with the challenges of urban life in Canada today? Use an example to support your position.

WHAT WAS LIFE LIKE IN
THE BACKWOODS?

Suppose that you move to a remote forested land to start a new life. You are surrounded by forests with wild animals such as deer and bear. There are no towns or roads, and your few neighbours live far away. This is what the settlers experienced when they arrived in **the backwoods** of Canada in the early 1800s.

the backwoods remote, uncleared, forested land

ARRIVING IN A NEW HOME

As you read in Chapter 4, British settlers known as Loyalists made their way to the British colonies in Canada after the American Revolution. Some took jobs in towns, but most settled in the backwoods and cleared land to start farms. The area we know today as southeastern Ontario had many forests and trails, but few buildings and roads. Many Loyalists took boats up the St. Lawrence River into Lake Ontario. They travelled by wagon along trails into the backwoods to their assigned pieces of land. Examine **Figure 5.14**, which shows a group of Loyalists on their way to Upper Canada after the American Revolution. What message do you think the artist is trying to convey about the Loyalist experience at that time?

FIGURE 5.14 C.W. Jefferys painted *Loyalists on Their Way to Upper Canada* in 1945. **Analyze:** What challenges has the artist chosen to show these Loyalists facing during their migration?

Loyalists settled in Upper Canada, in colonies in the Maritimes, and, to a lesser extent, in Lower Canada. Wherever they settled, the first year was very challenging. Most settlers arrived in spring in time to build a log cabin before winter. They would build a small one-and-a-half storey log cabin. A cabin was small enough to be heated by one fireplace. People slept in the attic.

Some early Loyalists were less prepared because they were fleeing war. Mary Barbara Fisher arrived in New Brunswick with her family in 1783 after Britain lost the American Revolution. In **Figure 5.15**, she describes the experience to her granddaughter Georgianna. What challenges did Fisher face?

WORKING IN THE FIELDS

Forested land in the backwoods needed to be cleared to build homes and create farmland. There were no tractors or machines to do the work. Trees had to be chopped by hand with an axe. Several men, horses, or mules were needed to haul logs once the trees were cut down. The logs then needed to be cut into planks to build homes.

After trees and large stones were removed, the soil needed to be turned so that seeds could be planted. Look at the farmer planting seeds between stumps in **Figure 5.16**. After a few years, the stumps rotted and were easier to pull out. Every year, a farm family would try to clear a little more land. Crops included wheat, pumpkins, squash, potatoes, and corn. Although most new settlers farmed, many also made a living from fishing and forestry.

"How we lived through that awful winter I hardly know. There were mothers [who] clasped their infants ... and tried by the warmth of their own bodies to protect them from the bitter cold. Sometimes a part of the family had to remain up during the night to keep the fires burning, so as to keep the rest from freezing. Some destitute people made use of boards, which the older ones kept heating before the fire and applied by turns to the smaller children to keep them warm."

— *Mary Barbara Fisher, backwoods settler*

FIGURE 5.15 In this quote, Fisher tells about her first winter in Canada in 1783, in which she and her family lived in a tent. **Analyze:** How prepared does it seem these settlers were for life in their new home?

FIGURE 5.16 C.W. Jefferys painted *The Pioneer, 1784* in 1926. **Analyze:** What evidence can you see of the labour that was done prior to the land being ready for seed planting?

WORKING IN THE HOME

At the start of the 1800s, the lives of settler women revolved around the home. The few that were employed outside the home had jobs such as domestic help for a wealthy family, or were teachers, nuns (in Catholic areas), dressmakers, or innkeepers. Working in the home was a woman's main responsibility. She looked after the children, the home, and the family finances. There were many challenging daily chores. They included sewing and knitting, washing clothes with a washboard, ironing, cleaning, and cooking over a fireplace or woodstove. Women spun wool, made candles, cared for farm animals, and planted and tended to vegetable gardens. They also made soap by combining animal fat with lye. Lye is made by boiling wood ash. Examine **Figure 5.17**, which shows a woman boiling lye in a large iron pot. How does this scene compare with household chores in Canada today?

FIGURE 5.17 C.W. Jefferys created this illustration in 1945 depicting a woman stirring a pot of boiling lye in the early 1800s. **Analyze:** Based on this illustration, what were some challenges of making soap?

SCHOOLING

Everybody, even children, had to pitch in to help with household chores or work on the farm. Families had an average of seven or eight children, all of whom had multiple chores every day. For example, they carried in wood for the fire or stove, peeled potatoes, churned butter, fetched water, and gathered eggs. During the harvest, they helped collect the hay and crops.

Few children went to school because they helped in the home and on the farm. Also, the private schools that existed charged fees that only wealthy families could afford. Some children learned to read and write from their parents. In 1807, a government act in Upper Canada approved funding for eight public schools located in towns. Each had room for 100 boys. This was the beginning of the public school system that we have in Ontario today.

CREATING COMMUNITIES

When possible, settlers tried to live close together so that they could form strong community connections. When they were part of a community, families were better able to meet the many challenges of living in the backwoods. Settler families worked hard to help each other in times of need. They hoped that eventually a community could support a mill, a general store, a church, and a school.

GOVERNMENT PLANNING

In many cases, the British government's planning of towns made it difficult to create connected communities. Robert Fleming Gourlay was a Scottish farmer who came to Upper Canada in 1817 to settle a plot of land. He wrote a guide to help other immigrant farmers. He noticed that government-controlled lands stood in the way of settlers being able to build roads that could connect them to villages and each other.

Look at **Figure 5.18**. This is how the land was assigned in a typical township in Upper Canada. The government kept **Crown reserves**, land which it sold off from time to time to bring in revenue. **Clergy reserves** were set aside to make sure that many Protestant churches were present in Upper Canada. Land was also set aside for other uses, such as providing timber to Britain's Royal Navy. How would this plan hinder the development of communities?

What other types of evidence could help you better understand Gourlay's concerns?

Crown reserve land set aside to finance the government

clergy reserve land set aside to finance Protestant churches

FIGURE 5.18 This diagram shows a government plan for dividing up land for settlement. Rows of lots were called concessions. **Analyze:** Who would be your neighbours if you lived on lot 3 in the third concession?

Typical Township in Upper Canada

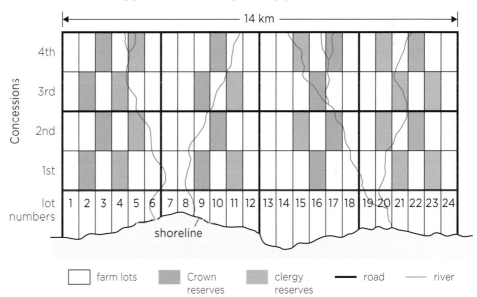

Gourlay surveyed the local farmers and brought complaints to the colonial government on their behalf. Colonial officials did not respond well to Gourlay's concerns. In 1819, they banished him from Upper Canada for encouraging rebellion. His banishment ended in 1839. However, Gourlay's concerns were shared by many people in Upper Canada. Read **Figure 5.19**. What were the consequences of the Crown and clergy reserves?

FIGURE 5.19 This quote by Buchanan was included in an 1839 British government report proposing reforms in Upper and Lower Canada. **Analyze:** Why does Buchanan describe settlers as being in an "almost hopeless condition"?

"These blocks of wild land place the actual settler in an almost hopeless condition, he can hardly expect during his lifetime, to see his neighbourhood contain a population sufficiently dense to support mills, schools, post-offices, places of worship, markets or shops; and, without these, civilization [erodes].... The inconvenience arising from the want [lack] of roads is very great."

— *Alexander Carlisle Buchanan, chief agent for the Superintendence of Emigration to Canada*

ANALYZING AND CONTEXTUALIZING
TEXT SOURCES

When you analyze text sources, it is important to contextualize, or study them in their historical context. Thinking about the time period in which a source was written, and who it was written by, can help you understand how and why it was created. It can also help you understand its significance today. For example, we know very little about the children of the past: what they did each day, what they thought about, and how they felt about their lives. Before there were public schools, only children who had a wealthy or well-educated family learned how to read and write. Letters, diaries, and drawings created by these children are treasured by historians because they reveal how the children saw their lives and offer different perspectives.

Eleanora Hallen, one of 10 children, was born in England in 1823. Her father was an Anglican clergyman. In England, the family had servants to cook and to care for the children, and a live-in governess to teach the children. The children studied reading and writing, arithmetic, Latin, geography, drawing, music, and dancing. To support such a large household, the family decided to move to Canada in 1835, where there would be new and possibly better opportunities to succeed.

In this activity, you will analyze and contextualize excerpts from Hallen's diary in **Figures 5.20** and **5.21**. Use the evidence to help you answer the following inquiry question: What was life like for some children in Canada during the 1800s?

HOW TO ANALYZE AND CONTEXTUALIZE A TEXT SOURCE

STEP 1

Start by closely reading **Figure 5.20** and **Figure 5.21**, using the steps outlined on page 57. What type of source is it? When and where was it created? Also examine the word choice the author uses and the details she includes. Compare the methods Hallen uses to record her thoughts and experiences with the technologies that you would use today.

STEP 2

Review the events and conditions occurring at the time. What was happening in Upper Canada in this period? Hallen rarely mentions events that were happening in the wider world in her diary. Why do you think this may be?

STEP 3

Examine what the source reveals about life at the time. What details does Hallen include about her daily life? How was her life in Upper Canada different from her life back in England?

STEP 4

Compare the source to the present day. How was Hallen's life as a settler in Upper Canada different from your life today? Are there ways in which her life sounds similar to yours?

STEP 5

Examine Hallen's position in society. What do these diary excerpts suggest about the ways in which boys' lives differed from girls' lives in settler families?

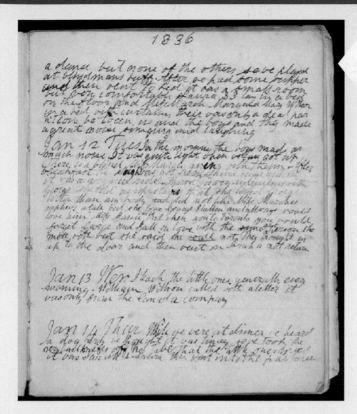

FIGURE 5.20 These excerpts from Eleanora Hallen's diary include entries from November 1835, when the Hallens first arrived at their new home in Upper Canada, and end several months later, in March 1836.

Excerpts from Eleanora Hallen's Diary

Nov. 5, 1835 I suppose it is a nice little log house, all with the bare logs

Nov. 13 We have 20 fouls [fowls] that I feed we have also two pigs

Nov. 16 We have only the sofa 3 rickety stools and two chairs to sit on

Nov. 18 My father and George are chopping in the wood

Jan. 13, 1836 ... I teach the little ones generally every morning

Jan. 19 It is my birthday we had some sauce for dinner I am thirteen

Jan. 22 In the morning I gett up be fore the rest generally and put breakfast after breakfast Mary washes the tea things Sarah generally puts dinner and then Sarah and Mary washes it up Mary and I make the beds. either of us put tea and I wash them up.

Jan. 31 we have but three dishes one of them very much cracked

Feb. 1 It is dreadfully cold we can hardly keep ourselfs warm.

Feb. 5 the oil is frozen in the lamps we had rice and aples for dinner The little ones have dinner in the parlour [as] the table cant hold all of us. The cat has burn her back quite brown

Mar. 8 In the morning I went into the wood with the sleigh and made a slide up & down a hill. When I came in their were too haunches of venison the Indian had come again & he had had some pork instead

Mar. 12 Saturday is a busy day as we have to make it tidy for Sunday

Mar. 14 I began to make a pair of mokasins for myself [as] I have no shoes to fit me

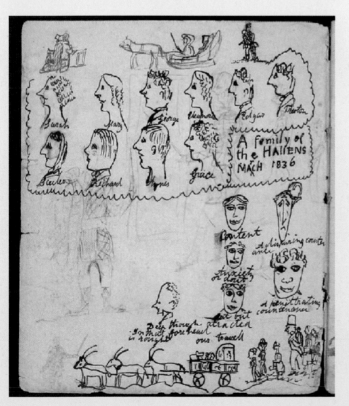

FIGURE 5.21 This page from Hallen's diary, written in March 1836, includes sketches of 10 of the Hallen children. The children are organized by age, from left to right. Sarah was the oldest, and Grace was the youngest. One child, Edith, died before the family moved to Upper Canada.

FIGURE 5.22 A logging bee is depicted in this lithograph of William P. Kay's 1834 painting called *Process of Clearing the Town Plot at Stanley*. It was published by George Ackermann in 1836.
Analyze: What can you learn about logging bees and the workers by looking closely at this painting?

working bee an occasion when neighbours work together to accomplish a major task for one member of the community

WORKING BEES

In some communities today, the school, community centre, or place of worship is where people come together to raise funds, socialize, and celebrate. Because there were few of these places in the backwoods of early Canada, social events were rare.

A **working bee** was an event that allowed early settlers to socialize while accomplishing a large task at the same time. Working bees were held for building barns, shearing sheep, picking apples, and cutting down trees. Twenty men with five oxen could clear about two hectares of land in one day (a hectare is about the size of a football field). Look at **Figure 5.22**, which shows a group of men working at a logging bee. What might make a logging bee different from other working bee events?

Preparing for a working bee took a lot of effort. Women would bake, cook, and clean for two to three days, preparing for the celebratory meal and party that often followed. In **Figures 5.23** and **5.24**, settler Susanna Moodie and historian Catherine Anne Wilson offer their views of working bees. How do these views compare?

"In the bush, where hands are few, and labour commands an enormous rate of wages, [working bees] are considered indispensable, and much has been written in their praise; but to me, they present the most disgusting picture of a bush life. They are noisy, riotous, drunken meetings, often terminating in violent quarrels, sometimes even in bloodshed. Accidents of the most serious nature often occur, and very little work is done."

— *Susanna Moodie, backwoods settler and author*

FIGURE 5.23 In her 1852 book, *Roughing It in the Bush*, Moodie describes her experience as a settler in Upper Canada in the 1830s. In this excerpt, Moodie gives her view of working bees. **Analyze:** Why would a historian studying working bees value Moodie's eyewitness account?

"Through reciprocal [mutual] labour, the farm family was able to [increase the value of their land]. It was also better able to cope with risks.... This was especially true in newly settled areas where population was highly dispersed and kin networks were not yet established. If your barn burnt, your fields were flooded, or your husband was killed, you needed to be able to rely on reciprocal aid rather than face these disasters on your own."

— *Catherine Anne Wilson, historian*

FIGURE 5.24 In 2001, Wilson, a historian, gives her view of working bees. **Analyze:** How is a historian's account different from an eyewitness account?

HISTORY AT WORK   RESEARCHER

Have you ever noticed a building in your neighbourhood that looks like it came from another era? Maybe it did. Some old buildings are protected from demolition because they are valuable evidence of our past. The government and other agencies, such as the Ontario Heritage Trust, help to determine which buildings to protect.

Erin Semande (**Figure 5.25**) is a researcher with the Ontario Heritage Trust. Her job is to assess the historical significance of a property and help determine if the government should protect it. To do this, Semande examines primary and secondary sources. She interviews people knowledgeable about the property and the time period when the building was constructed. Semande has travelled to almost every corner of the province to visit buildings she is assessing—sometimes even exploring buildings that have been boarded up for decades.

After her research is complete, Semande writes her assessment, which is called a Statement of Significance report. By using the same criteria for every property, Semande makes sure her assessments are fair. She has helped to preserve and protect many important buildings in Ontario, including many that date back to the mid-1800s.

Semande has always had a passion for history. She grew up visiting local museums and historical sites and studied history in university. She completed a Master's Degree in Public History. Semande's work highlights how an interest in Canadian history can lead to a satisfying career.

FIGURE 5.25 Semande poses in front of Barnum House in Grafton, Ontario. It was built around 1819.

MAKING CONNECTIONS

1. What criteria would you use to determine if a building is historically significant?

2. What skills would you need to assess the significance of a historic building?

CHOOSING NEIGHBOURS

Many settlers purposefully settled in areas where others from their extended family were living. They also tried to settle in areas with people who spoke the same language, practised the same faith, or had served in the same military regiment. These choices helped settlers achieve a strong sense of community with their neighbours. Settlers who made their requests before their lands were assigned could choose their neighbours. Those who tried to do it afterwards, however, had a more difficult time.

Richard Pierpoint was a Black Loyalist who fought for the British in the American Revolution. **Figure 5.26** is a depiction of Pierpoint in battle. Because of his loyalty to Britain, he, like other Black Loyalists, was given his **emancipation**, or freedom, from slavery. In 1788, Pierpoint received a land grant in the Niagara region, where he was one of the few Black Loyalist settlers.

Pierpoint travelled around Upper Canada as a storyteller in the Black community. Throughout his travels, he noticed that Black Loyalists had received land grants all across the province, making it difficult for them to form a close-knit community. Pierpoint and 18 other Black Loyalists wrote a petition to Lieutenant-Governor Simcoe. Pierpoint's petition came to be known as "The Petition of Free Negroes." Read the petition in **Figure 5.27**. What are the Black Loyalists asking for?

emancipation freedom from slavery

FIGURE 5.26 This 2005 painting by Malcolm Jones shows Black Loyalist Richard Pierpoint. **Analyze:** What personality traits of Pierpoint can you infer from this painting?

> Are petitions historically significant, even if they do not succeed?

"There are a number of negroes in this part of the country many of whom have been soldiers during the late war between Great Britain & America, and others who were born free with a few who have come into Canada since the peace.

Your petitioners therefore humbly pray that their situation may be taken into consideration, and if your Excellency should see fit to allow them a tract of country to settle on, separate from the white settlers."

— *Petition by Black Loyalists, including Richard Pierpoint*

FIGURE 5.27 This petition to the government was written in 1794 by a group of Black Loyalists, including Pierpoint. The request in the petition did not succeed. **Analyze:** Why would the petitioners ask for Black settlers to be separate from other settlers?

BECOMING A COMMUNITY OF EQUALS

There were many Loyalist families for whom life in Canada would have felt like a step backwards. They left behind established homes and farms, connected social circles, and an easier lifestyle.

For others, it was a step forward. Government land grants and assistance attracted many settlers. Read **Figure 5.28**, an excerpt from a letter written by Joseph Willcocks to his brother in Ireland. What reasons does Willcocks give for being happy with his new life in Upper Canada? As you read the quote, keep in mind that, in 1800, many societies had social rankings. Often, people with money and status did not treat those with less money and status very well.

> What were some intended and unintended consequences of settling in Canada in the early 1800s?

"Dear Brother

Remember me to all my friends, let me know particularly about my dear father's health. I wish he knew how much I am respected here, in fact I feel as if I was regenerated. I am here among rational beings, men though they are high in rank & fortune know themselves to be men & will be friendly & kind to you, [unlike officers, clerks, and busybodies in Dublin who] ... look down [upon] the rest of mankind with contempt."

— *Joseph Willcocks, settler in Upper Canada*

FIGURE 5.28 Willcocks wrote this letter to his brother in Dublin, Ireland, in 1800. **Analyze:** What differences does Willcocks describe between life in early Canada and life in Dublin, Ireland, at the time?

To survive in the backwoods, all settlers, no matter which social class they came from, had to work hard. Farming the land and other large tasks were tough work. In **Figure 5.29**, Loyalist John Kilborn gives his thoughts on the attractions of a settler's life. Although Kilborn is writing in the 1860s, he is reflecting on his 70 years living in Upper Canada. What does he remember fondly?

"[The] state of society, however humble was in many respects superior to the present. All the parties then were more or less dependent on each other for ... assistance, and all felt more or less interested in each others' condition and prosperity.... All were ... friends."

— *John Kilborn, settler in Upper Canada*

FIGURE 5.29 Kilborn reflects on growing up in Upper Canada in the early 1800s. **Analyze:** What does Kilborn think makes up for the "humble" circumstances of settler life?

CHECK-**IN**

1. **HISTORICAL PERSPECTIVE** Choose one first-person account of life as an early settler that you found interesting. What does it reveal about life in the early 1800s?

2. **HISTORICAL SIGNIFICANCE** How do you think the actions of early settlers shaped the community that you live in today?

3. **FORMULATE QUESTIONS** Develop a set of questions that would help you conduct an inquiry about how communities began in the backwoods. Your questions should ask how, who, what, when, where, and why.

WHAT WAS LIFE LIKE FOR
ABORIGINAL PEOPLE?

How would you feel if strangers claimed your neighbourhood as their own? Would you accept the situation, try to resist, or try to find a new home? In the early 1800s, more and more Aboriginal people were being displaced from their homelands, and their cultures were under threat.

DISPLACEMENT AND SETTLEMENTS

Some First Nations peoples were displaced from the United States to Canada. For example, in 1784, the Haudenosaunee Six Nations relocated from New York State to **reserves**, set-aside land, in Ontario. These reserves were given as compensation to First Nations for lands that they had lost. The British government had given First Nations lands to the United States at the end of the American Revolution.

When the Loyalists arrived, other First Nations were displaced within Canada. In some cases, the British government made land treaties with First Nations. For example, the government purchased land along the northwest shore of Lake Ontario (where the city of Toronto now stands) from the Mississauga First Nation in 1787. The Mississauga believed that they were renting the land to the government. To clarify the situation, the government negotiated a second treaty for the same land in 1805. It paid 10 shillings (about 10 cents) and set aside a small parcel of land for the Mississauga. In 2010, the unfairness of these old land transfers was acknowledged. The Canadian government paid a land claim settlement of $145 million to the Mississauga of the New Credit First Nation, located in southern Ontario.

Examine **Figure 5.30**. It is a watercolour of the Mohawk village on the Grand River, painted by Elizabeth Simcoe in 1793. It shows the kind of settled community that First Nations people were being encouraged to live in. Mohawk leader Thayendanegea approved the settlement, believing that First Nations people would benefit by adopting European-style farming. How does this image compare with what you have learned about traditional First Nations communities?

reserve an area of land set aside for the use of a specific group of Aboriginal people

FIGURE 5.30 Elizabeth Simcoe painted *Mohawk Village on the Grand River* in 1793. Thayendanegea lived in the house with the flag. **Analyze:** What European influences can you see in this painting?

FIGURE 5.31 This 1853 painting, *Indian Sugar Camp* by Seth Eastman, shows First Nations people making maple sugar. **Analyze:** According to this painting, what steps are involved in making maple sugar?

ADAPTING TO A NEW ECONOMY

Moving into settled communities made it very difficult for First Nations people to make a living off the land, as they had in the past. Hunting, fishing, and trapping were more difficult because the communities were far away from the best hunting grounds, fishing holes, and trap lines. First Nations people tried other ways to make a living in their changing world. Some found work in towns. Others focused on selling goods such as wild rice, baskets, or maple sugar.

The Anishinaabe (a-nish-i-nah-bay) people on Manitoulin Island are made up of nations that include the Ojibwe, Odawa, and Potawatomi. The Anishinaabe decided to focus on making maple sugar to earn a living. Look at the painting in **Figure 5.31**. It depicts some of the activities that were involved in making maple sugar. What challenges of making maple sugar do you see in the painting?

In 1845, a Catholic priest named Joseph-Urbain Hanipaux moved to Manitoulin Island to serve the Anishinaabe community. Read **Figure 5.32**, an excerpt from a letter that he wrote to his superiors. What injustice does Father Hanipaux describe?

FIGURE 5.32 This excerpt is from a letter written by Hanipaux to his superiors in 1846. **Analyze:** According to Hanipaux, what challenges did First Nations people face in trying to earn a living from maple sugar?

"Our native people have been busy in the woods making maple sugar.... The merchants with whom they deal claim, it is true, to buy the sugar from them at eight or nine cents a pound. But when it comes to paying them, instead of money they give them fabrics to which they attach any price they please, so that in the end the poor native receives only three or four cents for a pound of sugar.... They have had to make a great sacrifice when, to live their Catholic religion better, they came to settle in this village where they do not have any hunting."

— *Father Joseph-Urbain Hanipaux*

ADAPTING TO OR RESISTING CULTURAL CHANGE

Contact between two groups can result in cultural change. Sometimes cultural change is a positive experience, whereby both groups benefit from the best that each culture has to offer. Cultural loss happens when there is an imbalance: when one group gives up aspects of its own culture to embrace another group's culture. This is called assimilation.

Even after winning New France, the British still valued their strong military alliances with some First Nations. They needed First Nations forces to defend their colonies from any future conflict with the new American state to the south. As a result, the British tried to protect some First Nations lands.

However, the British also wanted to control First Nations populations by assimilating them. Many of the British believed that First Nations people should live in settled communities, speak English or French, and give up First Nations spiritual beliefs to practise Christianity. In Lower Canada, the Catholic Church was very active among First Nations people, teaching them the French language and Catholic beliefs. In Upper Canada, the Anglican and Methodist Churches worked to convince First Nations people to embrace a Protestant Christianity. All churches converted many First Nations people.

First Nations people were continuously being encouraged and pressured to adopt European habits and ways of life. Examine the painting in **Figure 5.33** that shows early examples of assimilation. Over many years of exposure to European culture, many First Nations people found that their connection to their own culture was weakened. What evidence of change do you see in this painting as a result of interactions with Europeans?

FIGURE 5.33 This painting, entitled *Costume of Domiciliated Indians of North America*, was created by E. Close in 1814. **Analyze:** Why does the title of the painting use the words *costume* and *domiciliated*?

THE END OF THE BEOTHUK

While some First Nations peoples assimilated or learned to co-exist with the Loyalist settlers, the Beothuk of Newfoundland did neither. They greatly valued their independence and traditions and did not allow anyone to interfere. The Beothuk had always relied on the river and ocean for food. When European fishers came to the island beginning about 1600, the fishers and the Beothuk did not get along. The Beothuk mostly kept their distance from the Europeans. Occasionally, they would leave furs for the European traders and then return to take the traded goods. However, often the Beothuk helped themselves to items the European fishing crews left behind in winter. The fishers viewed the Beothuk as thieves, and violence often broke out. The Beothuk fled to the interior for safety, where they began to starve because they no longer had access to their food resources from the coast.

Some Europeans tried to make alliances with the Beothuk. One of them was John Holloway, governor of Newfoundland from 1807 to 1809. Examine **Figure 5.34**. This is a reproduction of a painting requested by Governor Holloway in 1808. Holloway wanted the painting shown to the Beothuk in the hope of convincing them that the newcomer Europeans were friendly. It did not convince them. Why do you think this painting failed to convince the Beothuk to make an alliance with the Europeans?

Diseases spread among the Beothuk through changes in their diet and occasional contact with Europeans and the items they left behind. Some violence continued as the Beothuk raided settlements. Over time, the Beothuk culture and people could no longer survive. Records show that the last surviving Beothuk in Newfoundland, named Shanawdithit, died in 1829. Before her death, she drew illustrations to tell about her people, such as *Dancing Woman* in **Figure 5.35**. What makes her illustrations, such as this one, historically significant?

FIGURE 5.34 This engraving is a reproduction by John W. Hayward in 1915. He created it from the description of the picture painted for Governor Holloway in 1808. **Analyze:** What does Holloway try to communicate to the Beothuk through this image?

FIGURE 5.35 Shanawdithit drew this illustration, called *Dancing Woman*, in the 1820s. **Analyze:** According to this illustration and its title, what do you think Shanawdithit wanted others to know about her people?

A NEW NATION: THE MÉTIS

While changes in the early 1800s caused hardships for many First Nations peoples, the Métis were flourishing in Western Canada, where there were few settlers. The **Métis** are an Aboriginal people with both European and First Nations ancestry. Their roots lie in the fur trade. When Canadiens (and some Scottish traders) travelled west with the fur trade, they met and formed families with First Nations women, mainly Cree, Ojibwe, or Saulteaux. The children from these relationships became known as Métis. The word Métis originally comes from the Latin word *Miscere* meaning "to mix." It was used to describe the children of First Nations mothers and French fathers. Many of these Métis children also worked in the fur trade when they grew up.

Although these relationships had existed since the 1600s, it was not until the early 1800s that the Métis began to live together in established communities. They chose to live together because they did not feel that they were either First Nations people or European. Instead, they felt like a new people.

The early Métis communities were located near lakes and rivers on the fur trade routes, from the Great Lakes through to the Red River in Manitoba, into Saskatchewan, and toward the West Coast. The Métis farmed the land in long, narrow strips along the river, much like the Canadiens did in Lower Canada.

Examine the painting in **Figure 5.36**. It shows First Nations people, Métis, and Europeans all fishing with nets and spears through holes in the ice. How would you describe this community? The location was known as The Forks (present-day Winnipeg). On the ridge, you can see Fort Gibraltar, a key trading post in the early 1800s. The largest community of Métis families lived near the Red River, as seen in the painting.

Métis an Aboriginal person descended from a First Nations mother and a father of European descent

Why is it important to try to understand how the Métis thought and felt?

FIGURE 5.36 Peter Rindisbacher painted *Winter Fishing on the Ice of the Assynoibaine & Red River* in 1821. **Analyze:** What interactions do you see happening in this painting?

CONNECTIONS TO THE FUR TRADE

Most Métis worked at least part of the year in the fur trade. Some worked as voyageurs transporting furs and supplies, mainly by canoe for the North West Company. Since the North West Company was founded by Scottish immigrants in 1779, it had become a major player in the fur trade. The Métis navigated and translated for their Scottish employers. Other Métis made a living by supplying trading posts with fish, meat, and equipment, such as snowshoes.

An important source of income was the annual bison hunt. Every year, Métis hunters travelled westward as a community to hunt the great bison herds. Not only did the hunt provide food for their families, it was a source of income from making and selling pemmican. **Pemmican** is a food made of dried meat, animal fat, and berries that was highly valued by fur traders.

> In what ways were the early 1800s a period of progress for the Métis?

pemmican a preserved food made of dried meat and berries

A GROWING SENSE OF MÉTIS IDENTITY

Over time, the Métis began to develop their own identity as a distinct people. They developed *Michif*, a language that combines words from various languages, mainly French and Cree. The Métis followed their own beliefs, combining the Catholic religion with aspects of First Nations spirituality. They also developed a distinct style of clothing. Métis men, for example, wore long hooded coats, which they bound at the waist with a long sash. They created dances, such as the Red River jig, and songs that reflected their experiences. These dances and songs are still performed today.

As the century progressed, the Métis formed political bonds as well. They stood together, as a community, to resist attacks on their rights and way of life. What does the quote in **Figure 5.37** by a Métis Elder tell you about Métis identity? Today, the Métis are recognized in Canadian law as one of the three Aboriginal peoples of Canada.

> "If there was good food, there were stories, music and laughter, and from this came a richness that no amount of poverty or violence could completely take away. We were then and we continue to remain *kah tip aim soo chick*: the people who own themselves."
>
> — *Maria Campbell, Métis Elder*

FIGURE 5.37 In 2008, Métis Elder and writer Campbell explained how her people could survive challenging times. **Analyze:** What does Campbell mean when she says the Métis were "the people who own themselves"?

CHECK-IN

1. **HISTORICAL PERSPECTIVE** Create a chart listing some of the changes that Aboriginal peoples were experiencing in the early 1800s. Beside each change, note how an Aboriginal person and a Loyalist settler might view this change. How do their perspectives reflect the time period in which they lived?

2. **HISTORICAL SIGNIFICANCE** Choose one event or development from this section. How could you use it to explain a current issue?

3. **GATHER AND ORGANIZE** What types of sources might help you further explore the topic of Métis and First Nations community life in the early 1800s? Where could you find these sources?

WHY DID PEOPLE EXPERIENCE DIFFERENT CHALLENGES IN EARLY CANADA?

LEARNING GOALS

As you worked through this chapter, you had opportunities to

- identify the factors that affected how a variety of people lived in the early 1800s and the challenges they faced

- examine the significance of people, events, and developments from the early 1800s
- explore historical perspectives on debtors' prison
- analyze and contextualize text sources

In this chapter, you learned that people in Canada experienced life very differently, depending on where they lived and who they were. You learned that living in a town was very different from living in the backwoods. You also learned that not all people within one community led similar lives because of factors such as wealth, ethnicity, and gender.

Summarize Your Learning

Now that you have completed Chapter 5, you are ready to answer the Chapter Big Question: Why did people experience different challenges in early Canada? Select one of the following tasks to summarize your learning:

- Were people's lives more affected by where they lived or who they were? To help you decide on your answer, create a graphic organizer to compare life in town with life in the backwoods. Create another organizer with examples of life for different settlers and life for different Aboriginal peoples.
- Create a blog to help people understand the varied experiences of people living in Canada in the early 1800s. For your first post, present a collection of four quotes or images from this chapter. Make your selections and then explain how your chosen sources help us understand the past or the present.

APPLY **YOUR LEARNING**

1. **HISTORICAL PERSPECTIVE** List all the different groups of people mentioned in this chapter. For which of these groups was there a primary source quote or image to help you understand their lives? If you could add primary sources to this chapter, whose perspective would you like to hear more about? Explain your choice.

2. **CONTINUITY AND CHANGE** Of all the communities mentioned in this chapter, which most resembles the community where you live today? Which aspects of life in this early community continue today in your community? Which aspects have changed?

3. **GATHER AND ORGANIZE** Choose one type of community explored in this chapter. Create a digital scrapbook to tell the story of what life was like for the people who lived there. Look for sources online or in books.

4. **INTERPRET AND ANALYZE** Consider the primary sources used in this chapter, such as letters, diaries, and sketches. What are the challenges and benefits of working with such pieces of evidence? Use examples from this chapter to illustrate your points.

5. **HISTORICAL PERSPECTIVE** Did this chapter include more sources created by women than other chapters? What might explain what you observe?

6. **CONTINUITY AND CHANGE** You read on page 147 about the hardships one person experienced when she arrived in Canada in 1783. What connections can you make to the experience of newcomers to Canada today?

7. **CAUSE AND CONSEQUENCE** Create a movie trailer that features the triumphs or heartaches of a significant figure and their impacts from this period. Use editing software to pull together images, music, and text to create your trailer.

8. **EVALUATE AND DRAW CONCLUSIONS** In which community do you think children may have enjoyed the best quality of life? Extend your research outside this chapter to dig deeper into this question. Create a podcast that includes interviews with three fictional children from the past to share your findings and justify your conclusion.

UNIT 2 CHALLENGE CHECK-IN

1. Review the description of the Unit 2 Challenge on pages 134 to 135. To measure progress or decline during the early 1800s, you need to know what life was like at the beginning of the time period. That will be your baseline information. Make a list of the important characteristics of daily life that you have just learned about in this chapter. Consider characteristics such as health, food, employment, and education. What other characteristics could you add? These characteristics will be the criteria against which you will measure progress or decline in the following chapters. For example, consider whether or not a particular event or development created better employment opportunities for people. For which people?

2. Review the Focus On: Historical Perspective feature on pages 142 to 143. Think about the perspectives of the various groups of people presented in this chapter. Using the criteria you developed in question 1, make brief notes describing daily life from the perspective of each group. Are there any other criteria that you can add to the list you created in question 1? You will need to refer to these notes as you study each chapter in Unit 2, to gather evidence about whether or not events and developments represented progress for each of these groups.

NEL

CHAPTER 6

THE WAR OF 1812

WHAT IS THE SIGNIFICANCE OF THE WAR OF 1812?

LEARNING GOALS

As you work through this chapter, you will

- identify the causes of the War of 1812
- analyze the relevance of different battles and the significance of different individuals
- explore the impact of the War of 1812 on different groups and individuals
- create a story map about the War of 1812

In 2012, the Canadian government spent more than $28 million to celebrate the anniversary of the War of 1812. Why would the federal government spend so much money to celebrate a war that occurred over 200 years ago? Some historians argue that the War of 1812 was a key event in the development of Canadian identity and Canada as a nation separate from Britain and the United States. Others argue that the outcome of the war didn't lead to any major changes in Canada.

The War of 1812 lasted two and a half years. During that time, over 170 battles were fought and many heroes on both sides emerged. On this page, the 1896 painting by John David Kelly, entitled *The Battle of Queenston Heights, 13 October 1812*, focuses on the death of the British military leader Major-General Sir Isaac Brock. Brock is sometimes referred to as the Hero of Upper Canada. Why do you think the artist chose to paint the death of Brock, rather than one of his earlier victories?

As you read this chapter, you will explore causes, perspectives, and outcomes of the War of 1812 and determine its significance in Canadian history.

WHY DID THE UNITED STATES DECLARE WAR?

Wars are destructive and tragic. They are also messy and complicated, as are the reasons causing them. The War of 1812 is no exception. A number of factors caused the United States to declare war, once again, on Britain. Despite gaining their independence from Britain in 1783, many Americans felt that the British did not respect this independence. They believed that the British were still trying to interfere in American politics and government decision making.

THE NAPOLEONIC WARS

By 1812, Britain was already heavily engaged in a war with France. Napoleon Bonaparte, an ambitious military leader, had become the ruler of France. The Napoleonic Wars (1803–1815) pitted the French Empire against other European powers, including Britain and Spain. Napoleon was in a position to overtake Britain.

With Britain focused on fighting France in Europe, the Americans saw an opportunity to gain control of North America. Neither the Americans nor the British thought that Upper and Lower Canada would be significant in this conflict. However, both powers soon discovered the importance of these colonies in determining the outcome of the war.

Examine the painting in **Figure 6.1**. What does the painting reveal about how Americans viewed their relationship with Britain?

FIGURE 6.1 American artist John Archibald Woodside created this painting, entitled *We Owe Allegiance to No Crown*, in 1814. "Crown" is a reference to the British monarchy. **Analyze:** How does the artist indicate that the United States is independent from Britain?

ENFORCED MILITARY SERVICE

The British navy ruled the high seas. In times of war, however, sailors were often in short supply. During the French Revolution (1789–1799) and the Napoleonic Wars, the British Royal Navy authorized the search of port cities in Europe and in the colonies to round up men to serve in the navy. The men would have no choice but to join the navy. This practice was called **impressment**. The units that enforced this military service were called press gangs.

As well, British navy captains chased down American merchant vessels in search of British citizens who were trying to escape impressment by working for the United States. Since citizenship was often difficult to prove, American citizens were sometimes forced into service in the British navy. Estimates suggest that 10 000 American sailors were forced to serve on British ships between 1793 and 1812.

The United States viewed impressment as an offence to national pride and the personal freedom of Americans. This was apparent in an 1807 incident that occurred off the coast of Norfolk, Virginia. In June 1807, HMS *Leopard*, a British warship, fired on USS *Chesapeake*, an American ship, for failing to stop so that the British could search for deserters. **Deserters** are soldiers who leave military service without permission. Although the numbers vary, some sources indicate three men on the *Chesapeake* were killed and another 18 were wounded. Others were taken prisoner by the British and put on trial, including three Americans. The Americans were enraged. Examine an illustration of the incident, shown in **Figure 6.2**. Why was impressment a source of tension between the United States and Britain?

impressment the act of forcing individuals to serve in the military with or without notice

deserter a soldier who abandons military service without permission

FIGURE 6.2 This 1884 engraving by American illustrator Howard Pyle shows a British press gang from HMS *Leopard* investigating USS *Chesapeake* on June 22, 1807. **Analyze:** What does the body language of the inspectors and of the man being inspected tell you about the practice of impressment?

RESTRICTIONS ON TRADE

Britain's conflict with France also affected the ability of the United States to trade with other countries. As Britain gained the upper hand on the seas, Napoleon tried to destroy his enemy economically. In 1806, Napoleon ordered European nations under French control to stop trading with Britain. Britain responded by using its naval power to block cargo ships that were entering or leaving those European ports. In 1807, Britain issued laws, called Orders in Council, that called for neutral nations (those not taking sides in the war, such as the United States) to stop trading with France and its allies. Read the excerpt in **Figure 6.3** by Thomas Jefferson, the American president from 1801 to 1809. How do you think the United States reacted to the restrictions?

> What long-term impact do you think Britain's conflicts with France and the United States had on Canada?

FIGURE 6.3 This excerpt is from a letter written by former American president Jefferson to Consul James Maury on June 16, 1815. As an American consul in Great Britain, Maury represented the interests of the United States in England. **Analyze:** What British practices described in this excerpt do you think the Americans would view as grounds for war?

"[Britain] forbade us to trade with any nation without entering and paying duties in their ports on both the outward and inward cargo. Thus, to carry a cargo of cotton from Savannah to St. Mary's, and take returns in fruits, for example, our vessel was to go to England, enter and pay a duty on her cottons there, return to St. Mary's, then go back to England to enter and pay a duty on her fruits, and then return to Savannah, after crossing the Atlantic four times, and paying tributes [payments] on both cargoes to England, instead of the direct passage of a few hours. And taking ships not doing this, the [British say], is no aggression."

— *Thomas Jefferson, former American president*

Britain did not consider taking American ships that challenged its Orders in Council to be an act of aggression. The United States held a different view. In response, the United States passed its own laws to restrict trade involving Britain and France. The *Embargo Act, 1807* was intended to slow or stop the movement of American goods that supplied the British and French war efforts. The *Embargo Act, 1807* backfired, however. Rather than achieving its goal of getting Britain to back off, the legislation further harmed the American economy and its citizens. American farmers and merchants were not able to sell or trade their goods abroad.

CHALLENGE TO EXPANSION

Another source of tension was the British support for the creation of neutral First Nations territories. The Americans believed that they needed to protect American settlements on the southern and western frontiers, in places such as Ohio and Kentucky, from the Shawnee and other First Nations. The Shawnee and their allies were equally determined to stop the American expansion and drive out the settlers from First Nations lands. Some Americans believed that the British in Upper and Lower Canada were providing weapons to First Nations resisting American settlement west of the Appalachian Mountains.

TECUMSEH AND TENSKWATAWA

Tecumseh was a Shawnee chief and military leader. He opposed the expansion of American territories into the Ohio River Valley. His brother, Tenskwatawa, was a spiritual leader of the Shawnee. The brothers had similar goals for First Nations in America. Tenskwatawa wanted to unify First Nations peoples as one community. Tecumseh proposed an Indian Confederacy in which all First Nations would unite and live on protected lands. His goal was to reclaim territory for the confederacy that had been lost to American settlers. Look at **Figure 6.4**, which shows a confrontation in 1810 between Tecumseh and William Henry Harrison, governor of the Indiana Territory. Tecumseh was protesting Harrison's role in acquiring First Nations lands, which paved the way for expanding American settlements. What details has the artist used to suggest a peaceful resolution to the issue was not possible?

Tecumseh's confederacy was dealt a significant blow on November 7, 1811. Tenskwatawa and his warriors launched an attack against Harrison's forces, despite warnings from Tecumseh to wait until the confederacy was united and strong. The Americans defeated Tenskwatawa at the Battle of Tippecanoe. Tecumseh went on to lead First Nations warriors against the Americans during the War of 1812. Tecumseh's confederacy allied with the British in part to defend the First Nations way of life and lands from the ongoing expansion of the United States.

FIGURE 6.4 This undated engraving, called *Genl. Harrison & Tecumseh*, was created by American illustrator John Reuben Chapin. The colour was added at a later date. It depicts a clash between Shawnee Chief Tecumseh and Governor Harrison at Harrison's Indiana home in 1810. **Analyze:** With whose perspective—Tecumseh's or Harrison's—do you think the artist is more sympathetic? Why?

FIGURE 6.5 This 1872 painting by John Gast is entitled *American Progress* and represents American ideas of expansion into the West. **Analyze:** What symbols in this painting represent American ways of life?

THE CALL FOR WAR

Expanding American settlement farther and farther west was a priority for many American politicians throughout the 1800s. Many Americans viewed the takeover of North America as not only their duty, but also their right. They believed it was their mission to spread American culture and "civilization" throughout as much of the continent as possible. For some, this mission had a religious connection. Examine **Figure 6.5**. The angelic figure represents the spirit of America, leading settlers westward and driving First Nations peoples off their land.

> How might America's idea of westward expansion affect future relations with Canada?

WAR HAWKS

Several American politicians under President James Madison, Thomas Jefferson's successor, supported a war with Britain. They were concerned about Britain's interference in American shipping and exports. They were also concerned about Britain's challenge to westward expansion.

Nicknamed War Hawks because of their demand for armed conflict, these politicians pressured President Madison to take action. One particularly vocal War Hawk was Senator Henry Clay of Kentucky. Read the excerpt from one of his speeches in **Figure 6.6**. What reasons does Clay give for supporting a war with Britain?

> "The conquest of Canada is in your power.... Is it nothing to the British nation—is it nothing to the pride of her monarch to have the last of the immense North American possessions wrested [taken] from his dominion [control]? Is it nothing to us to extinguish the torch that lights up savage warfare? Is it nothing to acquire the entire fur trade connected with that country?"
>
> — *Senator Henry Clay*

FIGURE 6.6 This excerpt is from a speech delivered to Congress by Clay on February 22, 1810. **Analyze:** What does Clay mean by "extinguish the torch that lights up savage warfare"?

AMERICAN EXPECTATIONS

South Carolina congressman John C. Calhoun was another well-known War Hawk, like Clay. Based on his statement in **Figure 6.7**, what challenges does he anticipate from an invasion of Upper and Lower Canada?

> "I believe that in four weeks from the time a declaration of war is heard on our frontier, the whole of Upper Canada and a part of Lower Canada will be in our power."
>
> *— Congressman John C. Calhoun*

FIGURE 6.7 Calhoun delivered this statement in March 1812, three months before the United States declared war. **Analyze:** How are the statements in **Figures 6.6** and **6.7** similar?

On June 18, 1812, the United States officially declared war on Britain. In his proclamation released the next day, shown in **Figure 6.8**, President Madison mentions love of country as a motivating force.

> And I do moreover exhort [urge] all the good people of the United States, as they love their country ... that they exert themselves in preserving order, in promoting concord [harmony], in maintaining the authority and the efficacy of the laws, and in supporting and invigorating all the measures which may be adopted by the Constituted Authorities, for obtaining a speedy, just, and an honourable peace.

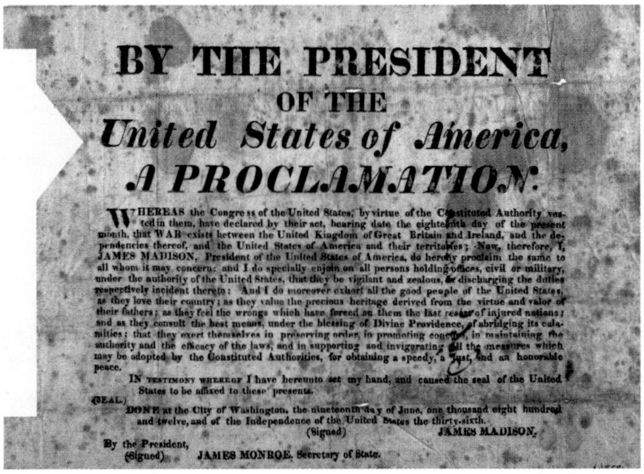

BY THE PRESIDENT
OF THE
United States of America,
A PROCLAMATION:

WHEREAS the Congress of the United States, by virtue of the Constituted Authority vested in them, have declared by their act, bearing date the eighteenth day of the present month, that WAR exists between the United Kingdom of Great Britain and Ireland, and the dependencies thereof, and the United States of America and their territories; Now, therefore, I, JAMES MADISON, President of the United States of America, do hereby proclaim the same to all whom it may concern: and I do specially enjoin on all persons holding offices, civil or military, under the authority of the United States, that they be vigilant and zealous, in discharging the duties respectively incident thereto: And I do moreover exhort all the good people of the United States, as they love their country; as they value the precious heritage derived from the virtue and valor of their fathers; as they feel the wrongs which have forced on them the last resort of injured nations; and as they consult the best means, under the blessing of Divine Providence, of abridging its calamities; that they exert themselves in preserving order, in promoting concord, in maintaining the authority and the efficacy of the laws, and in supporting and invigorating all the measures which may be adopted by the Constituted Authorities, for obtaining a speedy, a just, and an honorable peace.

IN TESTIMONY WHEREOF I have hereunto set my hand, and caused the seal of the United States to be affixed to these presents.

(SEAL.)

DONE at the City of Washington, the nineteenth day of June, one thousand eight hundred and twelve, and of the Independence of the United States the thirty-sixth.

(Signed) JAMES MADISON.

By the President,
(Signed) JAMES MONROE, Secretary of State.

FIGURE 6.8 President Madison issued this proclamation of war against Britain on June 19, 1812. **Analyze:** What do you think the terms of a "just, and an honourable peace" would be for the American people?

During his presidency, Jefferson had tried to avoid another war with Britain. On August 4, 1812, however, Jefferson wrote a letter to journalist and military officer Colonel William Duane. **Figure 6.9** is an excerpt from Jefferson's letter. How does he suggest that America could, once and for all, secure its independence?

> "I see, as you do, the difficulties & defects we have to encounter in war, and should expect disasters ... but the weakness of our enemy there will make our first errors innocent.... The acquisition [capture] of Canada this year, as far as the neighborhood of Québec, will be a mere matter of marching, and will give us experience for the attack of Halifax the next, and the final expulsion of England from the American continent."
>
> *— Thomas Jefferson, former American president*

FIGURE 6.9 This excerpt is from a letter written by Jefferson to Duane on August 4, 1812. **Analyze:** What threat did Jefferson think Upper and Lower Canada would pose to the United States?

REACTIONS IN UPPER AND LOWER CANADA

People in Upper and Lower Canada could sense that dangerous times were ahead. The Americans had fought for their independence from Britain in the American Revolution, but the American settlers in Upper and Lower Canada were mostly content to remain loyal to the British Crown.

However, within days of President Madison's declaration of war with Britain, the police in Québec City issued the notice shown in **Figure 6.10**, advising all American citizens to leave or face arrest. Under what circumstances do you think a notice like this could be issued in Canada today?

> Notice is hereby given, that all Subjects or Citizens of the said United States, and all persons claiming American Citizenship, are ordered to quit the City of Québec ... on pain of arrest.

FIGURE 6.10 This notice, issued on June 29, 1812, indicates that American citizens are no longer welcome in Québec City. **Analyze:** What impact do you think this notice had on families and communities?

CANADIAN EXPECTATIONS

The Americans were very confident that they would easily win the war. They did not consider that people in Upper and Lower Canada would stand up to them. Examine the words of the young British colonists in **Figures 6.11** and **6.12**. How do their perspectives compare with those of the American politicians in **Figures 6.6**, **6.7**, and **6.9**?

> "On this day I saw nothing before me but my Father's honour and glory. Although I knew how small a force we had to defend the Canadas, such was my confidence in his talents and fortune, that I did not feel the slightest apprehension [uneasiness] of any reverse. I thought those abominable [morally disgusting] Yankees deserved a good drubbing [beating] for having dared to think of going to War with England."

— *Anne Prevost, daughter of Sir George Prevost, commander-in-chief of Canada and commander of the British forces in North America*

FIGURE 6.11 Prevost was 17 years old when she wrote this entry in her diary on June 25, 1812. **Analyze:** What are Prevost's feelings toward the United States?

> "The Americans were in high spirits, and when I said I was Canadian, one of the officers laughed and said, 'You'll soon be under the Yankey government, my boy.' I was sassy, like most boys of my age, and I said, 'I'm not so sure about that.'"

— *Jacob Cline, British colonist*

FIGURE 6.12 Cline was only 13 years old when he stood up to the invading American soldiers in 1813. **Analyze:** Why might a young colonist stand up to the American soldiers?

UNDERWATER ARCHAEOLOGIST

We can learn a lot about past events by examining primary sources, such as the diary entry by Anne Prevost and the quote from Jacob Cline. We can also learn about past events by studying historical sites. Archaeology is the study of history through the excavation of sites and the analysis of artifacts and other physical remains.

Jonathan Moore, shown in **Figure 6.13**, is an underwater archaeologist with Parks Canada. He has a particular interest in the War of 1812. He and his team aim to protect "those parts of Canada's history found underwater." Many of the battles in the War of 1812 were fought on the water. Sunken ships still remain at the battle sites.

Moore has been interested in archaeology since he was very young. At 14, he began archaeological work through school programs. He participated in excavations throughout high school and learned how to scuba dive in university. He now spends half of the year conducting "diving fieldwork" all around Canada. He spends the other half of the year in his Ottawa office, researching sites and writing reports, to prepare for the next fieldwork season.

Recently, Moore led an underwater survey of two American warships, USS *Hamilton* and USS *Scourge*, both of which sank in Lake Ontario on August 8, 1813. These wrecks are well preserved at the bottom of the lake and were accessed by remotely operated vehicles. According to Moore, the survey was "like stepping back in time." The intact hulls of the ships contain a treasure trove of artifacts, such as cannons, that provide historians with evidence to help them understand the past.

FIGURE 6.13 Jonathan Moore, taking part in diving fieldwork

MAKING CONNECTIONS

1. How does archaeological evidence provide a more complete understanding of the past than just written or oral evidence alone?

2. What fields of study would help prepare someone for a career in underwater archaeology?

CHECK-**IN**

1. **CAUSE AND CONSEQUENCE** What reasons did the United States have for declaring war on Britain in 1812?

2. **COMMUNICATE** Identify what you think was the primary cause of the War of 1812. Debate your choice in a small group to reach an agreement.

3. **INTERPRET AND ANALYZE** How do you think the War of 1812 could have been avoided?

4. **HISTORICAL SIGNIFICANCE** For whom do you think the outbreak of the War of 1812 was most relevant: the Americans, the British, First Nations, or Canadians? Why?

HOW DID THE WAR PROGRESS?

The War of 1812 was fought on land and on water. However, the United States was at a disadvantage at sea. Britain had one of the largest and most impressive naval forces in the world. Because of this, the Americans needed to find another way to launch their attacks against British forces. They decided to focus on the colonies in Canada.

THE AMERICANS SEND A WARNING

Brigadier General William Hull was a high-ranking officer in the American military during the War of 1812. On July 12, 1812, he issued a proclamation to the colonists in Upper Canada. Read an excerpt from his proclamation in **Figure 6.14**. Like many Americans, Hull believed that the colonists in Upper Canada would not resist the American invasion, because the Americans would free and protect the colonists from British control. At the same time, he warned the colonists against joining the British soldiers in fighting against the Americans.

> If you were Hull, how would you have communicated to the Canadians to persuade them to join the American side in the fight against the British?

"Inhabitants of Canada!

After thirty years of peace and prosperity, the United States have been driven to arms. The injuries and aggressions, the insults and indignities of Great Britain have once more left no alternative but manly resistance or unconditional submission. The army under my command has invaded your country; the standard of the Union [the American flag] now waves over the territory of Canada. To the peaceful unoffending inhabitants, it brings neither danger nor difficulty. I come to find enemies, not to make them; I come to protect, not to injure you ... I have a force which will break down all opposition, and that force is but the vanguard of a much greater—If, contrary to your own interest, and the just expectations of my country, you should take part in the approaching contest, you will be considered and treated as enemies, and the horrors and calamities of war will stalk before you."

— *Brigadier General William Hull*

FIGURE 6.14 This excerpt is from Hull's proclamation to Canadians on July 12, 1812, in Sandwich (present-day Windsor), Upper Canada. **Analyze:** How do you think the Loyalists felt about the invasion and proclamation?

NEW BRITISH MILITARY STRATEGY

Major-General Sir Isaac Brock was a British military commander in Upper Canada during the War of 1812. Strengthening Upper Canada's defences was Brock's first priority. Read the quote in **Figure 6.15**. It is an excerpt from a letter Brock wrote to Lieutenant-Colonel Edward Baynes, four months before the Americans declared war. Baynes was the assistant to Commander-in-Chief Sir George Prevost. What is Brock's main message to Baynes?

Brock believed that the only way that Upper Canada could defend itself from an American invasion was to control Michilimackinac, an island in present-day northern Michigan. As you learned in Chapter 3, this was the location of a battle between First Nations and the British in 1763. Brock believed that controlling the island meant controlling the Upper Great Lakes. This would fend off an American invasion. Brock was right. A large group of 400 First Nations warriors, 200 fur traders, and 46 British officers gathered together as a show of British force. When they reached the island, the American commander was offered a chance to surrender before a full-on attack. He accepted. When Hull learned of this victory, he abandoned his invasion of Upper Canada and retreated to Detroit. **Figure 6.16** shows British troops and their allies preparing for battle. How would you feel if a window in your home overlooked this scene?

> "I set out with declaring my full conviction, that unless Detroit and Michilimackinac be both in our possession immediately at the commencement of hostilities, not only the district of Amherstburg, but most probably the whole country as far as Kingston, must be evacuated."
>
> — *Major-General Sir Isaac Brock*

FIGURE 6.15 This excerpt is from a letter written by Brock to Baynes on February 12, 1812. **Analyze:** Why does Brock believe that most of the country would need to be evacuated?

FIGURE 6.16 This 1997 painting by Keith Rocco, entitled *British Troops at Michilimackinac*, shows the rallying of British troops at Michilimackinac on July 17, 1812. **Analyze:** What evidence do you see in this painting that places the British at an advantage?

KEY EVENTS IN THE WAR OF 1812

Most of the battles in the War of 1812 took place in Upper and Lower Canada. The people in Upper Canada suffered the most because many key battles were fought on their soil, as the map and photos in **Figure 6.17** show. In total, there were over 170 battles, raids, skirmishes (unplanned fighting between small armies or fleets), and campaigns (series of military operations) during the War of 1812. **Figure 6.18** shows a timeline of some of the important events from the start of the war to its end in January 1815.

Battle of Crysler's Farm

FIGURE 6.17 To this day, we still see many monuments in commemoration of the War of 1812. Cities like Toronto have been built around the war's historic remains. **Analyze:** What do these photos tell you about the importance of the War of 1812? Why are memorials such as these important today?

Battle of York

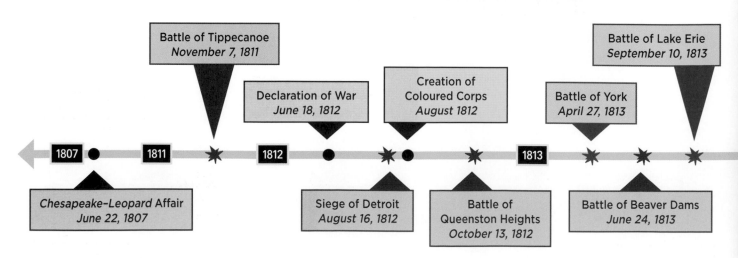

Battle of Tippecanoe
November 7, 1811

Declaration of War
June 18, 1812

Creation of Coloured Corps
August 1812

Battle of York
April 27, 1813

Battle of Lake Erie
September 10, 1813

1807   1811   1812   1813

Chesapeake–Leopard Affair
June 22, 1807

Siege of Detroit
August 16, 1812

Battle of Queenston Heights
October 13, 1812

Battle of Beaver Dams
June 24, 1813

FIGURE 6.18 This timeline shows several significant battles and events from the War of 1812. American victories are in blue, British victories are in red, and events are shown in black.
Analyze: What do you notice about the progression of the war?

Select Battles from the War of 1812

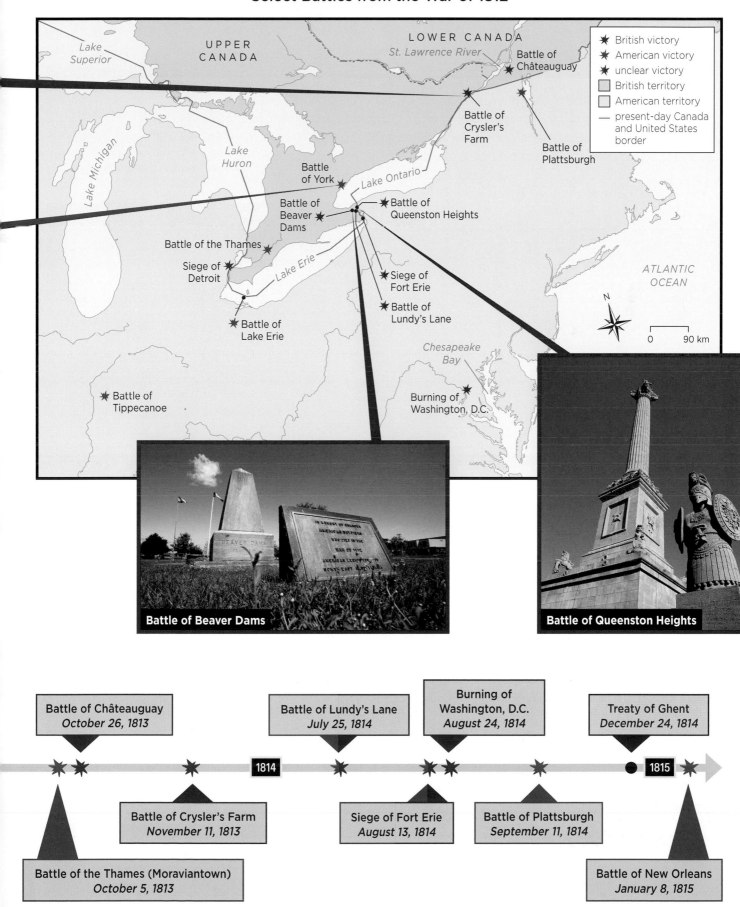

Battle of Beaver Dams

Battle of Queenston Heights

Timeline:

- **Battle of Châteauguay** *October 26, 1813*
- **Battle of the Thames (Moraviantown)** *October 5, 1813*
- **Battle of Crysler's Farm** *November 11, 1813*
- 1814
- **Battle of Lundy's Lane** *July 25, 1814*
- **Siege of Fort Erie** *August 13, 1814*
- **Burning of Washington, D.C.** *August 24, 1814*
- **Battle of Plattsburgh** *September 11, 1814*
- **Treaty of Ghent** *December 24, 1814*
- 1815
- **Battle of New Orleans** *January 8, 1815*

CREATING
A STORY MAP

A story map uses a combination of words and multimedia, such as photos and videos, to tell a story. A story map might be suitable to document and describe places you have visited, damage caused by natural disasters, current world affairs, or historical events, such as major battles in a war.

You can make a story map using online mapping technologies, such as ArcGIS Online. In the following activity, you will choose a battle from the War of 1812 and use ArcGIS Online to create a story map about this battle. You can choose one of the battles listed in **Figure 6.19** (referenced in the timeline on pages 176 and 177) or another battle that interests you. You will gather primary and secondary sources to help you document and describe your chosen battle in your story map.

FIGURE 6.19 This table lists some of the War of 1812's important battles, and their present-day location and coordinates.

Battle	Location	Coordinates
Siege of Detroit	Detroit, Michigan	42.33°N, 83.05°W
Battle of Queenston Heights	Niagara-on-the-Lake, Ontario	43.26°N, 79.07°W
Battle of York	Toronto, Ontario	43.70°N, 79.40°W
Battle of Châteauguay	Très-Saint-Sacrement, Québec	45.38°N, 73.75°W
Battle of Lundy's Lane	Niagara Falls, Ontario	43.12°N, 79.07°W
Siege of Fort Erie	Fort Erie, Ontario	42.92°N, 79.02°W
Burning of Washington, D.C.	Washington, District of Columbia	38.91°N, 77.02°W

HOW TO CREATE A STORY MAP

STEP 1
Choose a battle from the War of 1812. Research information about the battle. Then decide what you would like to document in your story map and develop a plan. For example, you could include a list of key dates and locations leading up to the battle, the names of important people, and the perspectives of different people and groups involved in the battle.

STEP 2
Gather primary and secondary sources to include in your story map. You could include images of people, places, or artifacts from the battle, quotes from people involved in or affected by the battle, or links to modern-day connections.

STEP 3
Start ArcGIS Online. Click on **Map** on the top toolbar to open the ArcGIS Online map viewer. Use the search box or zoom in to focus your map on the area of the battle. Choose a suitable basemap, such as the National Geographic basemap.

STEP 4
Add key locations and data to your map using **Add Map Notes**. You could add points to show the location of the battle and the locations of key events leading up to it. You could also add descriptions and images from your primary and secondary sources, as well as website links.

STEP 5
Save your map. Give your map a title and appropriate tags.

STEP 6
Click **Share**. You can now create your story map by clicking the **Create a Web App** button and using the **Story Map Tour** template. **Create** your story map, and share it with your classmates.

SIGNIFICANT BATTLES IN THE WAR OF 1812

The British, Americans, and allies from both sides, which included First Nations, fought to gain or defend territories. What were the human costs of this two-and-a-half-year war? There is no way to know exactly. Official records are vague. Thousands were killed in the battles and thousands more were killed due to diseases and other factors stemming from the battles. Some sources estimate a total of about 35 000 British soldiers, American soldiers, and First Nations warriors died in battle and from other causes related to the War of 1812.

The following are some of the key battles that took place during the War of 1812.

The Siege of Detroit

At the outset of the war, the Americans focused on Detroit as a key location from which to invade Upper Canada. Detroit lay between the British forces and their First Nations allies. By setting up camp in Detroit, the Americans hoped to interrupt communications between the British and their allies.

Hull's strategy of scaring colonists in Upper Canada into surrendering to the Americans (see **Figure 6.14**) did not work. In August 1812, under the leadership of Brock, a few hundred soldiers from Britain, British colonists from Upper and Lower Canada and the Maritimes, and First Nations allies, crossed the Detroit River to attack. Hull's 2500 troops vastly outnumbered Brock's forces. Despite this, the Americans believed Brock's forces were much larger than they actually were. Hull surrendered after heavy fire from British ships along the Detroit River. **Figure 6.20** shows the important role of the navy in the British victory.

This early win for the British helped to solidify alliances between the British and First Nations, especially between Brock and Tecumseh.

FIGURE 6.20 The *Bombardment of Fort Detroit, 1812* was painted in 1997 by artist Peter Rindlisbacher. Rindlisbacher is known for his historically accurate portrayals of naval battles. **Analyze:** How do you think fighting a battle on the water differs from fighting on land?

The Battle of Queenston Heights

FIGURE 6.21 This is a colourized image of an 1836 painting entitled *The Battle of Queenston Heights*. The original artist is unknown. **Analyze:** How does seeing this depiction of the battle help you to understand how the British won the battle?

The Americans considered Niagara in Upper Canada another strategic place to launch an invasion. If they conquered Niagara, they could cut off British access to Detroit.

The Americans invaded the town of Queenston in Niagara on October 13, 1812. Brock was awakened by the sound of guns being fired. He did not have the forces he needed to deal with such an invasion, but he gathered a small number of troops. As he led the troops up the hill (called the Heights), Brock was shot in the chest and killed. His troops withdrew. A few hours later, with a new major-general in place, more British troops arrived, along with Haudenosaunee Six Nations and Delaware warriors. The American forces were reduced when some members of the American militia, who were not strong supporters of the war, refused to fight on the Canadian side of the border. **Figure 6.21** shows the American forces crossing the Niagara River and scrambling up the embankment. British troops are assembled at the top of the hill, ready to face their attackers. The British won this battle, giving them a significant victory.

York (present-day Toronto) was the capital of Upper Canada. Its location was strategic since it was a site where weapons and gunpowder were stored. It also had a massive ship—HMS *Sir Isaac Brock*—under construction. The Americans thought that control of this ship would mean control of the Great Lakes.

Approximately 1700 American troops and a fleet of ships attacked York on April 27, 1813. The Americans beat the British and a group of Ojibwe and Mississauga warriors. They took the town, Fort York, and the dockyard. As the British retreated, however, they set off an explosion. The explosion blew up much of the fort and caused many deaths and casualties on both sides. The British also burnt HMS *Sir Isaac Brock* to prevent the Americans from capturing it.

In August 1814, the British retaliated for the loss of York. They attacked Washington, the capital of the United States. The British set fire to the White House, the Capitol building that held the Library of Congress, the treasury building, and the navy yard. When the fires were put out the next day, only one government building was left standing.

Figure 6.22 depicts the burning of the White House. Why would this be an important building for the British to destroy?

FIGURE 6.22 This image, entitled *The Burning of the White House, 1814*, was created by Tom Freeman in 2004. **Analyze:** How do you think both the British and the Americans felt as they watched the White House burn?

The Battle of Châteauguay

The Americans planned to invade Montréal and cut off British supply ties between Montréal and Kingston. Their goal was to hinder British war efforts in Upper Canada. However, leadership and communication were poor on the American side. Although American forces outnumbered the British by about eight times, they overestimated how large the British forces were.

The Battle of Châteauguay, shown in **Figure 6.23**, happened on October 26, 1813. The British forces in Lower Canada consisted of British soldiers, Canadian *Voltigeurs* (largely French-speaking soldiers from Québec), local militia, and Mohawk, Huron, and Abenaki warriors. The British blew horns in the woods as a tactic to trick the Americans into thinking they were outnumbered. The Americans were fooled and retreated. Montréal remained under British control. Of greater significance was that soldiers from both Upper Canada and Lower Canada joined forces in the battle. This meant that, for the first time in North America, the French and the English fought alongside each other.

FIGURE 6.23 This image, entitled *Bataille de Châteauguay, 1813*, was created by Henri Julien around 1884. **Analyze:** Would a colourized version of this image enhance your understanding of the Battle of Châteauguay? Why, or why not?

In the darkness of July 25, 1814, the Battle of Lundy's Lane began. Examine **Figure 6.24**. What does it tell you about this battle that took place near Niagara Falls? The lack of light led to much confusion on the battlefield. Both the British and the Americans accidentally killed some of their own men. The Americans withdrew and decided to build their defences at Fort Erie.

The British forces attacked Fort Erie on August 13, 1814. Their goal was to lay siege to the fort and force the Americans out of their defensive stronghold. Haudenosaunee Six Nations, Ojibwe, Mississauga, Odawa, Wyandot, and Delaware warriors fought alongside the British. Despite intense fighting, the British and their allies were unable to defeat the Americans and withdrew on September 21.

The Americans later decided to abandon the fort due to a shortage of supplies. They retreated across the Niagara River to American territory in Buffalo. Before leaving on November 5, 1814, they blew up the fort so that the British could not use it.

Because both the Americans and the British retreated, there was no clear winner in the battle. The British claimed victory from Lundy's Lane and the Americans claimed victory from Fort Erie.

FIGURE 6.24 This colourized image of an 1859 painting entitled *Lundy's Lane* by Alonzo Chappel depicts the Battle of Lundy's Lane on July 25, 1814. **Analyze:** Does this painting support the view that there was no winning side in this battle? Why, or why not?

CHECK-**IN**

1. **CAUSE AND CONSEQUENCE** What were some intended and unintended consequences of some of the significant battles in Upper and Lower Canada?

2. **HISTORICAL SIGNIFICANCE** Which battle do you think was most significant, and why? What criteria did you use to come to this conclusion?

3. **COMMUNICATE** Choose a battle from pages 179 to 181. Imagine you are a journalist reporting from the front lines of that battle. Create a news report covering the significant events of the battle. Remember to include a headline and answer the 5Ws in your report.

HOW WERE PEOPLE AFFECTED BY
THE WAR AND ITS OUTCOME?

Wars always have short-term and long-term effects. The people who fought in, and lived through, the War of 1812 were affected by its brutality. They lived with the trauma of the war, both mental and physical, for many years. As well, the war was a turning point in the relationships among Aboriginal peoples, the British, and the Americans. The long-term effects of the war on Aboriginal peoples are still being felt today.

> Who had the most to gain from a British victory in the War of 1812?

FIGHTING IN THE WAR

People fought in the war for many different reasons. Some were shipped over from Britain to fight in the war and defend the colony. Others were colonists who were already living in Canada. Some were eager to defend their country. Others felt obligated to fight in the war to protect their family and their property.

FIGURE 6.25 This 1971 painting entitled *The 104th (New Brunswick) Regiment of Foot* by Robert Marrion shows a pioneer of that regiment during the War of 1812. **Analyze:** What does this painting tell you about this soldier's role?

BLACK SOLDIERS

Some soldiers fought to keep their freedom. If the Americans succeeded in taking over Canada, Black Loyalists and other Black settlers could be forced back into slavery. As you learned in Chapter 5, Richard Pierpoint was a Black Loyalist who escaped slavery and fought for the British during the American Revolution. Wanting to fight in the War of 1812, he petitioned the military to create a company of Black soldiers. The Coloured Corps was the first all-Black company and fought in several important battles. At the time, the term *coloured* was used to refer to Black people, but it is not a term used today. Black soldiers also served in other ways. Each fighting unit had a team of about 10 men called pioneers. These pioneers were good with tools and, instead of fighting, they would build roads and bridges for the military and repair any damage to forts. Despite this, these soldiers still faced discrimination during their service. At the end of the war, they also were given less land and compensation than other soldiers. The soldier shown in **Figure 6.25** served in an all-Black group of pioneers. Why do you think the artist chose to portray the soldier in this stance?

THE EFFECTS OF THE WAR ON SOLDIERS

Soldiers who fought in the war experienced harsh battle conditions. In addition to injuries and the death of their fellow soldiers, they faced deadly epidemics of disease, such as measles, malaria, and smallpox, and endured terrible weather conditions. For some soldiers, these conditions caused them to flee the army. It is estimated that over 1500 British soldiers from units in Upper and Lower Canada deserted their troops during the War of 1812. If British deserters were captured, they were whipped or sentenced to hard labour as a penalty. Some were even executed.

LIVING IN A WAR ZONE

Soldiers were not the only ones to experience tremendous hardships during the war. Thousands of women and children were forced from their homes, including an estimated 2000 to 4500 First Nations women and children. They saw their family members and friends killed, their houses burned to the ground, and their food stolen by American soldiers. Estimates suggest that in Upper Canada, nearly 1 in 10 families lost property and 1 in 45 lost a family member in the war.

Invading American soldiers posed a real danger in Upper and Lower Canada. Read the quote in **Figure 6.26** by 16-year-old Amelia Ryerse. She describes the destruction of present-day Niagara-on-the-Lake by American soldiers. What does her experience tell you about what life was like for people during the war? Although the British government offered to compensate people for their lost property, the payments came years later and were far less than what was lost.

Many women took care of homes, children, and farms when the men went off to fight. Women also provided vital support to soldiers in camps and on the battlefield. They prepared meals and mended and washed uniforms. They nursed the wounded. Some women even took their children and followed their husbands to the battlefields. What does the image in **Figure 6.27** tell you about some women's involvement in the war?

FIGURE 6.26 The attack that Ryerse witnessed occurred on December 10, 1813. Almost all of the community's possessions were burned, and young and old alike were left to freeze in the snow. **Analyze:** Why do you think the invading American soldiers would burn homes and possessions?

"When I looked up I saw the hillside and the fields as far as the eye could reach covered with American soldiers.... Very soon we saw a column of dark smoke rise from every building and what at early [morning] had been a prosperous homestead, at noon there were only smouldering ruins."

— Amelia Ryerse, settler living in Niagara-on-the-Lake

FIGURE 6.27 This image from 1860 is entitled *A Soldier's Wife at Fort Niagara*. A woman is seen loading artillery with cannonballs during a battle at the fort during the War of 1812. **Analyze:** What might the artist want to convey about women's participation in the war effort?

HISTORICAL SIGNIFICANCE

How do you decide which stories to tell your friends, parents, or teachers? Are there some stories that you do not tell at all? Historians also make choices about what events, people, and developments are significant enough to research and retell.

When you think about the historical significance of various events, people, and developments, you can ask yourself the following questions:
- Did the event, person, or development create a long-lasting change?
- If so, how many people were affected, and were they affected profoundly or deeply?
- Was this the first time that an event such as this occurred or an idea such as this was introduced?
- Does this event, person, or development reveal something about the past that is different from the present?
- How did the significance of this event, person, or development vary for different people?
- Has the historical significance of this event, person, or development changed over time?

CASE STUDY: LAURA SECORD

Laura Secord is one of the most well-known women in Canadian history. Examine the evidence here and consider whether you think she is historically significant.

Secord lived in the Niagara region in Upper Canada. When the Americans occupied the area in 1813, Secord and her husband, James, were forced to take American soldiers into their home. She heard about the soldiers' plans to invade the British territory known as Beaver Dams. She walked more than 30 km through swamps and forest, avoiding American-occupied roads, to warn the British forces about the upcoming attack. When the attack came on June 24, 1813, the British and Mohawk were prepared. They defeated the Americans. Secord was not mentioned in British Lieutenant James FitzGibbon's official battle report.

Read **Figure 6.28**, which is a letter FitzGibbon wrote in 1827. Why do you think Secord might have been left out of the original 1813 report?

> "The weather on the 22nd day of June, 1813 was very hot, and Mrs. Secord, whose person was slight and delicate, appeared to have been and no doubt was very much exhausted by the exertion she made in coming to me, and I have ever since held myself personally indebted to her for her conduct upon that occasion."
>
> — Lieutenant James FitzGibbon

FIGURE 6.28 This excerpt from an 1827 letter was one of the first times FitzGibbon acknowledged Secord's efforts. **Analyze:** How does FitzGibbon describe Secord's actions?

Secord did not receive any recognition for her efforts until 1860 when a group of War of 1812 veterans were addressing the Prince of Wales. Secord insisted on being included. Impressed, the Prince sent Secord 100 pounds. What does **Figure 6.29** tell you about how Secord and her story were treated over time?

> "Perhaps Laura Secord's true importance lies in what her story tells us about how history treats women. The stubborn old lady who only wanted her fair share of the patronage rewards was too real and too much like a man. She had to be turned into a noble heroine."
>
> — Mona Holmlund and Gail Youngberg, historians

FIGURE 6.29 This excerpt is from a 2003 book which profiled women in Canadian history. **Analyze:** What do Secord's experiences reveal about attitudes toward women during this time period?

FIGURE 6.30 In Lorne K. Smith's 1920 painting, Secord is shown informing British soldiers of the American invasion plans in June 1813. **Analyze:** How does this depiction of Secord compare with what you know about the role of women during the War of 1812?

In 1913, Secord was chosen to be the public face of a chocolate company because she represented courage, devotion, and loyalty. Her portrait has been printed on stamps and she is the subject of many paintings, such as the one in **Figure 6.30**. As well, there have been plays and music praising her heroic act. Consider the perceptions of Secord at different times. What do the different sources tell you about her historical significance?

TRY IT

1. Is Laura Secord historically significant? Use at least two of the significance criteria questions to explain your answer.
2. How is Secord still relevant to us today?
3. What other person from the War of 1812 do you think is significant? Use the significance criteria questions to support your answer.

THE END OF THE WAR

When the Napoleonic Wars ended in Europe in the spring of 1814, more British resources became available to help fight the War of 1812. The end of the Napoleonic Wars also brought about an end to impressment and restrictions on American shipping and trade. These were two of the reasons why the Americans had declared war in the first place. With their hope of taking over Canada fading, the United States began to look for ways to end the conflict with Britain.

THE TREATY OF GHENT

Both sides wanted to end the war. The Americans realized they could not take over the colonies in Canada. Their goal was to protect the territory and independence that they had gained during the American Revolution. As shown in **Figure 6.31**, representatives from both the United States and Britain met in Europe to negotiate peace. These negotiations took months, however, and so the war continued. In fact, while they were negotiating peace in August 1814, the British burned down the capital in Washington, D.C.

The Treaty of Ghent was signed in Belgium on December 24, 1814, officially ending of the War of 1812. Despite the peace treaty being signed, Britain and the United States clashed again in the major Battle of New Orleans (see **Figure 6.18**).

The Treaty of Ghent essentially returned everything to the way it was before the war. Any territories that the British had won during the war were returned to the Americans. Any territories that the Americans had won were returned to the British. The border between the United States and Canada stayed the same. Both the British and the Americans walked away from the treaty believing that they had won the war.

FIGURE 6.31 This painting, *The Signing of the Treaty of Ghent* by Sir Amédée Forestier, was created in 1914. It shows representatives from the British and American governments shaking hands after signing the treaty. **Analyze:** Who is missing from these negotiations?

IMPACT OF THE WAR ON ABORIGINAL PEOPLES

In all, more than 10 000 Métis and First Nations warriors, including Tecumseh's confederacy, allied with the British to protect their lands and to prevent any further expansion by the Americans. Members of the Shawnee, Haudenosaunee Six Nations, Ojibwe, Dakota, and Mississauga nations, along with the Métis, fought in nearly every major battle during the war. Their significance to British victories on the battlefields cannot be overstated.

However, while there continues to be debate over whether the British or the Americans won the war, most historians agree that First Nations on both sides of the border suffered the greatest losses in status and territory. First Nations peoples endure to this day the consequences of the War of 1812. The war was the last conflict in which the involvement of First Nations as partners was critical. After the war ended, the British stopped creating military alliances with First Nations. They also began to focus on policies of assimilation, as well as continuing to obtain First Nations' land for new British settlers.

> What would motivate government policies to change how Aboriginal peoples are treated?

FIRST NATIONS AND THE TREATY OF GHENT

There were no representatives from First Nations present during the negotiations for the Treaty of Ghent. What does the quote in **Figure 6.32** tell you about the reaction of First Nations to the treaty? While the British did try to negotiate an established territory for First Nations peoples, the United States refused. With the stroke of a pen, First Nations lost their military and economic allies in North America. Promises made by the British before the war in order to secure First Nations alliances were also quickly abandoned and soon forgotten. What does the quote in **Figure 6.33** tell you about the perspective of First Nations peoples on the the treaty today?

> "After we have fought for you, endured many hardships, lost some of our people and awakened the vengeance of our powerful neighbours, you make peace for yourselves, leaving us to obtain such terms as we can."
>
> — *Chief Little Crow, Lakota First Nation*

FIGURE 6.32 This statement was made by Chief Little Crow in 1816 after the Treaty of Ghent was signed. He was angered by Britain's acceptance of Article 9 in the Treaty of Ghent. Article 9 offered no protection of First Nations' interests. **Analyze:** What are Chief Little Crow's concerns as a result of the Treaty of Ghent?

> "Our ancestors did contribute to building this nation, and it should be recognized and acknowledged. But it's also a story about betrayal, too. The British and the United States signed a peace treaty on the other side of the ocean—in Europe, in Belgium—and the First Nations, of course, weren't there to represent themselves. And all of the promises made at the beginning, like the creation of a homeland state for First Nations, that was gone. The United States pushed the negotiations to eliminate those promises. And the British abandoned their allies."
>
> — *Chief Darcy Bear, Whitecap Dakota First Nation*

FIGURE 6.33 This comment from Chief Bear appeared in a *National Post* article on June 17, 2012. **Analyze:** What one word, or few words, in this comment summarizes your understanding of the treatment of First Nations after the War of 1812?

TERRITORY LOSSES

First Nations fought in the War of 1812 to protect their lands from settlement by the Americans and to create an "Indian" state. In the summer of 1815, the United States signed treaties with different First Nations, guaranteeing those nations the land that had belonged to them in 1811. However, the United States never returned any of the land that First Nations had prior to 1811. In fact, the advance of settlers into First Nations' territory increased, pushing First Nations peoples north and west, off their land. Read the excerpt in **Figure 6.34** and examine the map in **Figure 6.35**, which shows First Nations lands in the United States before and after the War of 1812. What do these sources tell you about the outcome of the war for First Nations peoples and their lands?

> Why do you think the Americans and the British were able to ignore agreements they made with First Nations?

FIGURE 6.34 This quote from Macleod, curator of the Canadian War Museum's 1812 exhibit, appeared in a *National Post* article on December 12, 2012. **Analyze:** Why is the phrase "catastrophic defeat" an appropriate way to describe the outcome of the War of 1812 for First Nations peoples?

> "Native Americans that fought as British allies hoped that the support of a powerful European ally would allow them to roll back the American settlement frontier and secure their homelands and independence. Instead, they suffered a catastrophic defeat."
>
> — *Peter Macleod, Canadian War Museum curator*

FIGURE 6.35 This map shows the course of American expansion onto First Nations lands in under a century. **Analyze:** What does the map tell you about the loss of First Nations lands before and after the War of 1812?

First Nations' Land Losses in Northeastern United States, 1784–1850

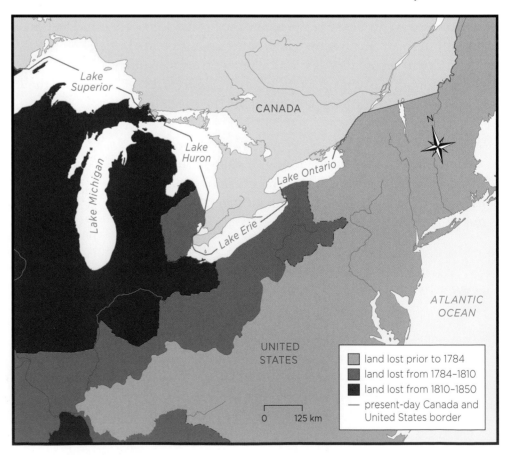

THE QUESTION OF WHO WON THE WAR

History often looks at war in terms of who won and who lost. So who won the War of 1812? There are many different perspectives on this question. Some people argue that it was a second war of independence for the United States, and that the Americans successfully defended themselves against the British. Others argue that the Canadians won, and see the war as a moment when we came together to defend ourselves as a nation, separate from the United States. There is a saying that states, "History is written by the victors." What do you think this means? Who do you think was victorious in the War of 1812? Consider **Figure 6.36**, which is one historian's viewpoint on the War of 1812.

> Can a war be considered significant if there is not a clear winner? Why, or why not? Explain.

"The War of 1812 is one of those episodes in history that makes everybody happy, because everybody interprets it in his own way. The Americans think of it primarily as a naval war in which the pride of the Mistress of the Seas was humbled.... Canadians think of it equally pridefully as a war of defense in which their brave fathers, side by side, turned back the massed might of the United States and saved the country from conquest. And the English are the happiest of all, because they don't even know it happened."

— *C.P. Stacey, Canadian military historian*

FIGURE 6.36 Stacey shared this viewpoint on the War of 1812 in a 1964 book about the war. **Analyze:** Whose viewpoint is missing in Stacey's quote?

Between 2012 and 2014, there were many celebrations and events in Canada to mark the 200th anniversary of the War of 1812, like the one shown in **Figure 6.37**. What do these celebrations say about the significance of the war for Canadians today?

FIGURE 6.37 The Niagara Parks Commission stages a re-enactment of the Siege of Fort Erie every August. **Analyze:** Why might someone participate in a historical re-enactment?

CHECK-**IN**

1. **CAUSE AND CONSEQUENCE** What were the consequences of the War of 1812 for First Nations? Which consequences do you think were unintended?

2. **HISTORICAL SIGNIFICANCE** In what ways is the War of 1812 relevant to Canadians today? Explain.

3. **EVALUATE AND DRAW CONCLUSIONS** Examine the experiences of Black people, women, and First Nations peoples during the war. Was the War of 1812 a period of progress or decline for each of these groups?

WHAT IS THE SIGNIFICANCE OF THE WAR OF 1812?

LEARNING GOALS

As you worked through this chapter, you had opportunities to

- identify the causes of the War of 1812
- analyze the relevance of different battles and the significance of different individuals
- explore the impact of the War of 1812 on different groups and individuals
- create a story map about the War of 1812

In this chapter, you learned that Canada could have become part of the United States as a possible result of the War of 1812. Instead, Canada's borders were defined and fortified, and Canada remained part of the British Empire. The United States never conquered British territory in North America, but it asserted itself again as an independent nation and won some significant battles. Canada managed to protect itself from an American invasion and came together as a nation. Today, both Canadians and Americans can find evidence to argue that they were victorious. You also learned the important role of First Nations in the War of 1812, and how the outcome of the war led to massive territory losses.

Summarize Your Learning

Now that you have completed Chapter 6, you are ready to answer the Chapter Big Question: What is the significance of the War of 1812? Select one of the following tasks to summarize your learning:

- On the basis of the evidence you have encountered and other sources you can find, come to a conclusion that answers the Big Question. Defend your position in a multimedia presentation. Use visuals and other sources to present your argument. Make sure that you take different perspectives into consideration.
- Was the peace created between the United States and Britain at the end of the War of 1812 worth the consequences of the war? With a partner, organize a debate to argue each side.

APPLY **YOUR LEARNING**

1. `CAUSE AND CONSEQUENCE` Identify two groups that were affected by the War of 1812. Were the consequences of war similar or different for both groups? Why?

2. `CONTINUITY AND CHANGE` Compare the experiences of the Black Loyalists when they first arrived in Canada to their participation in the Coloured Corps. Had anything changed for Black Loyalists? Did anything stay the same? Explain.

3. `FORMULATE QUESTIONS` What questions would you want to ask those who signed the Treaty of Ghent? Create the dialogue for an interview.

4. `INTERPRET AND ANALYZE` How does learning about the War of 1812 affect how you see wars that are occurring today?

5. `HISTORICAL SIGNIFICANCE` List the most significant events and battles of the War of 1812. Using the same two groups of people from question 1, determine whether each event and battle you have listed was significant for them or not.

6. `GATHER AND ORGANIZE` Research the War of 1812 from the perspectives of an American historian, a Canadian historian, a British historian, and a First Nations historian. Compare their perspectives. Based on your research, write a paragraph outlining your perspective on the War of 1812.

7. `HISTORICAL PERSPECTIVE` Whose voices do you think are missing from the narrative of the War of 1812? Why do you think those voices are not heard?

8. `COMMUNICATE` Write the script for a re-enactment of one of the key events or battles in the War of 1812. Create a podcast of the script. Incorporate excerpts from the primary and secondary sources in this chapter, where possible.

9. `HISTORICAL PERSPECTIVE` Create an artwork that conveys the experience of someone you learned about in this chapter. Your piece could be a poem, song, painting, diorama, or digital collage. Give your artwork an appropriate title.

10. `CONTINUITY AND CHANGE` Draw what you think the map in **Figure 6.35** should have looked like after the War of 1812 to reflect the promises made to First Nations.

UNIT 2 CHALLENGE CHECK-IN

1. Review the Focus On: Historical Significance feature on pages 184 to 185. Using the criteria provided, identify the most significant events or developments during the War of 1812.

2. What were the consequences of these events or developments? How did these events or developments affect different groups? Which groups gained and which groups lost as a result of the war?

3. Review the criteria and notes you made for the Chapter 5 Unit Challenge Check-In. Are there any other criteria you would like to add or any changes you would like to make, based on what you have learned in Chapter 6?

4. Now you are ready to set up your timeline. Review the description of the Unit 2 Challenge on pages 134 to 135. Rank the significant events and developments during this time period on your timeline. Place events and developments that represent progress above your timeline. Place events and developments that represent decline below your timeline. Use different colours to represent different groups. A single event or development might create progress for one group but may cause decline for another. Record all impacts. If there is no impact on any particular group, place the event or development in the middle (on the horizontal axis). Include evidence from sources in the chapter to support your rankings.

CHAPTER 7

THE CHANGING FACE OF CANADA:
1815-1836

HOW WERE PEOPLE AFFECTED BY SOCIAL CHANGE?

LEARNING GOALS

As you work through this chapter, you will

- examine the changing settlements and population in Canada after the war, and consider the perspectives of the people who arrived in Canada
- learn how conflicts shaped the West and impacted Aboriginal peoples
- analyze perspectives and tensions related to religious and racial differences in Canada
- use graphs to understand population growth in Canada

If you were thinking about moving to Canada in the 1800s, what would encourage or discourage you? After the War of 1812, Canada experienced a period of change and growth. Kingston grew rapidly after the war, quickly becoming the largest town in Upper Canada. *Kingston from Fort Henry* was painted by James Gray in 1828, during this period of growth. Can you tell from the painting what social changes were happening? Social changes can include anything that impacts a society and culture, such as political, economic, and legal changes. The buildings in the background or the boats on the river might indicate economic success. The soldiers might indicate a site of military importance. The number of people in the painting might suggest a large population.

After the War of 1812, waves of immigrants arrived and settled in Canada. This was also a period of economic growth and competition, particularly in the West. However, as the population increased and became more diverse, class, religious, and racial tensions grew.

As you explore this chapter, you will examine the factors and developments that contributed to this period of change and growth in Canadian history.

HOW DID SETTLEMENTS IN CANADA
CHANGE AFTER THE WAR?

Have you ever thought about the history of your community and what it would have been like to live there 200 years ago? What has stayed the same? What has changed?

The Treaty of Ghent, which ended the War of 1812, did not change the borders between Canada and the United States. However, decisions and developments made after the war affected the settlements and lives of the people who were living in Canada.

PROTECTING AND GROWING COMMUNITIES

The British government wanted to prevent any further conflict with the Americans. They also wanted to protect their colonies from possible American attacks. To do this, they built new forts and improved the existing forts throughout Upper Canada. They also encouraged settlement as a way to keep control over the land.

Kingston was one of the communities that was affected by the British government's decision to improve Canada's defences. With its position at the entrance to the St. Lawrence River from Lake Ontario, Kingston was the ideal location to build a fort. Fort Henry was built during the War of 1812 to protect the town and river from invading Americans. The fort was expanded and rebuilt in 1832. Why would the British expand and rebuild a fort during a time of peace? Today, Fort Henry is a National Historic Site. **Figure 7.1** shows a Sunset Ceremony of the Fort Henry Guard, who are Canadians trained to represent British soldiers.

In the same year the fort was expanded, the Rideau Canal opened. It is a 202 km canal that was built to link Kingston to Bytown (present-day Ottawa). As a result, Kingston became a military, economic, transportation, and political centre. The Rideau Canal was a major point of defence, a secure route for the shipment of goods, and a transportation route for immigrants who were arriving from Lower Canada to settle in Upper Canada.

FIGURE 7.1 This photo shows a Sunset Ceremony at Fort Henry. **Analyze:** Why do you think the fort holds ceremonies celebrating British soldiers of the past?

FROM SOLDIERS TO SETTLERS

The British government wanted former soldiers, or veterans, from the War of 1812 and the Napoleonic Wars in Europe to settle in the colonies. Former soldiers were given land grants in Upper and Lower Canada based on their rank and years of service. They were also given transportation to Canada, supplies, and food. The soldiers had to clear and cultivate a set amount of their land within a certain time period. If they failed, they had to give back the land. What does the artwork in **Figure 7.2** tell you about the challenges of clearing the land? Perth, located in present-day eastern Ontario, was one of these military settlements. Two-thirds of the town's original population was made up of soldiers. Read the excerpt in **Figure 7.3**. Why do you think the government wanted to give land to veterans of the war?

FIGURE 7.2 This mural, painted in 2000 by Becky Marr-Johnson, is called *Building the Richmond Road, 1818*. It shows former soldiers of the War of 1812 establishing a settlement in Richmond, Ontario. **Analyze:** According to this depiction, what was involved in creating a settlement?

> "Now, with the end of the war ..., Great Britain was overrun with discharged soldiers also seeking employment. Something had to be done quickly ... the British government had recognized that a loyal population must be established inland away from the St. Lawrence 'front' as a second line of defence in any future (American) threat."
>
> — Jean S. McGill, historian

FIGURE 7.3 In a book published in 1968, historian McGill explains some of the reasons for the settlement of veterans in Canada. **Analyze:** Why would having former soldiers living in a Canadian settlement help the British government?

Even with the free land, many soldiers had trouble starting a new life in Canada. The quality of the soil in the lots they were given was poor, compared with the more fertile soil around the St. Lawrence River and the Great Lakes. Also, the lots were spread far apart in order to protect as much land as possible against potential American attacks. Roads were poor or non-existent, so many soldiers and their families were isolated. As a result, the soldiers drifted to towns and cities in search of other work.

EVALUATE AND DRAW CONCLUSIONS

What do you do once you have gathered, organized, and analyzed your information? You need to evaluate and draw conclusions about your inquiry question. When you evaluate and draw conclusions, you make an informed and critical judgment based on your evidence.

To draw conclusions about your inquiry question,
- use your new understanding and what you already know
- evaluate your evidence to see if it does or does not support your conclusion
- determine whether you have enough evidence—you may need more sources

CASE STUDY: THE RIDEAU CANAL

The Rideau Canal opened in 1832 after six years of construction. It is considered one of the greatest engineering projects of the time, covering 202 km of water from southern Ottawa to the Kingston harbour. From a military perspective, the canal was important for improving Britain's defences against the United States. Look at **Figure 7.4**. What kind of labour do you think went into building the canal?

Use this inquiry question to help you learn more about the construction of the Rideau Canal: How did the Rideau Canal change the lives of the workers who built it? To answer the question, you first have to determine how you will evaluate or measure an improvement in workers' lives. What criteria will you use? Consider the following questions:
- What were some advantages of the construction for workers?
- What were some disadvantages of the construction for workers?
- What were some short-term effects of the construction?
- What were some long-term effects of the construction?

FIGURE 7.4 This photo shows locks on the Rideau Canal in Ottawa. The city of Ottawa (originally known as Bytown) was built around the canal. **Analyze:** How might the canal be important to the development of Ottawa?

To build such a massive canal, many labourers were needed. Thousands of Canadiens, along with Irish, Scottish, and English immigrants, worked on the canal. The Rideau Canal project provided much-needed jobs, especially to those who had been living in poverty.

Labourers worked for 14 to 16 hours a day, six days a week. Using only simple tools, they had to clear land, drill and blast rock, and construct locks and dams. Many of the construction sites were in marshy areas, which increased the risk of diseases such as malaria. Malaria is transmitted to humans by mosquitoes. It is estimated that about 2 percent of workers died from malaria and another 60 percent became ill.

FIGURE 7.5 This painting by C.W. Jefferys was painted in the early 1930s. It shows Lieutenant Colonel By watching the workers building the canal in 1826. By was responsible for overseeing the construction of the Rideau Canal. **Analyze:** Why do you think the artist chose to place By in the foreground instead of the background?

Look at **Figure 7.5**, which shows a construction site for the Rideau Canal. The workers tried to protest the unfair and often dangerous conditions on these sites. However, they were stopped by troops or British soldiers sent to end the unrest.

Many workers and their families lived in nearby towns. However, many others lived on the actual work sites in construction camps that often consisted of roughly built log cabins. In the camps, women were sometimes able to find domestic jobs, such as housekeeping. Boys were sometimes used to deliver supplies. Read **Figure 7.6**. Most of the workers' low salaries went toward paying the high cost of living in the construction camps.

Some canal workers, as well as other newcomers to Canada, settled along the canal route. Between 1834 and 1851, the population of the land around the Rideau Canal tripled. What effect do you think these new communities had on the workers after construction was complete?

"The cost of living in the camps would have taken most of the earnings of a common labourer. Expenses were high not only because of the difficulty of transporting provisions over long distances, but because of determination of many contractors to make a profit on supplies as well as construction."

— *William N.T. Wylie, historical researcher*

FIGURE 7.6 This excerpt is from a 1983 article by Wylie about the construction of the Rideau Canal. **Analyze:** How does this excerpt help you answer your inquiry question?

TRY IT

1. What conclusions can you draw about the impact of the construction of the Rideau Canal on the lives of the workers? What evidence supports your conclusions?
2. What other questions would you ask to help you evaluate your evidence? Research to find information that would answer these questions. How does this additional information affect your conclusions?

BLACK COMMUNITIES

Much like the Black Loyalists who fought for Britain during the American Revolution, many of the Black veterans from the War of 1812 were also given land grants in Canada. However, when they tried to claim the rewards for their service, they often faced discrimination. When land grants were distributed in 1821, they received only 100 acres, half of what the other soldiers were given. Despite this, these land grants helped to establish the first Black settlements in Canada, such as the one in Oro Township.

> What do the land grants suggest about the government's view of Black soldiers?

ORO TOWNSHIP

Oro Township, in present-day Simcoe County, Ontario, was established in 1819. The settlement was created for the veterans from the War of 1812, including the Coloured Corps. For the most part, land grants given to soldiers were spread out, far apart from one another. However, Black soldiers were allowed to settle together in one area. Oro Township was the only government-sponsored Black settlement in Upper Canada at the time. Why do you think the Black soldiers settled together in one area?

Eventually, the settlement reached a maximum of 100 people. In 1831, white settlers were allowed to move to Oro, as well. The increase in population made the land worth more money, so many families sold their grants. The Black population of Oro grew smaller and smaller as people left to find work on nearby farms and in towns. However, some descendants of the first settlers remained in the township for 130 years.

One of the important landmarks of the Black settlement in Oro is the Oro African Methodist Episcopal Church. Built in 1849, the church became a community centre. In **Figure 7.7**, you can see that the church is still standing today. In 2015, descendants of Private Samuel Thomas, who was given land in Oro in 1819, worked together with their community to restore the church. Do you know of a building in your community that is historically significant?

FIGURE 7.7 The Oro African Methodist Episcopal Church is a National Historic Site. In 2015, work began to preserve and restore the building. **Analyze:** What is the historical significance of the Oro African Methodist Episcopal Church?

RICHARD PIERPOINT'S 1821 PETITION

As you learned in Chapters 5 and 6, Richard Pierpoint fought for the British during the American Revolution and the War of 1812. When it came time to receive his land grant in return for his military service, 71-year-old Pierpoint requested instead to go back to his homeland in Senegal, Africa. Read **Figure 7.8**, an excerpt from his petition in 1821 to Peregrine Maitland, the lieutenant-governor of Upper Canada. Why did Pierpoint want to return to Senegal?

> "That Your Excellency's Petitioner is a native of Bondon [Senegal] in Africa; that he was conveyed to America about the year 1760 and sold to a British officer; that he served his Majesty during the American Revolutionary War ... and again during the late American War [War of 1812] in a Corps of Color raised on the Niagara Frontier. That your Excellency's Petitioner is now old and without property that he finds it difficult to obtain a livelihood by his labour; that he is above all things desirous to return to his native country."
>
> — *Richard Pierpoint's 1821 petition*

FIGURE 7.8 This excerpt is from Pierpoint's petition to Lieutenant-Governor Maitland in 1821. **Analyze:** Why do you think Pierpoint included in his petition that he is "now old"?

Lieutenant-Governor Maitland denied Pierpoint's request. Pierpoint was given land near present-day Fergus, Ontario. Having no other options, and despite the challenges of clearing the land while in his 70s, he was settled by 1826. He became a leader in his community by helping people escape slavery in the United States. Examine **Figure 7.9**, which is a poster of Pierpoint created in 2014. Why is Pierpoint celebrated as a hero today?

FIGURE 7.9 Historica Canada commissioned this poster of Pierpoint, which was created in 2014 by artist Christopher Hemsworth. **Analyze:** What clues does the artist provide about Pierpoint's life?

CHECK-**IN**

1. **HISTORICAL PERSPECTIVE** What was life like for Black soldiers and other Black settlers in Canada at this time?

2. **CONTINUITY AND CHANGE** How were settlements changing in Upper Canada? What forces were creating change?

3. **GATHER AND ORGANIZE** What types of evidence might help you understand more about the challenges that soldiers faced after the War of 1812?

HOW WERE COMMUNITIES AFFECTED BY IMMIGRATION?

What pushes people to leave one country for another, and what is the impact of their arrival in a new country? The immigrants who came to Canada after 1815 left their homes hoping for a better life. The large wave of immigration to Canada in this time period had many consequences for community life.

IMMIGRATION TO CANADA FROM BRITAIN

In addition to former soldiers, thousands of people moved to Canada after 1815. This caused a huge population boom. Between 1815 and 1840, the population of Upper Canada grew from 100 000 to over 400 000. Lower Canada experienced similar population growth. Most people came from England, Ireland, Scotland, and Wales.

Poverty and overcrowding were an increasing problem in Britain. The **Industrial Revolution** led to the rapid growth of technology and changes in how goods were manufactured. Tasks that had required manual labour could now be completed using machines and other technologies. Living conditions deteriorated as more and more people left their rural communities to find work in towns and cities. The British government saw Canada as a way to rid Britain of poverty and overcrowding. Potential immigrants saw Canada as a way to get ahead economically or socially.

> Industrial Revolution the rapid transition to new manufacturing processes in the 1700s and 1800s

TRAVELLING BY SHIP FROM BRITAIN TO CANADA

Crossing the Atlantic Ocean by ship was the only way to travel from Britain to Canada. Many travelled by timber ship. Timber ships were built to carry lumber. But during the immigration boom, these ships were often used to carry immigrants from Britain to Canada. Immigrants would live for weeks in parts of the ship that were designed to hold timber, not people. The ships would then be loaded with timber and head back to Europe. Look at the painting in **Figure 7.10**. It shows the Montréal harbour in 1830 and the loading of a timber ship. How do you think immigrants felt knowing they were boarding a large ship that was not built for passengers?

FIGURE 7.10 *View of the Harbour, Montreal, 1830* was painted by Robert Auchmuty Sproule in the same year. **Analyze:** How different do you think this scene would have looked when immigrants were disembarking the same ship?

Until the mid-1820s, the British government provided some financial aid and free land grants to encourage immigration to Canada. However, most immigrants paid for the move with their own money. The fee for first-class sea travel was expensive. Thousands of people who could not afford first class braved terrible living conditions to get to their new home. The journey to Canada could take four to eight weeks. Up to 250 passengers could be packed into a ship at a time. One in every 28 immigrants died on board from disease. Read the account in **Figure 7.11** by Stephen E. De Vere. De Vere was a British official who travelled on a ship to investigate and report on the living conditions on board. Why do you think the British government would allow people to travel in such terrible conditions?

> "Hundreds of poor people ... huddled together without light, without air, wallowing in filth and breathing a fetid [stinking] atmosphere, sick in body, dispirited in heart.... The food is generally ill selected and seldom sufficiently cooked.... The supply of water, hardly enough for cooking and drinking, does not allow washing."
>
> — *Stephen E. De Vere, British official*

FIGURE 7.11 De Vere describes his 1847 voyage to Canada in this excerpt from a letter he wrote to a British official. **Analyze:** What might have led people to call these vessels "death ships" or "coffin ships"?

CHANGES IN UPPER AND LOWER CANADA

By 1840, the population boom was affecting the population makeup in Lower Canada. In Montréal, the increase in British immigrants meant that less than half of Montréal's population was now made up of Canadiens.

Québec City was the most popular landing destination in Canada, but thousands moved on after their arrival. Those who planned to settle in Upper Canada had to pay for another boat ride to get to their "free" land. The Rideau Canal was a favourite route for people travelling to Upper Canada. Examine **Figure 7.12**, which shows people on boats passing through Jones Falls, which is part of the Rideau Canal. How do you think the canal influenced the growth of communities along its route?

> What consequences do you think the British immigration had for Canadien culture?

FIGURE 7.12 This 1838 painting, *Jones Falls* by Philip John Bainbrigge, shows people travelling along the Rideau Canal. **Analyze:** What challenges could immigrants have faced travelling in small boats rather than in large ships?

READING A
POPULATION GRAPH

A graph can be used to show a change in population over a period of time. A population can increase due to births or immigration (people moving to a country from another country). A population can also decrease due to deaths or emigration (people leaving a country to live in another country). On a population graph, the *x* (horizontal) axis usually shows a period of time. The *y* (vertical) axis usually shows the population. By plotting data on a line graph, we can get a visual picture of any changes in population:

- An increase is shown by an upward trend from left to right.
- A decrease is shown by a downward trend from left to right.
- No change is shown by a flat horizontal line.

The population of Canada grew significantly after 1815. We can use a graph to look at the change in total population, the change in the population of a specific region or city (for example, Upper Canada or Montréal), the change in the population of a specific group (for example, British or French), or the country where immigrants have come from. **Figure 7.13** shows the changes in population in two Canadian cities from 1800 to 1850.

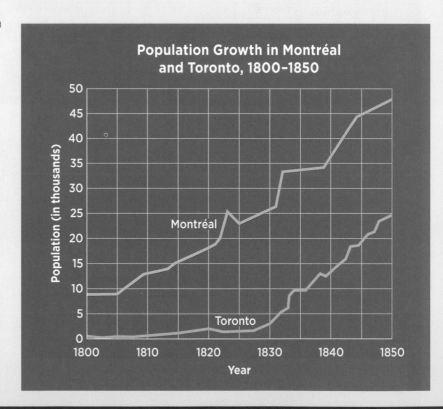

Population Growth in Montréal and Toronto, 1800–1850

FIGURE 7.13 This graph shows the population growth in Montréal and Toronto from 1800 to 1850.

HOW TO READ A POPULATION GRAPH

Look at the graph in **Figure 7.13**. What does the title of the graph tell you? What data is shown?

STEP 1

STEP 2

Look for patterns in the graph. Do the lines show an upward trend or a downward trend, or do the lines stay the same? What does this tell you?

Identify any years that had significant changes in population. What do you think caused these changes in population?

STEP 3

THE CHOLERA EPIDEMIC

Cholera is a contagious and often-fatal disease that results in fever, diarrhea, and dehydration. In 1832, cholera was one of the diseases that was carried to Canada on immigrant ships.

The outbreak of cholera prompted a wave of panic. At the time, no one knew what caused cholera or how to prevent and treat it. Some people thought that it was caused by an invisible bad air, and that burning fires could destroy it. Others thought that it was caused by bad living conditions. By the end of October 1832, the disease had claimed 7500 lives in Québec City and Montréal. It wasn't until the 1850s that it was discovered that cholera was caused and spread by contaminated water or food.

Health boards were established to care for those with the disease and also to inspect immigrant ships. Examine the cholera bulletin in **Figure 7.14**. What impact do you think news of the cholera epidemic had on the people who were living in Canada and the people who were arriving to start a new life?

John Capling moved to Canada with his wife and 11 children. Read the quote in **Figure 7.15** by Capling. How did the cholera epidemic impact him and his family?

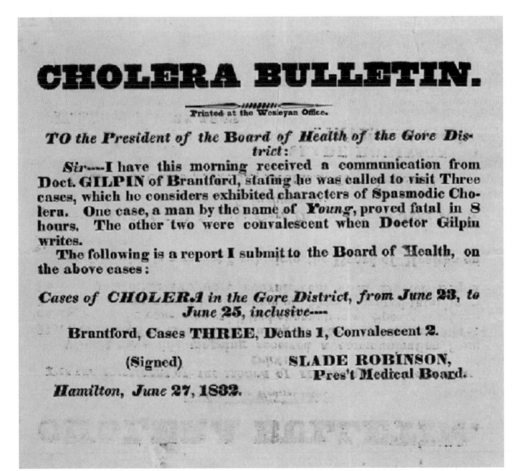

CHOLERA BULLETIN.

Printed at the Wesleyan Office.

TO the President of the Board of Health of the Gore District:

Sir——I have this morning received a communication from Doct. GILPIN of Brantford, stating he was called to visit Three cases, which he considers exhibited characters of Spasmodic Cholera. One case, a man by the name of Young, proved fatal in 8 hours. The other two were convalescent when Doctor Gilpin writes.

The following is a report I submit to the Board of Health, on the above cases:

Cases of CHOLERA in the Gore District, from June 23, to June 25, inclusive——

Brantford, Cases THREE, Deaths 1, Convalescent 2.

(Signed)   **SLADE ROBINSON,**
                         Pres't Medical Board.

Hamilton, June 27, 1832.

FIGURE 7.14 This bulletin was sent to a board of health in Upper Canada on June 27, 1832. It describes the effects of cholera in the community. **Analyze:** Why do you think the boards of health were unsuccessful in stopping the disease?

"I lost my poor little Mary for the first, then my poor dearest wife, then my two youngest, and little Edmund, all in the space of eight days.... The complaint was the cholera morbus; they all die in the space of a fortnight.... But I will not persuade any one to come, tho' I can see much better prospects here than in England."

— *John Capling, immigrant from England*

FIGURE 7.15 After moving to Canada in 1832, Capling wrote this letter to his brother who lived in England. **Analyze:** What reasons do you think Capling may have had to feel that Canada was a better place to live than England, despite the tragedy of losing so many members of his family?

CHALLENGES OF CREATING COMMUNITIES

The increase in population meant that more people were clearing new land. However, settlers and immigrants were not always prepared for life in Canada. As you learned in Chapter 5, rural life in the backwoods of Canada meant long days of hard labour. There was little time for socializing, and homes were often separated by several kilometres of forest. For weeks at a time, settlers might see no one except their immediate family. Examine the cartoon in **Figure 7.16**. How was the experience of these immigrants living in Canada the same as or different from your own?

FIGURE 7.16 *The Emigrants' Welcome to Canada, 1820* shows an immigrant arriving, unprepared for life in Canada. **Analyze:** What is the artist's view of immigrants who are coming to settle in Canada?

THE EMIGRANTS WELCOME TO CANADA.

ISOLATION AND HARDSHIP

Once they had arrived, many immigrants wrote letters to their family and friends back in Europe. These letters help us understand what everyday life was like. They also give us a unique and personal glimpse into the past.

When sisters Catharine Parr Traill and Susanna Moodie came to Canada, they began to record their experiences for their loved ones back in England. The sisters moved to Upper Canada with their husbands around the same time, in 1832. Parr Traill and Moodie are two of Canada's first female authors. They turned their diaries and letters about their new life in Canada into books that became popular in Canada and Britain.

The Backwoods of Canada by Parr Traill and *Roughing It in the Bush* by Moodie detail the isolation and difficulties that many settlers faced. Although they did not immigrate together, the sisters lived on neighbouring farms. Compare Parr Traill's impression of Canada in **Figure 7.17** to Moodie's account in **Figure 7.18**. What do these two excerpts suggest about the sisters' experiences when they settled in Canada?

"Much as I had seen and heard of the badness of the roads in Canada, I was not prepared for such a one as we travelled along this day. Indeed, it hardly deserved the name of a road.... Sometimes I laughed because I would not cry."

— *Catharine Parr Traill, backwoods settler*

FIGURE 7.17 This excerpt was written upon Parr Traill's arrival in Canada in 1832. The letter was included in her book *The Backwoods of Canada*, published in 1836. **Analyze:** Why would Parr Traill write to her family in England about the roads in Canada?

"I was rendered so weak by want of proper nourishment ... with kindly presents from neighbours—often as badly off as ourselves—a loin of a young bear, and a basket containing a loaf of bread, some tea, some fresh butter, and oatmeal, went far to save my life."

— *Susanna Moodie, backwoods settler*

FIGURE 7.18 This excerpt from Moodie's book *Roughing It in the Bush*, published in 1852, is about an incident that occurred after she gave birth. (The word "bush" is another term for the backwoods.) **Analyze:** Why do you think neighbours sometimes relied on each other to survive?

In 1837, Anne Langton emigrated from England with her parents and aunt. Upon their arrival, they stayed with Anne's brother John, who had moved to Upper Canada in 1833. Langton and her parents soon built their own home nearby. To record her surroundings, Langton wrote journals and letters and created sketches. **Figure 7.19** shows a sketch of her brother's house in 1837. Why do you think Langton created all these records?

FIGURE 7.19 *End view of John's house, Canada, 1837* was sketched in the same year by Anne Langton. **Analyze:** What details in this illustration tell you what life was like for settlers in the 1830s?

CHAPTER 7: *The Changing Face of Canada: 1815–1836*

ECONOMIC GROWTH AND WORKING LIFE

The population boom resulted in rapid economic growth. In particular, the timber and wheat industries were very successful. The Industrial Revolution eventually reached Canada. Canada's first bank, the Bank of Montréal, was founded in 1817 in response to the growing economy. Read another excerpt from Parr Traill's book in **Figure 7.20**. Why do you think she had this optimistic view of her new home?

The influence of the Industrial Revolution can also be seen in the construction of Canada's first public railway in 1836. A huge celebration marked the occasion. The Champlain and St. Lawrence Railroad was built in Lower Canada to connect the St. Lawrence River Valley with Lake Champlain. Lake Champlain is located in present-day Québec, as well as Vermont and New York in the United States. Look at the engraving in **Figure 7.21**. How do you think the introduction of the railway changed life for people living in Canada at the time?

People began moving to the growing cities to find jobs. Workers were in high demand, especially in Upper Canada. Because of this demand, some poor immigrants were welcomed as a source of cheap labour. Labourers, such as those who worked on the Rideau Canal, were often the poorest immigrants from Ireland and Scotland.

However, William Robinson, an established settler in Upper Canada, had trouble finding workers for his farm. Many immigrants were escaping bad working conditions in Britain and wanted to run their own farms. Read **Figure 7.22**, an excerpt from a letter that Robinson wrote to an emigration society in England to ask for help finding employees.

FIGURE 7.20 Parr Traill wrote this comment in her book *The Backwoods of Canada*, published in 1836. **Analyze:** What does Parr Traill mean when she describes Canada as "the land of hope"?

"Canada is *the* land of hope. Here, everything is new; everything going forward; it is scarcely possible for arts, sciences, agriculture, manufactures, to retrograde [move backward]; they must keep advancing."

— *Catharine Parr Traill, backwoods settler*

FIGURE 7.21 This engraving is based on an 1836 drawing by John Loye of the Champlain and St. Lawrence Railroad, the first public railway in Canada. **Analyze:** What are some advantages of travelling by train versus travelling by horse or wagon?

"I will give employment to two men who have wives and children who are of good reputation for sobriety, honesty, and diligence. The wages that I offer to these men are 30 pounds per annum [year], with a house rent-free, as much fuel as they wish and the keep of a cow winter and summer."

— *William Robinson, settler in Upper Canada*

FIGURE 7.22 This excerpt is from an 1836 letter that Robinson wrote to an emigration society in England to help him find labourers. **Analyze:** What can you infer are the problems he has had finding reliable workers in Canada?

IMPACTS OF SETTLEMENT ON FIRST NATIONS COMMUNITIES

First Nations peoples continued to struggle after the War of 1812. By 1815, they were already outnumbered, 10 to 1. Much of their land had been taken for the new immigrant settlements in the colonies. The economic growth and development during this period also affected their relationship with the land. The Mississauga Nation, in Upper Canada, was one of the First Nations affected by the increase in settlers. They wrote to the lieutenant-governor of Upper Canada for help. Read **Figure 7.23**. What problems are the Mississauga describing?

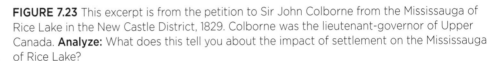

"White men seize our furs, and take them from us by force, they abuse our women and violently beat our people.... That we are poor in lands ... much of our hunting grounds are covered by white settlement, and the small remainder left to us are invaded by the hunters from Lower Canada."

— *Mississauga Nation of Rice Lake*

FIGURE 7.23 This excerpt is from the petition to Sir John Colborne from the Mississauga of Rice Lake in the New Castle District, 1829. Colborne was the lieutenant-governor of Upper Canada. **Analyze:** What does this tell you about the impact of settlement on the Mississauga of Rice Lake?

FIGURE 7.24 This portrait of Peter Jones was painted by English artist Matilda Jones in 1832. **Analyze:** What do you notice about how Jones is dressed in this portrait?

Mississauga Ojibwe Chief Peter Jones (known in Ojibwe as Kahkewaquonaby) is shown in **Figure 7.24**. He converted to Christianity in 1823 and became a Methodist minister. The Mississauga were close to collapse due to the impact of European settlement. Jones helped his people adjust to the presence of Europeans. He was the first to make Ojibwe a written language, and he translated the Bible and various hymns into different First Nations languages. How do you think these kinds of changes affected community life among the Mississauga?

CHECK-**IN**

1. **COMMUNICATE** Create a memorial or plaque to recognize the efforts of an individual or a group of people from this time period. Why is the individual or group worthy of remembering? What memorials already exist? How does your memorial contribute to educating the public about our heritage?

2. **CONTINUITY AND CHANGE** How was life changing for First Nations peoples at this time? How was it staying the same?

3. **INTERPRET AND ANALYZE** Did the rewards outweigh the challenges for immigrants and settlers at this time? Make a t-chart to analyze the evidence.

HOW WAS CONFLICT CHANGING
THE WEST?

When two rival businesses are competing today, what do they do? They may try to attract more customers through advertising or lower their prices. Two hundred years ago, however, competition between two important companies, Hudson's Bay Company and the North West Company, resulted in violent conflict.

THE RED RIVER AREA

The West was home to Aboriginal peoples, fur traders, and a few Europeans in settlements. Several Aboriginal groups, including the Saulteaux and Métis, lived in the Red River area near present-day Winnipeg, Manitoba. Many Métis worked in the fur trade for the North West Company. They used the Red River as an important trading route and relied on the buffalo hunt for their livelihood. The Métis also supplied the North West Company with buffalo meat and valuable pemmican (a preserved food made from dried meat and berries).

In 1811, Lord Selkirk, a Scottish noble and a shareholder in Hudson's Bay Company, wanted to establish an agricultural settlement for farmers who were losing their land in Scotland. Hudson's Bay Company gave him a large land grant in Rupert's Land to create the Red River Settlement. The Saulteaux were allies of Hudson's Bay Company. Saulteaux Chief Peguis signed a treaty with Selkirk that would allow settlers on their land. The Saulteaux even helped the settlers survive the difficult winter of 1812. Examine **Figure 7.25**. What information about the importance of the Red River area can you gather?

FIGURE 7.25 This map shows the Red River area after the establishment of the Red River Settlement. The Aboriginal settlements shown on the map represent only one settlement from each nation. These nations had many settlements and many were not permanent. **Analyze:** Why do you think the North West Company and the Métis felt threatened by the Red River Settlement?

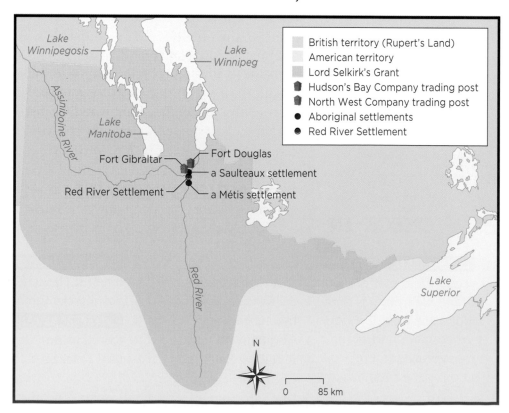

Red River Area, 1811

Legend:
- British territory (Rupert's Land)
- American territory
- Lord Selkirk's Grant
- Hudson's Bay Company trading post
- North West Company trading post
- Aboriginal settlements
- Red River Settlement

Lake Winnipegosis
Lake Winnipeg
Assiniboine River
Lake Manitoba
Fort Gibraltar
Fort Douglas
Red River Settlement
a Saulteaux settlement
a Métis settlement
Red River
Lake Superior

N

0   85 km

FIGURE 7.26 This painting, *The Fight at Seven Oaks, 1816*, was painted by C.W. Jefferys in 1914, almost 100 years after the battle took place. **Analyze:** Why might a one-day fight, involving fewer than 100 people, be significant enough to inspire a painting decades later?

> How do you think a similar conflict would be handled today?

COMPETITION AND CONFLICT

Hudson's Bay Company and the North West Company were in competition for years. This competition intensified as both companies moved west in search of new trading routes. Selkirk's settlement also increased conflict in the area. He hoped that the settlement would help Hudson's Bay Company traders by providing them with food from the agricultural settlement. However, the settlement was located in the Red River area used by the North West Company for its pemmican supply and trading route. Because of this, the North West Company opposed the Red River Settlement. They worried that the buffalo hunt would be disrupted by the settlement and cut off their essential food supply. The Métis feared the settlement would disrupt their close ties with their trading partner. The Scottish settlers were in the middle of a dangerous conflict between the two largest fur trading companies. Interactions between the rival traders started to become more violent. Forts for each company were burned down, Selkirk's settlements were attacked, and skirmishes between the traders were common.

THE BATTLE OF SEVEN OAKS

The conflict came to a head on June 19, 1816, at the Battle of Seven Oaks. Seven Oaks was located near Hudson's Bay Company's Fort Douglas. Led by Métis leader Cuthbert Grant, 61 Métis who worked for the North West Company attacked 25 Hudson's Bay Company employees and settlers from the Red River Settlement. The battle resulted in the deaths of 20 of these men and one Métis. Examine **Figure 7.26**, which shows a scene from the battle. Does this depiction hint at who the winners of the battle were? Why, or why not?

THE PEMMICAN PROCLAMATION

What was the final straw in the rivalry that led to the Battle of Seven Oaks? Miles Macdonell was the governor of the Red River Settlement. He attempted to solve a food shortage in the area by issuing the Pemmican Proclamation in 1814. This proclamation outlawed the export of pemmican from the Red River area. Another proclamation banned the buffalo hunt, since it drove buffalo, an important food source, away from the settlement. As the Métis relied on pemmican and the buffalo hunt for their survival, banning both would hurt their livelihood. Then Macdonell ordered the North West Company to leave the area, which was still claimed by Hudson's Bay Company. As you read the quote in **Figure 7.27** by Duncan Cameron, a North West Company agent, consider the importance of pemmican to the livelihood of all the inhabitants of the area. Cameron encouraged the Métis to destroy the Red River Settlement. Soon after, the settlement was under siege.

"Macdonell is now determined not only to seize our pemmican but to drive us out of the Assiniboia district [the Red River area] and consequently out of the north west. Hostilities will no doubt begin early spring."

— *Duncan Cameron, agent for the North West Company*

FIGURE 7.27 Cameron's reaction to the Pemmican Proclamation was a prediction that things would turn violent. **Analyze:** What does this quote reveal about the reaction of the North West Company and the Métis to the Pemmican Proclamation?

IMPACT ON THE MÉTIS

Examine the song in **Figure 7.28**, called "la chanson de la Grenouillère." The Battle of Seven Oaks is also called *la Grenouillère*, meaning "frog plain," which is what the Métis called the location of the battle. Métis Pierre Falcon was a fur trader, poet, and songwriter. He fought in the Battle of Seven Oaks, and it has been said that he wrote this song that same night. The song remained popular among the Métis for decades. The Métis saw the battle as a defining event in establishing their identity as a people. The Selkirk settlers saw the battle as a massacre. The government said that both sides were to blame—that it was a private war between two companies, not the business of the government. Why do you think the government did not want to get involved?

Why do the Métis, the Selkirk settlers, and the government have such different views of the battle?

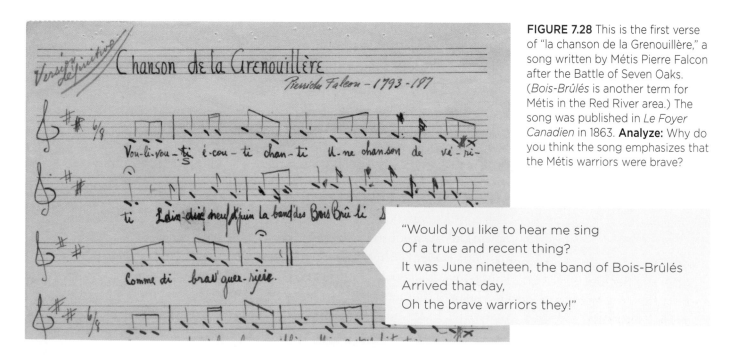

"Would you like to hear me sing
Of a true and recent thing?
It was June nineteen, the band of Bois-Brûlés
Arrived that day,
Oh the brave warriors they!"

FIGURE 7.28 This is the first verse of "la chanson de la Grenouillère," a song written by Métis Pierre Falcon after the Battle of Seven Oaks. (*Bois-Brûlés* is another term for Métis in the Red River area.) The song was published in *Le Foyer Canadien* in 1863. **Analyze:** Why do you think the song emphasizes that the Métis warriors were brave?

THE MERGER OF HUDSON'S BAY AND NORTH WEST COMPANIES

In 1821, only five years after the Battle of Seven Oaks, Hudson's Bay Company and the North West Company merged (combined) together. Over time, the British government had pressured them to end the competition and violence once and for all. The new company kept the name "Hudson's Bay Company" and now had the most trading power in the West. New policies were introduced to make the company more efficient. Half of the employees were let go and 73 forts were closed. Trading relationships with Aboriginal peoples changed after the merger, as well. Hudson's Bay Company favoured trading with the Métis and the Ojibwe and was reluctant to renew trade relationships with other First Nations, such as the Sioux. This had a huge impact on the ability of the Sioux to make a living. They responded by attacking both Hudson's Bay Company forts and Ojibwe settlements. Look at **Figure 7.29**, which shows two company forts on the Red River in 1822 after the merger. A First Nations group is shown attacking the Hudson's Bay Company fort on the left. What does this say about the impact of the merger and the closure of 73 forts on some First Nations peoples?

FIGURE 7.29 This 1822 painting by Peter Rindisbacher is entitled *View of the two Company Forts on the level prairie at Pembina on the Red River, and surprise by the savages at nightfall of May 25, 1822.* It shows Hudson's Bay Company's Fort Daer on the left and former North West Company's Fort Pembina on the right. **Analyze:** What do the positions of the forts tell you about the relationship between the two companies before the merger?

CHECK-**IN**

1. **INTERPRET AND ANALYZE** Do you think the painting in **Figure 7.26** is an accurate portrayal of the battle and the people involved? Explain why, or why not.

2. **HISTORICAL PERSPECTIVE** Write a short bio poem or diary entry about an event in this section from the perspective of one of the following: a fur trader, a Métis, or a settler from the Selkirk settlement.

3. **CAUSE AND CONSEQUENCE** What impact did Hudson's Bay Company and the North West Company have on First Nations and Métis?

4. **HISTORICAL SIGNIFICANCE** What do you think was the most important development or event in the West during this time period? Use evidence to support your answer.

HOW DID TENSIONS BETWEEN GROUPS AFFECT COMMUNITIES?

As immigration to Canada increased, the population became more diverse. While many came to Canada to find opportunity, they discovered that social tensions created barriers to getting ahead. Tensions were caused by differences in religion, political beliefs, and social class, as well as racism and prejudice. Conflicts between different groups played a large role in the daily life and development of communities.

RELIGIOUS AND POLITICAL TENSIONS

Have you ever wondered why Canadian towns and cities have so many different religious buildings? As the population of Canada grew and became more diverse, the number of different religions increased. What does the painting in **Figure 7.30** tell you about the importance of religion to people living in Canada in the 1800s?

The Church of England was the official church in Britain. Many Loyalists who had immigrated to Canada belonged to other Protestant churches, such as Methodist, Baptist, and Lutheran. Although these are all Christian churches, they have different beliefs and rituals.

People in rural areas were often served by itinerant preachers. **Itinerant** preachers travelled to different communities and only stayed for a short time before moving on to the next place. Methodist itinerant preachers gained a wide following in Upper Canada. They dissented, or disagreed, with the established Protestant churches of England and Scotland, which mostly catered to the upper classes.

itinerant a person who travels from place to place, especially as a minister

FIGURE 7.30 This 1830 painting by James Cockburn is entitled *Winter View of the Upper Town Market showing the Catholic Cathedral and Seminary*. You can see the Catholic cathedral and seminary in the heart of Québec City. **Analyze:** What details in the painting tell you about the role of the Catholic church in this community?

STRACHAN AND RYERSON

In the 1820s, John Strachan and Egerton Ryerson became very influential in Upper Canada. Strachan arrived in Canada from Scotland in 1799 and became a priest of the Church of England in 1804. Soon after, he started teaching boys from the influential families of Upper Canada. For Strachan, education was about training the elite to become British patriots, good Christian gentlemen, and the future leaders of society. Ryerson, on the other hand, was the son of Loyalist immigrants. He started his career as a Methodist itinerant minister, travelling and preaching in the York region around Yonge Street. He believed that religion should guide people in their personal life, but that no one religion in Canada should have a privileged place in education or politics.

Why might Strachan and Ryerson be considered historically significant?

The two men were rivals and held opposing religious and political views. Both Strachan (**Figure 7.31B**) and Ryerson (**Figure 7.32A**) had strong views on how to improve conditions in and unite the colonies of Canada. Examine the quotes in **Figure 7.31A** and **Figure 7.32B**. What do these quotes tell you about these men's opposing visions for Canada?

"It is by reasoning, by early instruction and example, that the unity of the Empire is to be maintained ... it is only through the Church and its institutions, that a truly English character and feeling can be given to, or preserved among the population"

— *John Strachan, Anglican priest and politician*

FIGURE 7.31 (A) This excerpt from an 1826 sermon by Strachan outlines his vision for unifying the colonies of Canada. (B) A portrait of Strachan from 1847 is shown. **Analyze:** What might Strachan mean by the term "English character"?

"Have the dissenters [people who differ in religious opinion] in this country ever shown a disposition in any way hostile to the true interests of the colony? Have they not been quiet in times of peace and bold in time of war? ... they are slanderers and liars, who say that the religious any more than the political dissenters in Canada, are not true to 'the political institutions of England'!"

— *Egerton Ryerson, Methodist minister and politician*

FIGURE 7.32 (A) A portrait of Ryerson from 1838 is shown. (B) Ryerson's response to Strachan's sermon was published in *The Colonial Advocate* in 1826. **Analyze:** What is Ryerson saying about Strachan and religion in Canada?

SOCIAL TENSIONS AND PREJUDICE

People were divided in Canada not only by religious and political beliefs but also by ethnicity and class differences.

FIRST NATIONS

As you learned in Chapter 5, the British government believed that First Nations populations needed to be converted to Christianity and taught the agricultural way of life. After arriving in Upper Canada from Ireland in 1822, settler Frances Stewart exchanged many letters with her relatives back home. Read **Figure 7.33**, in which Stewart's cousin Harriet Beaufort retells a story about Stewart's church in Upper Canada. What can you tell about Stewart's attitude toward the First Nations churchgoers?

IRISH IMMIGRANTS

From 1845 to 1851, a devastating famine forced Irish families to leave their homeland to escape starvation, disease, and poverty. In 1847, after surviving the "coffin ships," tens of thousands of destitute Irish immigrants arrived in Canada. Some residents and religious groups were sympathetic and helped settle the newcomers. Others, however, were not very welcoming. Read **Figure 7.34**, an excerpt from *The Globe* newspaper. Irish immigrants were often met with these kinds of hostile attitudes. Even though the Irish immigrants spoke English, most were Roman Catholic. The increasing number of Irish Catholics in Upper Canada caused tensions with the primarily Protestant population. In 2007, Ireland Park (**Figure 7.35**) opened in Toronto to commemorate the thousands of Irish famine victims who arrived in 1847. What does the creation of Ireland Park tell you about how attitudes toward the Irish immigrants have changed over time?

> "They [First Nations] were converted to Christianity in the course of the summer by a country man of their own who had been taught by an English missionary; and ... have since their conversion become quite ... well mannered."
>
> — Harriet Beaufort, cousin of settler Frances Stewart

FIGURE 7.33 This excerpt is from a letter written by Beaufort in 1827. In this letter, Beaufort retells a story from her cousin, Frances Stewart, who lived in Upper Canada. **Analyze:** How does Beaufort's letter reflect the British policy of assimilation?

> "Irish beggars are to be met everywhere, and they are as ignorant and vicious as they are poor. They are lazy, improvident [thoughtless], and unthankful; they fill our poorhouses and our prisons."
>
> — The Globe

FIGURE 7.34 This quote is from an 1858 editorial in Toronto's *The Globe* newspaper. **Analyze:** What does this excerpt reveal about attitudes toward the Irish in Upper Canada in the mid-1800s?

FIGURE 7.35 The sculptures in Ireland Park in Toronto, Ontario, represent the thousands of Irish famine victims who came to Toronto in the mid-1800s to start a new life. **Analyze:** Why would the City of Toronto choose to commemorate victims of the Irish famine?

BLACK SETTLEMENTS

In 1833, Britain outlawed slavery in the *Slavery Abolition Act*. Although the act ended the practice of slavery in Canada, it did not end the discrimination, hardship, and isolation that many Black Canadians faced in the 1830s. Discrimination was common in schooling, housing, and employment, and many were victims of racist petitions and riots.

Recall the settlement in Oro Township, which you read about on page 198. Mary O'Brien was a white settler in Oro. She was married to a British official in charge of the area around Oro Township. O'Brien witnessed the hostility that Black people often encountered in Canada. Read an excerpt from her journal in **Figure 7.36**. What other sources might be available to help us understand what life was like for Black settlers in Canada?

"I am provoked to see that some of our wise members have resolved that the [Black] settlement is likely to disturb the peace of the neighborhood, but I hope that no notice has been ... taken of such nonsense."

— *Mary O'Brien, settler from Oro Township*

FIGURE 7.36 This is an excerpt from O'Brien's 1830 journal. **Analyze:** What does the use of the word *likely* tell you about the attitude of some settlers toward people in the Black settlement?

THE UNDERGROUND RAILROAD

Once slavery was outlawed in Canada, the number of immigrant and refugee Africans and African-Americans increased. This led to the creation of the Underground Railroad. The Underground Railroad was not actually a railroad, but a network of routes and safe houses to help enslaved people escape from the United States into Canada.

Very few written records exist about the Underground Railroad. Oral tradition tells us that there were many secret codes used by **abolitionists**, people who were actively involved in ending slavery, to communicate with people escaping slavery. For example, the word *conductor* referred to an abolitionist who helped to bring enslaved people across the border. Why do you think it was hard to communicate directions to everyone who wanted to flee?

abolitionist a person who wants to end slavery

While many people escaped slavery with the help of the Underground Railroad, some escaped and arrived in Canada without any help. Read William Wells Brown's account of his experience fleeing slavery in the United States in **Figure 7.37**.

"When I escaped there was no Underground Railroad. The North Star was, in many instances, the only friend that the weary and footsore fugitive found on his pilgrimage to his new home among strangers."

— *William Wells Brown, author, poet, and playwright*

FIGURE 7.37 Kentucky-born Wells Brown recounts his experience fleeing slavery in 1834. **Analyze:** Why do you think it was difficult to find help to get into Canada?

Those who escaped slavery by coming to Canada began to create successful communities, building homes and establishing businesses. Initially, these settlements were welcomed. But racism and discrimination increased throughout the latter half of the 1800s as the population continued to grow.

MEGAN LAMBKIN: HONOURING HER HERITAGE

Megan Lambkin (**Figure 7.38**) first started volunteering at Uncle Tom's Cabin Historic Site when she was just seven years old. Uncle Tom's Cabin Historic Site is a museum located in Dresden, Ontario. It is dedicated to remembering the life of the renowned Reverend Josiah Henson (1796–1883). Reverend Henson was born into slavery in Maryland, United States. He made important contributions to the movement for the abolition of slavery in Canada and to the Underground Railroad. In a dangerous six-week journey, he and his family used the Underground Railroad to flee to Canada. They arrived on October 28, 1830. In Upper Canada (present-day Ontario), Reverend Henson established a community called the Dawn Settlement, where former enslaved people and anti-slavery workers could come together and share their skills and resources to help one another. Those who remained in Ontario after the end of slavery in the United States in 1863 were central to the development of the significant Black community in the province. Uncle Tom's Cabin explores and celebrates the unique heritage of that community.

> "I GET TO HEAR AND SEE WHAT SOME OF MY ANCESTORS WENT THROUGH AND HOW THEY CAME TO CANADA."

For Lambkin, volunteering at Uncle Tom's Cabin began as a way to work with her grandmother and learn more about their heritage. Lambkin is the seventh-generation descendant of an ancestor who was enslaved. Through her work at the museum, she has the opportunity to learn about her family history. "I get to hear and see what some of my ancestors went through and how they came to Canada," she shares. Apart from this personal connection, Lambkin enjoys sharing the life story of Reverend Henson with others. Her position as a volunteer at Uncle Tom's Cabin allows her to use her various skills to learn more about others, herself, her family, her community, and her country. She says, "Seeing people from all around the world makes my day, and, if I'm lucky, someone might come from Québec and I can speak French to them." Through her volunteer work, she cultivates values that are important to her, such as equality for all the people in her community. Finally, she believes that she can learn from watching her grandmother teach young people, which will help her teach others in the future.

FIGURE 7.38 Megan Lambkin at Uncle Tom's Cabin Historic Site

A CALL TO **ACTION**

1. How could you learn more about the experiences of your ancestors? Are there resources in your community that could help you?

2. What would you have to do if you wanted to volunteer with a local museum or cultural centre in your community?

POVERTY

The upper class included governors and other officials from Britain, as well as people who became wealthy through industries, such as the timber trade and shipping. People in the upper class saw poverty as a danger to a stable society. They considered poverty to be a moral problem and the fault of poor people.

Waves of poor immigrants were arriving in Upper Canada, which created problems in existing communities. By the 1830s, the policy of providing land grants to all immigrants had ended, leaving some immigrants with no land and little to no money.

Relief for poor people was often provided by charities and religious organizations, such as churches. In 1817, the Society for the Relief of Strangers was founded to help alleviate the misery of poor immigrants. Strachan was a member of this organization. In many cases, however, only people who were both sick and destitute were able to receive charity.

While churches provided relief to some, the legal system would frequently put poor people in jail. This was a seen as a valid way to deal with people considered to be social outcasts. Examine **Figure 7.39**, which shows a jail and courthouse along King Street in Toronto in 1835. Why might a jail be built in the middle of the city?

> How might different perspectives on poverty lead to tensions in Upper Canada in the 1830s?

FIGURE 7.39 This 1835 painting by John George Howard is entitled *North side of King Street East, from Toronto to Church Streets*. It shows a jail, firehall, courthouse, and church in Toronto at the time. **Analyze:** What does this painting tell you about the needs of growing cities?

CHECK-IN

1. **CONTINUITY AND CHANGE** How has the role of religion in people's lives changed in Canada since the 1830s?

2. **FORMULATE QUESTIONS** Write a question that would help you investigate a particular group's experience of racism or discrimination.

3. **HISTORICAL PERSPECTIVE** Explain how Strachan and Ryerson differed in how to "fix" the problem of diversity in Upper Canada. Which view do you think was closer to a modern perspective?

HOW WERE PEOPLE AFFECTED BY SOCIAL CHANGE?

LEARNING GOALS

As you worked through this chapter, you had opportunities to
- examine the changing settlements and population in Canada after the war, and consider the perspectives of the people who arrived in Canada

- learn how conflicts shaped the West and impacted Aboriginal peoples
- analyze perspectives and tensions related to religious and racial differences in Canada
- use graphs to understand population growth in Canada

In this chapter, you learned that a large wave of immigration occurred in Canada after the War of 1812. This population boom was a result of decisions made by the British government, economic hardship in Britain, and slavery in the United States. You learned that both challenges (such as hard work and disease) and rewards (such as opportunities for economic and social improvement) awaited immigrants in their new home. You also learned that immigration and settlement often had a dramatic impact on First Nations and Métis people. Finally, you examined the role of religion in Canada, and looked at the issues of race and discrimination in the 1800s.

Summarize Your Learning

Now that you have completed Chapter 7, you are ready to answer the Chapter Big Question: How were people affected by social change? Select one of the following tasks to summarize your learning:
- Look back through the chapter and categorize the events or developments discussed as either social, economic, political, religious, or demographic changes using a graphic organizer. Some events or developments may involve more than one kind of change.
- Choose four historical figures that you think represent a diversity of viewpoints. Create a role-play comparing their viewpoints to your viewpoint on the same or a similar issue today.

APPLY YOUR LEARNING

1. **HISTORICAL PERSPECTIVE** Choose three primary sources from this chapter that you think effectively express a historical perspective. Explain what each source reveals about the time period.

2. **CONTINUITY AND CHANGE** Compare the changes in immigration from 1815 to 1836 with immigration in the 1700s and with immigration today. How did immigration change from 1815 to 1836? How did it remain the same? How is immigration similar and different today?

3. **CAUSE AND CONSEQUENCE** List the consequences of the War of 1812 on the development of Canada. Explain which consequence you think had the most impact at the time and which has had the most impact on Canada today.

4. **FORMULATE QUESTIONS** In this chapter, you learned about the Battle of Seven Oaks, the cholera epidemic, and the Underground Railroad. Which of these historical events would you like to learn more about? Write questions that could help you start an investigation of your own.

5. **COMMUNICATE** Write a bio poem or create a drawing from the point of view of any historical figure in this chapter.

6. **INTERPRET AND ANALYZE** Choose two quotes or excerpts from this chapter. Explain what words show that person's perspective and how those words might be different from the words of similar people or sources today. How are the two perspectives similar to or different from each other?

7. **HISTORICAL SIGNIFICANCE** Which person, event, or development do you think was the most significant of this time period? Use the historical significance criteria on page 12 to support your answer.

8. **COMMUNICATE** Choose three primary or secondary sources from this chapter, and design a museum exhibit or display that depicts what stayed the same and what changed after 1815. Write a caption for each image or use a quote that explains how it shows change or continuity.

9. **EVALUATE AND DRAW CONCLUSIONS** If you had to name the period in Canadian history from 1815 to 1836, what would you call it? Support your title with evidence from this chapter.

UNIT 2 CHALLENGE CHECK-IN

1. What impact did the War of 1812 have on settlement or demographic patterns? How did the war affect different groups? Why was the war a significant development?

2. Review the Focus On: Evaluate and Draw Conclusions feature on pages 196 to 197. Using the criteria, evaluate and draw conclusions about which events during this time period improved life in Canada. What sources provide the best evidence of the improvements? What other types of sources would provide new perspectives?

3. What groups or individuals were significant during this time period? Why? Which groups prospered, and which groups did not?

4. Review the criteria and notes you made for the Chapter 5 Unit Challenge Check-In. Are there any other criteria you would add or change, based on what you have learned in Chapter 7?

5. Review the description of the Unit 2 Challenge on pages 134 to 135. Using your responses to questions 1 to 4 and other information from the chapter, rank the significant events and developments during this time period on your timeline, showing either progress or decline. Include evidence from sources in the chapter to support your rankings. Look back at the events and developments you added to your timeline in Chapter 6. Update your timeline as needed.

CHAPTER 8
DEMANDS FOR **CHANGE:**
1837–1850

HOW DID PEOPLE PUSH FOR POLITICAL CHANGE?

LEARNING GOALS

As you work through this chapter, you will
* examine and communicate the key causes of political conflict during the 1800s
* describe how different groups envisioned the government's responsibilities in the 1800s
* analyze the impact of the actions people took to create political change
* corroborate primary sources

In the 1830s, Canada was entering a period of great change. A growing population was changing the social and economic structure in many cities and towns across the colony. These social and economic changes led people to demand political changes.

What would you do today if you wanted political change? Would you create an online campaign, start a petition, or organize a protest? In the 1800s, people who wanted change used the methods that were available to them, such as organizing protests, delivering speeches, and holding public rallies. This painting, entitled *The Assembly of the Six Counties*, was created in 1890 by Charles Alexander Smith. It shows a two-day public rally in Lower Canada in 1837. The rally was attended by over 5000 Canadiens who were frustrated with the British-controlled government. In the painting, Louis-Joseph Papineau, a celebrated Canadien politician, is speaking to the crowd and calling for change. What does the audience's reaction tell you?

As you read this chapter, you will discover why and how people in Canada were challenged to make changes. You will also examine and evaluate the consequences of those changes.

WHAT CAUSED UNREST IN
UPPER AND LOWER CANADA?

Have you ever heard about a conflict in Canada or another part of the world and wondered how and why the conflict started? All conflicts have root causes. Political conflicts are caused by different ideas and beliefs about who should be in power and how power, territory, and resources should be used. These conflicts can sometimes become violent. Tensions in Canada were rising throughout the 1830s between those in power and those who wanted change. In 1837 and 1838, the political conflict in Upper and Lower Canada exploded into violent **rebellions**, or uprisings, throughout the colony. What caused these rebellions to break out when they did?

rebellion an act of violent or open resistance to an established government or ruler

ECONOMIC CONFLICTS

After the War of 1812, much of the best unfarmed land was given to wealthy British immigrants. The clergy land reserves, which you learned about in Chapter 5, took good farmland away from other immigrants and Canadiens. As a result, many Canadien and Loyalist farmers were forced to farm on land with poor soil, where it was hard to grow crops. Crop failure left families in poverty, and sometimes near starvation. Many Canadien farmers were forced to leave their farms to take low-paying jobs in nearby cities.

Poverty in Upper and Lower Canada was growing. In Lower Canada, most of the wealthy families were British. What does the quote in **Figure 8.1** tell you about the inequality in Lower Canada in the early 1830s? In both Upper and Lower Canada, many poor people felt that rich people were ignoring their suffering. At the same time, a growing middle class of professionals (doctors, lawyers, and journalists) were making more money and wanted to have more power and influence. However, the existing government structure kept these people out of positions of power.

Why would the growing middle class want more power?

"The [British] conquerors have a firm hold on commerce, jobs, wealth, and power. They form the upper classes, dominating the entire society. In every locality where the French Canadians do not have the upper hand in terms of their sheer strength in numbers, the dominated people is gradually losing its culture, its language, and its national identity."

— Alexis de Tocqueville, political philosopher and author

FIGURE 8.1 This is a quote from de Tocqueville, during his visit to Lower Canada in 1831. **Analyze:** According to de Tocqueville, what was the impact of the British on the Canadiens?

RISING TENSIONS

Daniel Tracey, an Irish immigrant and newspaper editor, was resentful of Britain's power over the Irish and Canadiens in Montréal. He founded two newspapers, *The Vindicator* and *The Canadian Advertiser* and published stories critical of the British-run government. In January 1832, he criticized the government of Lower Canada in his newspaper, *The Vindicator*, and called for an end to British control of the government. Tracey was jailed for 40 days for his printed attack. After he was freed from jail, Tracey decided to take further action. He wanted to change the governing system, so in the spring of 1832, he ran for office in the Montréal election. His opponent was a candidate who was backed by the British and who supported British control of Montréal.

On May 21, as crowds gathered to vote, fights broke out. British troops, who were stationed in Montréal, fired into the crowd, claiming that the voters were rebelling. Three Canadiens were killed. Tracey ended up winning the election, but he died of cholera before he could take office. Tracey's death highlights another issue that created tension in the 1830s.

As you learned in Chapter 7, the cholera epidemic, brought to North America by immigrants arriving at the time, was causing panic among the people in Upper and Lower Canada. As well, the immigration boom created other conflicts.

On November 6, 1837, tensions came to a head between a Canadien political group and a group of British Loyalists. A newspaper at the time called *Journal Le Canadien* reported that the Canadien group were gathered peacefully in a courtyard at their monthly gathering when a large group of Loyalists arrived and started throwing stones. Once the Canadiens left the courtyard, the Loyalists bombarded them with stones. Then, a full-blown fight broke out between the two groups. Examine **Figure 8.2**, which shows a scene from the riot. Whose perspective of the riot is the artist showing?

FIGURE 8.2 This 1890 illustration, entitled *L'Émeute du lundi 6 novembre 1837* (The Riot of Monday, November 6, 1837) by Georges Tiret-Bognet, shows a clash in Montréal between a Canadien political group and Loyalists. **Analyze:** What details about the conflict does the artist include?

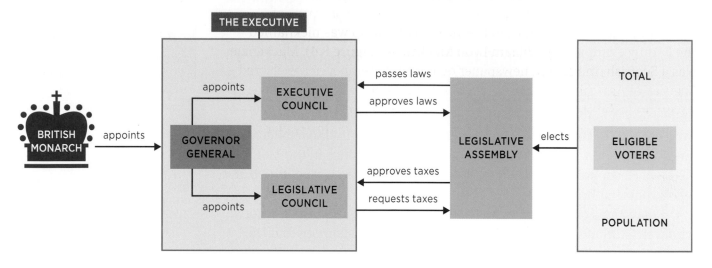

Government Structure in Upper and Lower Canada, 1830s

THE EXECUTIVE

BRITISH MONARCH → appoints

GOVERNOR GENERAL

appoints → EXECUTIVE COUNCIL

appoints → LEGISLATIVE COUNCIL

passes laws
approves laws
approves taxes
requests taxes

LEGISLATIVE ASSEMBLY

elects

TOTAL
ELIGIBLE VOTERS
POPULATION

FIGURE 8.3 This diagram shows the main groups in the government during the 1830s. This government structure was created in 1791. **Analyze:** Did this government structure represent the total population fairly?

GOVERNMENT STRUCTURE IN THE 1830s

When the *Constitutional Act, 1791* created Upper and Lower Canada, it also created separate governments in each colony. Examine **Figure 8.3**, which shows the government structure in Upper and Lower Canada. Why do you think people like Daniel Tracey felt frustrated with this structure?

The governor general was appointed, or chosen, by the British monarch. The governor general then appointed members of the Executive Council and Legislative Council. These appointments were for life, meaning that the people in these positions could not be removed from office. Together, the governor general, the Executive Council, and the Legislative Council were referred to as the Executive.

Separate from the Executive was the Legislative Assembly, which was made up of elected representatives. Each colony had its own Assembly. In Upper and Lower Canada, only white, male property owners could vote for, or run for, the Legislative Assembly. Which groups of people were not able to vote?

The Legislative Assembly could create and pass laws. However, the Executive could stop any laws that the Legislative Assembly passed. In turn, the Executive needed the Legislative Assembly to approve taxes. These taxes helped to fund projects supported by the Executive. The elected members of the Legislative Assembly did not want to raise taxes to fund Executive projects, so they would block Executive requests to increase taxes. In response, the Executive would refuse to approve laws passed by the Legislative Assembly.

> What influences from the government structure in the 1830s exist in Canada's government today?

THE FAMILY COMPACT AND THE CHÂTEAU CLIQUE

In Upper Canada, a group of wealthy, upper-class, white men who made up the Executive controlled the economy and government of Upper Canada from the 1790s to the 1830s. This group was nicknamed the **Family Compact** by William Lyon Mackenzie (**Figure 8.4**). Mackenzie was a Scottish immigrant, newspaper owner, and member of the elected Legislative Assembly in Upper Canada. Even though he was part of the government, he was unhappy with how it worked. Examine **Figure 8.5**, which is his description of the Family Compact. What are the reasons why he was upset?

> "The family connection rules Upper Canada. A dozen nobodies, and a few placemen, pensioners and individuals of well-known narrow and bigoted [prejudiced] principles: the whole of the revenue of Upper Canada are in reality at their mercy;—they are paymasters, receivers, auditors, King, Lords, and Commons."
>
> — *William Lyon Mackenzie, member of the Legislative Assembly*

FIGURE 8.5 This critique of the Family Compact appeared in Mackenzie's newspaper, the *Colonial Advocate*, in 1833. **Analyze:** How does Mackenzie describe the Family Compact?

FIGURE 8.4 This portrait of William Lyon Mackenzie was painted by John Wycliffe Lowes Forster in 1931. **Analyze:** Why do you think Mackenzie was painted with documents in his hand?

Family Compact a small group of men who controlled most of the political and economic power in Upper Canada

Château Clique a small group of men, mostly merchants, who controlled most of the political and economic power in Lower Canada

In Lower Canada, a similar group of men controlled the Executive from the 1810s to the 1840s. They were nicknamed the **Château Clique**. The main difference between these two groups was that the men in the Château Clique were English-speakers who were governing a French majority population. The Château Clique pushed to unite Upper and Lower Canada so that English-speakers would be the majority population. What could be some other consequences of this union?

THE REFORMERS

By the 1830s, many people within the government, not just Mackenzie, were critical of the government system. These critics were called **Reformers**. Many felt that Executive members made decisions that benefited mainly themselves and their friends and family. The appointed Executive often ignored the wishes of elected Legislative Assembly members. Members of the Legislative Assembly felt that they had no real power since Britain could overrule any law, at any time.

Reformer critic of the government system in Canada during the early 1800s

Reformers like Mackenzie were tired of appointed officials making most of the decisions. They grew more frustrated that their requests for government reform were rejected repeatedly by the governor general and the Executive. As tensions grew, politicians were divided into two camps. The Reformers were on one side and the Conservatives who supported the existing system were on the other. The Conservatives were often called "The Tories."

COMMUNICATE

Now that you have evaluated your information and drawn conclusions, the next step is to communicate and share your findings with others.

When communicating your findings, include
- your inquiry question
- the evidence you found
- your conclusion
- a delivery that will engage your audience

To find the right way to communicate your findings, begin by determining who your audience is. Then, choose the best format to engage your audience. **Figure 8.6** below lists different formats that you can choose.

While you are creating your presentation, keep in mind the following questions to make sure you are communicating clearly to your audience: What language and format are appropriate for my audience? Am I using historical terms and other vocabulary correctly? Am I citing my sources of information correctly?

Type of Communication	Examples
Written	• Written report • Slide show • Poem • Annotated map
Visual	• Photo essay • Infographic • Poster • Artwork
Performance	• Oral report • Dance • Skit • Documentary

FIGURE 8.6 These are just a few examples of ways to communicate your findings. **Analyze:** Which formats are more appropriate for a presentation to your classmates? To your teacher?

CASE STUDY: THE ROLE OF NEWSPAPERS IN LOWER AND UPPER CANADA POLITICS

In this case study, you will examine the role of newspapers during political conflicts in the 1830s. As you read, consider the following inquiry question: Were newspapers an effective way for politicians in the 1830s to communicate their ideas and beliefs? In the 1800s, newspapers were the main tool that people used to communicate news and public opinion. Many politicians even owned their own newspapers. Daniel Tracey, whom you read about earlier in the chapter, owned a newspaper called *The Vindicator*. On January 3, 1832, he published an article calling for the annihilation, or total destruction, of the Legislative Council in Lower Canada. **Figure 8.7** shows what the front page of the newspaper looked like on that day.

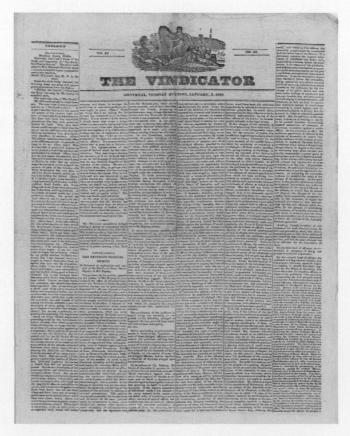

FIGURE 8.7 This is the front page of Tracey's newspaper, *The Vindicator*, on January 3, 1832. **Analyze:** Would a newspaper name like this be effective for today's audience?

A Canadien newspaper called *La Minerve* was also used to communicate political frustrations to the public. In 1832, journalist Ludger Duvernay published an article that demanded the abolition, or closing, of the Legislative Council. Both Tracey and Duvernay were imprisoned because of the opinions they published in their newspapers. However, this made them heroes in the eyes of the Reformers.

As mentioned on page 225, William Lyon Mackenzie published his own newspaper, the *Colonial Advocate*, in Upper Canada. Mackenzie believed that all people should have access to information, particularly information about their government. He also believed that his newspaper could be used by the public to express opinions about controversial issues in Upper Canada, including politics. The excerpt in **Figure 8.8** is from the first edition of the *Colonial Advocate*. In this excerpt, Mackenzie states the purpose of his newspaper.

"[The purpose of the *Colonial Advocate* is] to do the people's business and check and expose speculation and official knavery [dishonesty]."

— *William Lyon Mackenzie*

FIGURE 8.8 This excerpt is from the September 22, 1831, edition of the *Colonial Advocate*. "Knavery" refers to the actions of a dishonest person, or knave. **Analyze:** Do you think that the purpose of newspapers and other news media today is the same as the purpose of the *Colonial Advocate*?

Using his newspaper, Mackenzie advocated for responsible government, or government that was answerable to the people. One barrier to achieving this was the government's system for appointing officials. Mackenzie frequently used the *Colonial Advocate* to attack members of the Family Compact, who became enraged.

They fired back at Mackenzie, calling his newspaper a "poisonous paper." They also fired back with lawsuits, threats, and even an attack on Mackenzie's printing office in 1826, which destroyed his printing press.

The actions of the Family Compact, and, in particular, the destruction of Mackenzie's printing press, caused many people to see Mackenzie as a victim of the Family Compact. This motivated them to support the push for responsible government. Two years after the destruction of his printing press, Mackenzie was elected to the Legislative Assembly.

In addition to promoting responsible government, Mackenzie wanted to see changes in many aspects of life in Upper Canada, such as banking, taxes, investment in the economy, and education. He also brought these issues to the attention of the public through his newspaper.

TRY IT

1. Review your inquiry question: Were newspapers an effective way for politicians in the 1830s to communicate their ideas and beliefs? Use evidence presented in this feature and in the chapter to support your answer.

2. Select an audience to whom you can communicate your findings from question 1. Write a brief plan, outlining the information you will share with your audience. Use the criteria on page 226 to help you develop your plan.

3. Decide on the best format to communicate your findings from questions 1 and 2 to your audience. Prepare your presentation and share it with a partner. Use your partner's feedback to improve your presentation.

THE TORONTO YOUTH CABINET

Over the years, Canada has been through a variety of conflicts over issues related to its government. Today, more than ever, the government remains a vital part of how changes are made in our society.

The Toronto Youth Cabinet (TYC) is a group of young people who are doing important political work in the city of Toronto. Established in 1998 by the Toronto City Council, the TYC is run entirely by youth and encourages young people to participate in government. The TYC represents Toronto's diverse 320 000 youth at City Hall and advocates for an equitable and youth-friendly city. **Figure 8.9** shows two members of the TYC at Toronto City Hall. Through volunteer work, the TYC strives to empower young citizens, inspire them to get involved, and, ultimately, make changes in their community. The TYC works to establish valuable relationships with government officials and community groups and to voice opinions and concerns on issues that affect youth in Toronto. Working groups are created to explore issues such as community safety, municipal policy development, and community outreach.

> "WE ALWAYS TALK ABOUT 20 YEARS FROM NOW. I WANT TO KNOW ABOUT 20 DAYS FROM NOW. I WANT TO KNOW HOW WE'RE GOING TO IMPROVE THE NEXT 20 MINUTES."

The TYC structures its mission around these working groups, which form the foundation of the TYC's mandate to bring about change. A yearly work plan is collectively developed by the TYC's co-chairs, working group leaders, and members. All decisions are made through consensus or formal voting, and every member has one vote. All youth in Toronto, from 13 to 24 years of age, are encouraged to join the TYC.

A youth member of the TYC was quoted as saying, "We always talk about 20 years from now. I want to know about 20 days from now. I want to know how we're going to improve the next 20 minutes." The Identify 'N' Impact (INI) Awards, given out by the TYC, are presented to youth who make valuable contributions in Toronto communities. These awards celebrate the importance of youth as visionaries and agents of social change.

Organizations like the TYC play a very important role in society. They give voice and power to youth and help to build a city that values the lives and voices of young people. They remind us about the importance of governance and how it can be used to make positive changes.

FIGURE 8.9 Members of the Toronto Youth Cabinet at Toronto City Hall

A CALL TO **ACTION**

1. What are some ways that you can participate in government, either in your school or in your community?
2. What changes would you like to see in your community? How can you make these changes happen?

THE PARTI PATRIOTE

Reformers in Lower Canada organized into the *Parti Patriote*. The *Patriotes* believed that French-speaking people, not the British, should be in control of Lower Canada. The Patriotes were led by Louis-Joseph Papineau, a Montréal-born lawyer and politician, shown speaking to a crowd in **Figure 8.10**. What does this painting tell you about public political meetings during this time? In 1834, the Patriotes wrote a document called the "92 Resolutions," which was sent to Britain. The document listed the issues that the Patriotes had with the existing government and their demands for more power for the elected Legislative Assembly. Read Papineau's statement in **Figure 8.11**. Why did he think political change was needed?

FIGURE 8.10 This painting, *A Political Meeting in Lower Canada* by Kyle Fergus, was created in 1938. It shows Papineau leading the Parti Patriote in the 1830s. **Analyze:** Based on how Papineau is portrayed in this painting, what characteristics do you think he had?

> "We will not cease our demands for full political rights and power. And though we feel uneasy, we hope that the British government will at last grant us justice. In this hope, we shall ... lead the people towards that day, which will know neither monarchy nor aristocracy."
>
> — *Louis-Joseph Papineau, leader of the Parti Patriote*

FIGURE 8.11 This quote from Papineau was likely recorded in 1834, around the time he wrote the 92 Resolutions. **Analyze:** Based on this quote, how do you think the British government would have responded to Papineau's statement?

REFORMERS DIVIDED

All of the Reformers wanted **responsible government**. With responsible government, the main decision makers in both Upper and Lower Canada would be the elected Legislative Assembly, rather than the appointed members of the Executive. The Legislative Assembly would then control the government, not the governor general. However, the Reformers disagreed on how to achieve responsible government.

Egerton Ryerson and Robert Baldwin, politicians in Upper Canada, were Reformers. They were willing, however, to work on a compromise with the Executive. Papineau and Mackenzie did not want to compromise. Mackenzie and his supporters decided that they wanted an American-style political system in Upper Canada and would use violence to achieve it.

responsible government a government that is responsible to its voters, not to appointed members

CHECK-**IN**

1. **INTERPRET AND ANALYZE** How do you think the 1832 and 1837 riots in Montréal affected the relationships among the Canadiens, the British supporters, and the new immigrants?

2. **CAUSE AND CONSEQUENCE** What do you think would be a positive consequence of being a radical Reformer? What could be a negative consequence?

3. **GATHER AND ORGANIZE** List the main issues people living in Upper and Lower Canada had with the system of government in the 1830s. Rank the issues in order of importance. Provide reasons for your ranking.

WHAT WERE THE CONSEQUENCES OF POLITICAL UNREST?

By 1837, tensions in Lower and Upper Canada were reaching a boiling point. Drawing inspiration from the American Revolution and the French Revolution in the late 1700s, the Reformers pushed for action against the British.

In Lower Canada, the Parti Patriote saw all of its 92 Resolutions rejected by the British government in March 1837. This rejection fuelled Patriote anger and pushed more radical Patriotes, such as Dr. Wolfred Nelson, to support the idea of a rebellion. Based on Dr. Nelson's quote in **Figure 8.12**, why do you think violence was the Patriotes' next step?

In Upper Canada, the Tories and the Reformers were locked in a constant struggle for political power. The divisions among the Reformers made them less effective against the Tories. These divisions led to a Tory victory in the 1836 election. The Tory victory caused frustration for both moderate and radical Reformers.

LOWER CANADA REBELLIONS

After the riot between French Reformers and British Loyalists on November 6, 1837, described on page 223, the Patriotes began to organize rallies and prepare for a rebellion. They also began to boycott British goods. British troops were sent into Lower Canada to stop the unrest. On November 16, 1837, the government in Lower Canada tried to arrest some of the leaders of the Parti Patriote. About 800 Patriotes replied with an armed uprising at Saint-Denis on November 23, winning the battle when the British retreated. Two days later, after the British army added 400 more soldiers, the Patriotes were defeated during the battle of Saint-Charles, depicted in **Figure 8.13**. With most of the Patriote fighters dead, the British imprisoned the rest of the rebels around Saint-Charles and set fire to the surrounding farms.

After the battles at Saint-Denis and Saint-Charles, the Patriotes regrouped and took their last stand north of Montréal, in Saint-Eustache. On the morning of December 14, 1837, about 1280 British soldiers and 220 Loyalist volunteers faced the remaining 200 Patriote fighters. Examine **Figure 8.14**, which shows a battle scene from Saint-Eustache. Does the painting reveal who won the battle? Why?

After a short fight in Saint-Eustache, the armed rebellion in Lower Canada was over. The victorious British army then looted and burned the houses of the rebels. Papineau and the other leaders of the rebellion fled to the United States. The remaining Patriote fighters who were unable to flee were either killed or taken prisoner by the British.

"It is time to melt down our dishes and tin spoons to make bullets."

— Dr. Wolfred Nelson, Patriote

FIGURE 8.12 In 1837, Patriote Dr. Nelson called for a rebellion. **Analyze:** How do you think Reformers in Upper Canada would have reacted to Nelson's words?

What would have motivated the Patriotes to keep fighting?

FIGURE 8.13 *Attack on St. Charles* was painted by Charles Beauclerk in 1840. Beauclerk was a commanding officer in the British army during the battle at Saint-Charles. **Analyze:** How might Beauclerk's role in the battle have influenced his depiction of the event?

FIGURE 8.14 *Back View of the Church of St. Eustache and Dispersion of the Insurgents* was painted by Charles Beauclerk in 1840. The British, on the left, are shown fighting the Patriotes in Saint-Eustache. **Analyze:** What does the painting show about the organization of the British soldiers compared to the organization of the Patriotes?

CORROBORATING
SOURCES

No one source can provide a complete picture of the past. Historians crosscheck, or **corroborate**, the inferences they have made from a source. They can confirm or challenge their inferences using other sources. To corroborate information from different sources, historians ask questions like the ones in the table in **Figure 8.15**.

The speakers in **Figures 8.12** and **8.17** argued for armed resistance against the British. From these two sources, you might infer that the rebels' cause enjoyed widespread support.

In this activity, you will analyze a primary source written by a British settler, Susanna Moodie. Moodie's stories about life in the backwoods were described in Chapter 7. You will compare her poem, shown in **Figure 8.16**, with the sources in **Figures 8.12** and **8.17**. You will then use the questions in **Figure 8.15** to decide whether these three sources support the inference that there was widespread support for armed resistance against the British.

FIGURE 8.16 "The Oath of the Canadian Volunteers," by Susanna Moodie appeared in newspapers like the Montréal *Herald* in 1838.

Questions to Ask When Corroborating Sources

Type of Communication	Examples
Similarities and differences	• What is similar about these sources? How do they differ? • Why are they similar or different? • Is one source more reliable?
Support for inferences	• Does this source give evidence to confirm what I have already learned? • Does it extend what I know about the topic? • Do I now have enough evidence to answer my historical question?
Challenges to inferences	• Does this source challenge what I have already examined? • Does it contradict inferences I made using other sources?
Importance	• What makes this source an important piece of evidence?

FIGURE 8.15 These questions will help you corroborate information from different sources.

"Huzza for England! – May she claim
Our fond devotion ever ...
We swear to die, or save
Her honour from the rebel band
Whose crimes pollute our injured land!"

— *Susanna Moodie, British settler*

HOW TO CORROBORATE SOURCES

STEP 1
Read **Figure 8.16**. Compare the poem to the quotes in **Figures 8.12** and **8.17**. How are the sources similar and how are they different?

STEP 2
Does Moodie's poem support or challenge your inference? Use the questions in **Figure 8.15** to help you determine the answer.

STEP 3
Is Moodie's poem an important piece of evidence? Based on your corroboration, is the inference that the rebels' cause had widespread support *probably* or *definitely* correct, or *possibly* or *likely not* correct? Explain your reasoning.

RIOTS IN UPPER CANADA

As in Lower Canada, after many years of trying to create peaceful change, politics in Upper Canada had become increasingly violent. William Lyon Mackenzie was a major supporter of the Patriotes during the unrest in Lower Canada. He campaigned for the Reformer cause, giving fiery speeches. Read the quote in **Figure 8.17** from one of his speeches. What does this quote tell you about Mackenzie's perspective on the rebellions?

In Upper Canada, the Tories had used the support of recent British immigrants to win the 1836 election. However, they had also used bribery and corruption to win. They had gained the support of the new British immigrants by branding the Reformers as dangerous radicals. As a result, riots broke out between Mackenzie's Reformers angered by the Tory campaign and the supporters of the Tories during the election. This was much like the riot that had broken out during the 1832 election in Montréal. Examine **Figure 8.18**. What is the artist trying to tell you about the political tensions during this time?

"To die fighting for freedom is truly glorious. Who would live and die a slave? Never ... Never ... Never ..."

— *William Lyon Mackenzie, member of the Legislative Assembly and Reformer*

FIGURE 8.17 This quote is from a speech made by Mackenzie in November 1837 to rally support for rebellion in Upper Canada. **Analyze:** Why do you think Mackenzie uses the word "slave" in his speech?

FIGURE 8.18 This undated illustration by C.W. Jefferys, entitled *An election during the struggle of responsible Government*, shows an election in Upper Canada. At the time, votes were made in public, unlike the secret ballots that are used today. **Analyze:** What are the risks of public voting as shown by the artist?

FIGURE 8.19 This undated sketch of C.W. Jefferys's *The March of the Rebels upon Toronto in December, 1837* shows the Reformers walking down Yonge Street. **Analyze:** What mood is the artist trying to convey?

> Was 1837 a time of continuity or change for people in Upper Canada?

UPPER CANADA REBELLION

When Lieutenant-Governor Sir Francis Bond Head found out about the uprising in Lower Canada, he sent the troops who were stationed in Upper Canada to help defeat the rebels. Mackenzie realized that the conflict in Lower Canada was distracting the British. He saw an opportunity for Reformers in Upper Canada to stage their own rebellion.

On December 5, 1837, Mackenzie and about 800 supporters marched down Yonge Street in Toronto. Examine a sketch of this march in **Figure 8.19.** How are the Reformers portrayed? They eventually stationed themselves at Montgomery's Tavern, just north of present-day Eglinton Avenue in Toronto. The next day, they marched toward the downtown area to obtain more guns and ammunition. A small group of about 30 Loyalists, who were fighting for the British, managed to scatter the rebels.

Later that evening, the rebels were able to regroup and reorganize under the command of an experienced military leader. However, the British forces were able to gather more troops, and they now numbered 1000 men. Two days later, the rebels were defeated, and the British burned down Montgomery's Tavern. Another group of rebels, from the London, Ontario, area, tried to join Mackenzie, but they, too, were easily defeated by government forces. Tory supporters burned homes and farms belonging to known rebels and even those belonging to people who were only suspected supporters.

PUNISHMENT OF THE REBELS

The rebellion of Upper Canada was over. Mackenzie managed to escape to the United States, but some of his followers were captured. Two of them, Samuel Lount and Peter Matthews, were tried and then hanged. Examine **Figure 8.20**, which shows the day of Lount and Matthews's execution. Why do you think they were publicly hanged?

Over the next year, Mackenzie tried to gather supporters in the United States. The rebels carried out a number of destructive raids from their safe haven in the United States. They hoped that their actions would convince others to join their uprising against the government. Aside from a few sympathizers, however, the rebels could not gain enough support. They eventually gave up.

In the end, more than 1000 people were jailed on the suspicion of treason, 100 were exiled, and 15 were hanged. What could have been done to prevent this violence? What would the future now hold for Canada?

FIGURE 8.20 An unknown artist's undated illustration of the public hanging of Samuel Lount and Peter Matthews. The hanging took place in Toronto on April 12, 1838. **Analyze:** What does this image tell you about people's attitudes toward punishment at the time?

CHECK-**IN**

1. **CAUSE AND CONSEQUENCE** Think about all of the causes of the Lower and Upper Canada rebellions. Which cause do you think triggered the rebels to fight? Why? Support your answer with evidence.

2. **HISTORICAL SIGNIFICANCE** Do you think the British government benefited from these rebellions? Why, or why not?

3. **FORMULATE QUESTIONS** Review the instructions for creating inquiry questions on page 26. Create an inquiry question about either the Lower or Upper Canada rebellion.

4. **HISTORICAL PERSPECTIVE** Why did most of the new immigrants arriving from Britain not support the rebels?

WHY DID THE SYSTEM OF GOVERNMENT CHANGE?

The Upper and Lower Canada rebellions forced the British government to realize that Canada's system of government was not working. However, the British government did not want to give more power to the Reformers. So how would this situation be resolved?

THE DURHAM REPORT

John George Lambton, Lord Durham, shown in **Figure 8.21**, arrived in Canada from England in May 1838. He was sent by Queen Victoria and the British government to find ways to calm the tensions in the Canadian colony following the rebellions in Upper and Lower Canada. The Upper and Lower Canada rebellions had occurred in 1837, which was also the first year of Queen Victoria's reign. Queen Victoria is seen in **Figure 8.22** at her first meeting with senior politicians. As Queen, she was able to impose any new law onto the governments of Upper and Lower Canada. How would the perspectives of the people in Upper and Lower Canada be represented in such a meeting?

Upon his arrival to Canada, Durham learned about the main political conflict between the Executive and the Legislative Assembly. This conflict was especially a problem in Lower Canada, where the mainly French-speaking elected Legislative Assembly refused to approve budgets for projects that could boost British business. Durham's report had three main recommendations that focused on political and cultural changes to Upper and Lower Canada. He submitted his report to Queen Victoria in 1839.

FIGURE 8.21 An undated portrait of Lord Durham, drawn by J. Stewart and engraved by H.B. Hall. **Analyze:** What elements of this portrait show Durham's social status?

FIGURE 8.22 Sir David Wilkie's 1838 painting entitled *The First Council of Queen Victoria* shows Queen Victoria meeting with some of the senior politicians in the British government. **Analyze:** What does this painting reveal about the British monarchy and politicians who influenced Canada's government overseas?

DURHAM'S RECOMMENDATION ON RESPONSIBLE GOVERNMENT

Durham observed that the public opposed the Executive members of government because they were not elected. Durham recommended in his report that the Executive and Legislative Councils should no longer be appointed. What does **Figure 8.23** reveal about his opinion on the Executive? Durham suggested that members should be elected, but elected by white men who owned property and other forms of wealth. How do you think others, including women, would have felt about his suggestion?

DURHAM'S RECOMMENDATION OF UNIFICATION

Durham spent most of his time in Lower Canada, observing the relationship between the Canadiens and the British. His next recommendation was to unite Upper and Lower Canada into one province, called the United Province of Canada. Read Durham's quote in **Figure 8.24**. What is his solution for peace?

> "[the Family Compact is a] petty, corrupt, insolent [rude] Tory clique"
>
> — Lord Durham

FIGURE 8.23 This quote about the Family Compact is from the Durham Report. **Analyze:** How do you think Reformers would have reacted to Durham's words?

> "I believe that tranquility can only be restored by subjecting the province to the vigorous rule of an English majority; and that the only [effective] government would be that formed by a legislative [government of] union."
>
> — Lord Durham

FIGURE 8.24 This quote from the Durham Report offers a solution for peace. **Analyze:** Do you think this was a fair solution? Why, or why not?

DURHAM'S RECOMMENDATION ABOUT THE CANADIENS

Durham believed that tensions were caused not only by political conflicts, but by cultural differences as well. Durham's third recommendation was that the Canadiens be assimilated. This meant that the Canadiens would lose their own culture and adopt British ways. How does Durham justify his reason for assimilation in **Figure 8.25**?

> "They [the Canadiens] are an old and stationary society, in a new and progressive world ... They are a people with no history, and no literature."
>
> — Lord Durham

FIGURE 8.25 This quote from the Durham Report describes Durham's view of the Canadiens. **Analyze:** What does Durham mean when he says the Canadiens have "no history, and no literature"?

Consider all three main recommendations from Durham's report. Why might his report be considered controversial?

THE *ACT OF UNION*

The British government rejected Durham's recommendation of responsible government, but it adopted his suggestion of uniting Upper and Lower Canada. The *Act of Union* of 1840 joined Upper and Lower Canada into one colony, named the Province of Canada. The government for this new province was made up of representatives from Canada West (former Upper Canada, present-day Ontario) and Canada East (former Lower Canada, present-day Québec), beginning in 1841. The following list highlights some of the main points in the *Act of Union*:

- The capital was Kingston, Canada West (present-day Kingston, Ontario).
- The use of French was banned in the government. English was now the official language of the new government.
- Canada West and Canada East were given equal numbers of elected representatives. (In 1841, Lower Canada's population was 650 000; Upper Canada's population was 500 000.)

> What does the ban on speaking French in the government reveal about how the British government cooperated with the Canadiens?

ACHIEVING RESPONSIBLE GOVERNMENT

The response of the Canadiens to the *Act of Union* was outrage. Many leaders in Canada East wanted to end the *Act of Union*. Despite this, Louis-Hippolyte LaFontaine, a Reformer leader from Canada East, disagreed. As attorney-general, LaFontaine was in charge of making sure the government and the public followed the law. He did not support the violence of the 1837 rebellions. Instead, LaFontaine joined Robert Baldwin, a Reformer from Canada West, to pursue responsible government.

The partnership between Baldwin and LaFontaine led many Canadiens to view LaFontaine as a traitor. He eventually gained their confidence by standing up for them. Read the quote in **Figure 8.26** from his first speech.

> "I must inform the honourable members that even if I knew English as well as French, I would still make my first speech in the language of my French Canadian countrymen, if only to protest solemnly the cruel injustice of that part of the *Act of Union* which aims to [ban] the mother tongue of half the population of Canada. I owe it to my countrymen, I owe it to myself."
>
> — *Louis-Hippolyte LaFontaine, attorney-general and Reformer*

FIGURE 8.26 This quote is from LaFontaine's first speech to the members of the Province of Canada in 1842. **Analyze:** What parts of this quote support the idea of responsible government?

In 1848, LaFontaine and Baldwin's Reformers won a majority government. This was the first time the English and the French had achieved a common political goal peacefully. By 1849, the LaFontaine-Baldwin government had convinced the British government to give political power to the elected Legislative Assembly, not the Executive. Responsible government had finally become a reality.

THE *REBELLION LOSSES BILL*

On the evening of April 25, 1849, a group of radical Tories took to the streets and threw rocks and rotten eggs at the carriage of Lord Elgin, the new governor general. Then, they set fire to the parliament buildings in Montréal, which had become the capital in 1844. A painting of the massive fire is shown in **Figure 8.27**. The representatives were still inside when the building was torched. They had to run for their lives. What could have caused the Tory demonstrators to carry out such a violent act?

Earlier, in February 1849, the Baldwin-LaFontaine government had introduced the *Rebellion Losses Bill* to compensate people in Canada East who had lost property during the rebellions. As estimates of the costs increased, so did the English-speaking public's opposition to paying them. In time, public protests by the Tories turned into riots. It was up to Lord Elgin to decide whether to sign the bill as law. If he did sign it, he would anger the Tories even further. If he did not sign it, he would damage the foundation of responsible government. On April 25, 1849, Lord Elgin signed the bill. Was the new government acting responsibly to the people by passing this bill?

FIGURE 8.27 This 1849 painting entitled *The Burning of the Parliament Building in Montreal* is by Joseph Légaré. It shows the destruction of the Montréal parliament buildings by fire. **Analyze:** What message did the protesters send by burning down the parliament buildings?

BROKEN RELATIONSHIPS

The fire reduced the Montréal parliament buildings to a burnt pile of rubble. Valuable items, such as rare paintings and documents, were ruined, as was the relationship, once again, between the English and the French. William Rufus Seaver, a pastor who witnessed the riot, blamed prejudice for the disaster. Read **Figure 8.28**, a quote from Seaver. What did he think were some of the consequences of this conflict?

The *Rebellion Losses Bill* and resulting riot also further damaged the relationship between the Tories and Britain. The Tories felt betrayed that the British government had not stopped the bill. This added to their frustrations over Britain's new economic policy. Britain was still the major industrial power in the world and dominated global trade. In 1846, the British government adopted a **free trade** system. Previously, Britain had not taxed goods, such as fish, fur, minerals, timber, and wheat, from merchants in the colonies. However, goods from other countries were charged extra taxes. Under the free trade system, goods from the colonies were no longer given better tax rates. Merchants from other countries could then compete with colonial merchants by offering products at the same or lower prices. Examine **Figure 8.29**, which is a political cartoon commenting on Britain's free trade system. How do you think merchants in Canada would have reacted to this cartoon?

> "The quarrel is a war of Races—English speaking people will not be ruled by a Canadian government, and none can see what the end of these things will yet be—But we are in trouble enough now, and blood will be shed worse yet than in the Rebellion of '37."
>
> — *William Rufus Seaver, pastor*

FIGURE 8.28 Seaver, a witness to the burning of the parliament buildings in 1849, described the state of the English-French conflict. **Analyze:** Do you think a Canadien would have agreed with Seaver's perspective?

free trade a system in which every country can trade goods without having to pay extra taxes

FIGURE 8.29 This cartoon from 1850 shows a lion, the symbol of Britain, fat and comfortable as a result of Britain's free trade agreement. **Analyze:** How do you think the cartoonist may have drawn Canada in this scenario?

THE BRITISH LION IN 1850;

OR, THE EFFECTS OF FREE TRADE.

WITHDRAWAL FROM POLITICS

The Reformers at the heart of the responsible government movement were worn down by the continued conflict. Papineau decided to move back to Canada from the United States. He returned to politics in 1848 and immediately called to cancel the *Act of Union*. However, he could not find many supporters. Many of his former supporters had joined LaFontaine. Papineau eventually left politics in 1854. Examine **Figure 8.30**, a quote from Papineau. What kind of emotions can you detect from his words?

In 1849, Mackenzie returned from exile and was elected to Parliament. However, he found that people no longer paid attention to his criticisms. Bitter, he retired from politics in 1859. Both Baldwin and LaFontaine, memorialized in the statue shown in **Figure 8.31**, retired from politics in 1851. The struggles had taken a toll on their mental and physical health.

"You will believe me, I hope, when I tell you: I love my country ... Did I love her wisely? Did I love her foolishly? ... I believe I can say that I have loved her the way she ought to be loved."

— *Louis-Joseph Papineau, former leader of the Parti Patriote*

FIGURE 8.30 This quote is from a speech made by Papineau to the *Institut Canadien* in 1867. The Institut Canadien was a public library and debating room for young professionals in Montréal. **Analyze:** Based on the evidence in this chapter so far, do you think Papineau's love for his country was wise or foolish?

FIGURE 8.31 This statue of Baldwin and LaFontaine is located on Parliament Hill in Ottawa, Ontario. **Analyze:** Why would a statue of Baldwin and LaFontaine be on Parliament Hill, where the federal government of Canada meets?

CHECK-**IN**

1. **CAUSE AND CONSEQUENCE** Think back to Lord Durham's recommendation to unify Upper and Lower Canada. What would be the consequences of this unification for the Canadiens?

2. **INTERPRET AND ANALYZE** Who benefited more from the *Act of Union*, Canada East or Canada West? Why?

3. **HISTORICAL SIGNIFICANCE** How was Baldwin and LaFontaine's willingness to work together an important achievement in Canadian history? Why is their work to create responsible government still relevant to Canadians today?

4. **GATHER AND ORGANIZE** What evidence is there that the Tories were unhappy with both Canada's new government and the British government?

HOW DID DIFFERENT GROUPS TRY TO OVERCOME POLITICAL CHALLENGES?

Politicians are not the only people who can create changes to the political system. Often, it's people outside of the government who can help to trigger change.

FIRST NATIONS LAND RIGHTS

First Nations continued to meet resistance from the government regarding land rights. The millions of acres around the Great Lakes were prime agricultural land. The arrival of thousands of European settlers during the 1800s led to the Canadian government taking this land away from First Nations. Ojibwe Chief Shingwaukonse spoke to Lord Elgin, governor general of Canada, in 1849 about the increasing pressure on First Nations to give up their land. What does **Figure 8.32** suggest about Chief Shingwaukonse's perspective on the Ojibwe's situation?

First Nations leaders continued to demonstrate that they were as entitled to the land as Europeans. Sometimes, this meant that they used the land in the same way that Europeans did—for farming. Look at **Figure 8.33**, which is a painting of the Wikwemikong community on Manitoulin Island. The painting shows an example of a First Nations farming community. What European influences on this First Nations settlement do you see depicted in this painting?

> "Father, time wore on and you have became a great people, whilst we have melted away like snow beneath an April sun; our strength is wasted, our countless warriors dead, our forests laid low ... you have swept away all our pleasant land, and ... you tell us 'willing or unwilling, you must now go.'"
>
> — *Ojibwe Chief Shingwaukonse*

FIGURE 8.32 Chief Shingwaukonse led many campaigns for First Nations rights. This is part of his speech to Lord Elgin in 1849. **Analyze:** Look at Shingwaukonse's use of verbs in this excerpt. What feelings is he trying to emphasize?

FIGURE 8.33 This 1908 painting, called *Numbering the Indians, Wikwemikong, Manitoulin Island* by William Armstrong, shows the Wikwemikong community on August 16, 1856. **Analyze:** What information about the Wikwemikong community can you gather from this painting?

CATHERINE SUTTON'S CAMPAIGN

Despite actions by leaders like Chief Shingwaukonse, over time, First Nations were continuously forced to give up most of their territories. They were placed onto smaller reserves, often on land that had poor soil for farming. **Figure 8.34** shows a portrait of Nahnebahwequay, also known as Catherine Sutton, an Objiwe from Ontario. In the mid-1800s she campaigned for First Nations land rights. She gained support from First Nations groups, as well as non-Aboriginal people, in Canada, the United States, and Britain. After many years of campaigning, she and her husband finally met Queen Victoria in 1860. Queen Victoria promised to help the First Nations. She sent the Duke of Newcastle to meet with the Canadian government. After meeting with the government, however, the duke felt that there was nothing he could do for the First Nations. The duke believed that the Canadian government had all the decision-making power. Does this decision reflect the ideas of responsible government?

FIGURE 8.34 This is a photo of Catherine Sutton. **Analyze:** What is the significance of having Sutton pose with an open book?

CHANGING VIEWS ON WOMEN'S RIGHTS

As you learned earlier, Canada went through many political struggles during the 1800s. Like many people concerned about the government, women wrote to newspapers to voice their concerns. During this time, however, women were not included in the political process. Their opinions were not always welcome. Many women wrote to newspapers under a different name to protect their identity. For example, a Canadien woman, calling herself "Adelaide," published an article in the newspaper *La Minerve*. Read the excerpt in **Figure 8.35** from her article, in which she asks the Patriotes to defend women's equality as a traditional feature of French society. She felt that British traditions threatened women's rights. Have the attitudes about women described in **Figure 8.35** changed or stayed the same compared to today?

The laws of England view the wife in a less favourable manner, and place her in an inferior category. She ceases to have a life of her own, from the moment she is contracted into marriage [married]; she loses her name and takes that of her husband, exclusively.

FIGURE 8.35 This excerpt is from a letter written by "Adelaide" to the newspaper *La Minerve* on February 2, 1837. **Analyze:** Why does "Adelaide" see women changing their last name as a loss of independence?

WOMEN'S RIGHT TO VOTE

Women's right to vote was an ongoing issue in the 1830s and 1840s. Under the *Constitutional Act, 1791* certain landowners and tenants were allowed to vote, with no mention of whether they had to be male or female. Some female landowners in Lower Canada took advantage of this and voted in elections, something that was unheard of at the time. How might the Reformers have reacted to this? Read **Figure 8.36**, which is a quote from Papineau in 1834. In his quote, he refers to "hustings," which are public speeches made before an election.

In 1849, reforms to the provincial **statutes**, or laws, of Canada included a section that affected women's right to vote. According to **Figure 8.37**, how did the reforms affect women's rights? Other British colonies followed this practice so that no women, even the few who owned property in their own name, could vote. As a result, women were not able to vote in federal elections in Canada until 1918. In Québec, women had to wait until 1940 to vote.

PUBLIC DEMANDS FOR EDUCATION

In the early 1800s, free public education was not available for all children. There was very little government funding for a few public schools, and some communities could not even afford to pay the salary of one teacher. Many schools did not have proper supplies. Examine **Figure 8.38**, which shows recommended school supplies during this time. Do you think most schools would have had all of these supplies?

"It is revolting to see women dragged by their husbands and daughters, by their fathers, often against their will, to hustings [public speeches]. Public interest, decency, and the modesty of women demand that these scandals never reoccur."

— *Louis-Joseph Papineau, Patriote*

FIGURE 8.36 Papineau expressed his opinion on women's rights in a February 1834 issue of *La Minerve*. **Analyze:** What does Papineau's description reveal about society's expectations of women at the time?

statute written law passed by a government

"And be it declared and enacted, That no woman is or shall be entitled to vote at any such Election, whether for any Count or Riding, City or Town."

— *Law from Baldwin-LaFontaine government*

FIGURE 8.37 This 1849 law, which took away women's right to vote, was passed by the Baldwin-LaFontaine government. **Analyze:** How might the female landowners have reacted?

FIGURE 8.38 An image from Ide & Dutton's 1855 catalogue of school supplies. Teachers could order these supplies for their school. **Analyze:** See if you can identify any of the supplies shown here. Are any of these supplies used in your classroom today?

Education was often available only through tutors or in private schools. One of the first private schools in Canada was Upper Canada College, which still exists today. Private schools were mostly attended by children of the upper classes, who could afford to pay tuition fees. Governments in New Brunswick and Prince Edward Island began to partially fund schools in the early 1800s. However, the majority of schools in all the colonies still required parents to pay a fee in exchange for their child's education. Examine the poster in **Figure 8.39**. What does it tell you about the approach to education at this time?

> What could happen to people's attitudes toward education if people have to continue to pay for it?

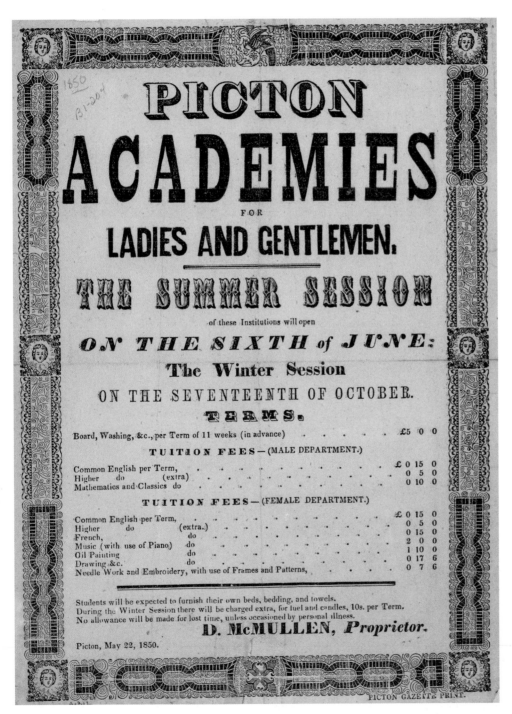

FIGURE 8.39 This poster for the 1850 summer session of Picton Academies, located in Picton, Ontario, shows the school's tuition fees in British currency. **Analyze:** What are some similarities and differences between the education offered in this poster and the way that education is offered today?

CHAPTER 8: *Demands for Change: 1837–1850*

PUBLIC EDUCATION REFORM

During the 1820s, demands and petitions for a public school system grew. Once again, people used newspapers to communicate their demands and frustrations publicly. **Figure 8.40** is an example of the kind of public comments that appeared in local newspapers. What does this quote tell you about public opinion on education?

"What a disgrace it is to Upper Canada, a colony inhabited by Christians, that the education of youth should be so little attended to. [Gambling], and other practices prevail in a great degree, which is entirely owing in the want of education."

— *Andrew Heron, bookseller and librarian*

FIGURE 8.40 Heron wrote to the *Gleaner and Niagara* newspaper in 1825 to complain about the state of the education system. **Analyze:** What problems does Heron believe that education can fix?

People continued to campaign for more school funding throughout the 1830s and 1840s. Ryerson was the Reformer politician in charge of developing public education in Canada. He received many letters from parents and teachers, criticizing the existing school system. Ryerson agreed that changes were necessary. Examine **Figure 8.41**. Why did he believe that education should be available to everyone?

"[Education] is as necessary as the light—it should be as common as water, and as free as air.... Education among the people is the best security of a good government and constitutional liberty.... An educated people are always a loyal people to good government; and the first object of a wise government should be the education of the people."

— *Egerton Ryerson, Reformer politician*

FIGURE 8.41 An excerpt from Ryerson's editorial in the *Christian Guardian* in 1829. **Analyze:** Do you think that the struggle for responsible government influenced Ryerson's views on education? Why, or why not?

> **What is the significance of the Common School Act?**

Eventually, because of public demand and Ryerson's own passion for education reform, the Province of Canada passed the *Common School Act* in 1846. This act created a system of free schools, with standards for teacher training, funding, and textbooks. It was the foundation for Canada's present-day public school system.

BARRIERS TO EDUCATION

Despite the *Common School Act*, there were still barriers to education for certain groups. In 1844, the Canadian government recommended that First Nations children should attend boarding schools based on farms. This was a government strategy to assimilate First Nations peoples. This system separated First Nations children from their parents. What do you think would be the consequences of separating First Nations children from their parents?

Black children attended **segregated** schools where schools were separated by racial group. Black children were also not free to go to any school they wanted. Mary Ann Shadd, shown in **Figure 8.42** in a painting created by her great-great-grandniece, was a Black Canadian activist working on increasing access to education for Black children. **Figure 8.43** is a quote from Shadd that describes the kind of conditions Black children and teachers had to face. How do you think segregation affected Black children's education? Shadd lobbied her own community, as well as the governments of both Canada and the United States, to end racist educational practices. She eventually opened the first **desegregated** school in Chatham, Ontario, which meant that different racial groups could attend school together.

FIGURE 8.42 This is an undated portrait of Mary Ann Shadd by Artis Lane. **Analyze:** What do you think is the meaning behind the facial expression that the artist chose to portray on Shadd?

segregation the deliberate separation of different racial groups in a society or institution

desegregation the elimination of the separation of different racial groups in a society or institution

> "The children of the colored school are not promoted to the grammar school, neither are they led to hope that they may be ... that disgrace of the place the little colored school house should be left to rot down, or to stand as it is a monument of the injustice the colored people sustain."
>
> — *Mary Ann Shadd, Black Canadian activist*

FIGURE 8.43 Shadd started her own newspaper, the *Provincial Freeman*. This quote is from an 1855 editorial she wrote for the newspaper. **Analyze:** Did the state of education for Black children match Ryerson's belief that education "is as necessary as the light—it should be as common as water, and as free as air"? Why, or why not?

CHECK-IN

1. **CAUSE AND CONSEQUENCE** Choose one person featured in this section who created change. Create a placemat diagram and list a positive, negative, intended, and unplanned consequence in each section. Why do you think this person was able to create change?

2. **CONTINUITY AND CHANGE** How does the letter written by "Adelaide" in the newspaper *La Minerve* provide evidence that women's roles in Canada were different than in England? How did some women rise above the barriers to equal rights?

3. **EVALUATE AND DRAW CONCLUSIONS** Examine some of the ways First Nations peoples responded to territory losses. Were these responses effective?

4. **GATHER AND ORGANIZE** Compare the actions of two women featured in this section. What are the similarities and differences between the methods they used to try to accomplish their goals?

HOW DID PEOPLE PUSH FOR POLITICAL CHANGE?

LEARNING GOALS

As you worked through this chapter, you had opportunities to

- examine and communicate the key causes of political conflict during the 1800s
- describe how different groups envisioned the government's responsibilities in the 1800s
- analyze the impact of the actions people took to create political change
- corroborate primary sources

In this chapter, you learned how different people tried to improve their lives through political change in the 1800s. Sometimes, this meant trying to change the society in which they lived and the way it was governed. Other times, this meant trying to gain the right to live like their neighbours. You also learned about different forces that worked against people's best efforts. These included opposing goals and values held by different groups, as well as attitudes and beliefs about what was best for other people.

Summarize Your Learning

Now that you have completed Chapter 8, you are ready to answer the Chapter Big Question: How did people push for political change? Select one of the following tasks to summarize your learning:

- Create a news broadcast on either the Lower Canada or Upper Canada rebellion. Your broadcast message should include the main facts of the rebellion, including the main reasons why the rebellion failed.
- Think of some of the opposing groups of people covered in this chapter: Reformers and Tories, men and women, British and French, First Nations and non-Aboriginal peoples, and so on. Each group had its own perspective on what political changes needed to be made. Choose one pair and create an advertisement for each side that explains why people should support its goals. Your advertisement should be able to answer this question: Why did some people want to change the government system, while other people did not?

APPLY YOUR LEARNING

1. **INTERPRET AND ANALYZE** Carefully review two ways that people tried to create change, including private campaigns, participation in the government, and violence. Which actions were most successful? Why?

2. **CONTINUITY AND CHANGE** With a partner or small group, debate whether the mid-1800s was a turning point in Canadian history or not. Some questions to consider as you prepare for your debate are: What were the most drastic changes at this time? Which groups of people were most affected by these changes? Which groups do you think experienced the fewest changes?

3. **COMMUNICATE** You are in charge of the Reformers. Write a letter to Lord Durham explaining why government reform is needed in both Upper and Lower Canada.

4. **HISTORICAL PERSPECTIVE** Identify some biased behaviours and decisions that existed in the mid-1800s. Explain how different attitudes and values promoted these behaviours and decisions.

5. **HISTORICAL PERSPECTIVE** Imagine you are part of the Family Compact or the Château Clique. You have just read William Lyon Mackenzie's attack on your family and friends. How will you respond? Defend your position and your actions in a letter to another newspaper.

6. **EVALUATE AND DRAW CONCLUSIONS** List the reasons why the rebellions in Upper and Lower Canada failed. Examine the reasons you have listed. What could the rebels have done differently?

7. **COMMUNICATE** Many people during the 1800s wrote to newspapers to communicate their frustrations and demands. Choose a person who is featured in this chapter and write a letter in that person's voice. Your letter should include his or her main concerns, based on evidence presented in this chapter.

8. **FORMULATE QUESTIONS** Suppose you were investigating how the government structure changed from 1837 to 1850. Create an inquiry question that would help you focus your research.

UNIT 2 CHALLENGE CHECK-IN

1. What were the impacts of the rebellions in Upper and Lower Canada? Which groups were affected, and why?

2. How did the system of government change during this time period? How did that affect life in Canada? Which groups benefited, and which groups did not?

3. Review the description of the Unit 2 Challenge on pages 134 to 135. Using your responses to questions 1 and 2 and other information from the chapter, rank the significant events and developments during this time period on your timeline, showing either progress or decline. Include evidence from sources in the chapter to support your rankings. Look back at the events and developments you added to your timeline in Chapters 6 and 7. Has your thinking changed? Make any necessary updates on your timeline.

4. Review the Focus On: Communicate feature on pages 226 to 227. Examine the suggested formats for communicating the results of your inquiry. What other formats would you add to the list? Identify your audience. What will be the best format for sharing your conclusion about whether the 1800s was a period of progress or decline for Canada? What will be the best format for presenting the evidence you gathered to support your conclusion? How will you cite your sources?

DID CANADA PROGRESS AS A RESULT OF THE CONFLICTS AND CHALLENGES FROM 1800 TO 1850?

The War of 1812 begins.

The Treaty of Ghent ends the War of 1812.

Shanawdithit, last surviving Beothuk in Newfoundland, dies.

| 1800 | 1812 | 1814 | 1819 | 1829 |

British Major-General Sir Isaac Brock dies during the Battle of Queenston Heights.

First government-sponsored Black settlement in Upper Canada is established in Oro Township.

WAR OF 1812 MILITARY FORCES

Britain 48 000
United States 35 000
First Nations 10 000

Percentage of immigrants coming to Canada from Ireland, 1830–1849 **64.2%**

UNIT 2 CHALLENGE

CREATE A PROGRESS AND DECLINE TIMELINE

Throughout Unit 2, you have been identifying significant events or developments that occurred and deciding whether they represented progress or decline.

Now, examine your timeline and the evidence you collected in each chapter. Formulate a conclusion about the overall impact. Was Canada a better place to live by 1850? Was it a better place for some groups but not for others? Go back to the description of the Unit 2 Challenge on pages 134 to 135, and review the features that should be included in your final timeline.

Next, communicate your conclusion. Consider who your audience will be. Design your presentation so that it clearly states your viewpoint. You should convince your audience that you have made a sound judgment by supporting your conclusion with evidence. Select a format to present your conclusion: a persuasive speech, a debate with a classmate who has an opposing view, a multimedia presentation, or another format of your choosing.

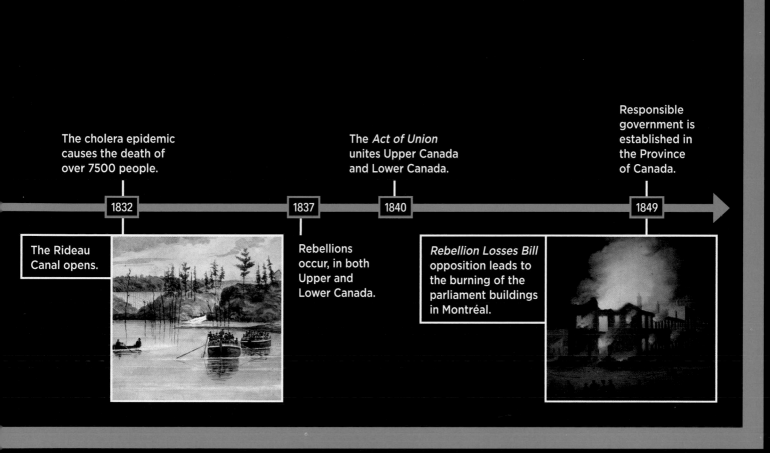

The cholera epidemic causes the death of over 7500 people.

1832

The Rideau Canal opens.

Rebellions occur, in both Upper and Lower Canada.

1837

The *Act of Union* unites Upper Canada and Lower Canada.

1840

Rebellion Losses Bill opposition leads to the burning of the parliament buildings in Montréal.

Responsible government is established in the Province of Canada.

1849

Estimated population in **1848**

Upper Canada 725 879
Lower Canada 765 797

Travel time between Toronto and Montréal in 1850
4 DAYS

Self-Check List

Use the following to check that you have met all the criteria for your timeline.

Knowledge and Understanding

☐ I identified significant events and developments during the time period.

☐ I described the impact of those events on various groups.

Thinking

☐ I selected criteria to evaluate the events and developments as progress or decline.

☐ I selected and used a variety of appropriate sources as evidence.

☐ I used the inquiry process and historical thinking concepts to plan and develop my timeline.

Communication

☐ I selected an appropriate method of communication for my purpose and my audience.

Application

☐ I developed a timeline of events and developments and included my judgment on whether each event or development represented progress or decline.

☐ I used the information on my timeline to decide if this time period represented overall progress or decline for Canada.

GLOSSARY

abolitionist: a person who wants to end slavery

Acadian Expulsion: the historical event in which thousands of Acadians were forced from their homeland in Acadia by the British

alliance: a type of agreement between people or groups to achieve a common goal

assimilate: to bring into conformity or adapt to the customs and attitudes of a group

British North America: the remaining British colonies in North America, north of the United States in what is known as Canada today, after the American Revolution ended in 1783

Château Clique: a small group of men, mostly merchants, who controlled most of the political and economic power in Lower Canada

class structure: a system for ordering society based on social or economic status

clergy reserve: land set aside to finance Protestant churches

coureur de bois: an independent French Canadian fur trader who travelled deep into the forests of New France

Crown reserve: land set aside to finance the government

desegregation: the elimination of the separation of different racial groups in a society or institution

deserter: a soldier who abandons military service without permission

disputed territory: area of land that different groups claim belongs to them

emancipation: freedom from slavery

Family Compact: a small group of men who controlled most of the political and economic power in Upper Canada

free trade: a system in which every country can trade goods without having to pay extra taxes

guerilla warfare: a type of fighting using small groups of soldiers to carry out surprise attacks against an opponent

habitant: French settler who farmed a small plot of land in what is now Québec

imperialism: the policy of extending a country's power and influence by creating colonies or conquering other countries

impressment: the act of forcing individuals to serve in the military with or without notice

Indigenous: native to the area; to do with the original inhabitants of Canada (First Nations, Métis, and Inuit)

Industrial Revolution: the rapid transition to new manufacturing processes in the 1700s and 1800s

itinerant: a person who travels from place to place, especially as a minister

land grant: an area of land given by the government in exchange for settling the land

Lower Canada: created by the *Constitutional Act, 1791*, a region of the lower St. Lawrence River and the Gulf of the St. Lawrence (roughly the region of southern Québec today) that was part of the former colony of the Province of Québec

Loyalist: a person living in the Thirteen Colonies who remained loyal to Britain during the American Revolution

mercantilism: an economic system that increases wealth by increasing exports and by limiting imports through taxes

Métis: an Aboriginal person descended from a First Nations mother and a father of European descent

military allies: two or more parties that agree to support one another in case of war

New England: a region in present-day northeastern United States, made up of the states of Connecticut, Maine, Massachusetts, New Hampshire, Rhode Island, and Vermont

oral history: a method of obtaining information about the past by gathering and interpreting voices and memories from people, communities, and past participants in events

Patriot: a person living in the Thirteen Colonies who supported the rebellion against Britain during the American Revolution

pemmican: a preserved food made of dried meat and berries

Planter: a British settler (colonist) from New England who migrated to Atlantic Canada between 1759 and 1774

proclamation: an official announcement, statement, or declaration

pull factor: a social, political, economic, or environmental benefit that draws migrants to an area

push factor: a social, political, economic, or environmental force that drives migrants out of an area

rebellion: an act of violent or open resistance to an established government or ruler

Reformer: critic of the government system in Canada during the early 1800s

representation: the act of speaking or acting on behalf of an individual or group

reserve: an area of land set aside for the use of a specific group of Aboriginal people

responsible government: a government that is responsible to its voters, not to appointed members

segregation: the deliberate separation of different racial groups in a society or institution

seigneurial system: the system used by the government to divide land among settlers in New France

statute: written law passed by a government

stronghold: a fortified place, or fortress, that is difficult to attack

the backwoods: remote, uncleared, forested land

Thirteen Colonies: the 13 British colonies on the east coast of North America, south of Nova Scotia, which eventually joined together to form the United States of America

treason: the act of betraying one's country

treaty: an agreement signed between different countries, in which promises are made

United Kingdom of Great Britain: the kingdom of Great Britain, or Britain, was formed when England and Scotland united in 1707

Upper Canada: created by the *Constitutional Act, 1791*, a region of the upper St. Lawrence River and the Great Lakes (roughly the region of southern Ontario today) that was part of the former colony of the Province of Québec

voyageur: a professional canoeist who transported furs

wampum: beads made of shells, used as currency or as a method of recording messages

working bee: an occasion when neighbours work together to accomplish a major task for one member of the community

INDEX

pull factor for Planters, 105
Land settlements. *See also* Farmland/
farming
    after War of 1812, 206, 222
    in Ohio Valley, 62–63
    and working bees, 152–53
Language
    Abenaki-French dictionary, 42
    canadien-français dialect, 48
    English official; French banned, 238
    First Nations sign language, 26
    Michif of Métis, 161
    Ojibwe written, 207
La Vérendrye, Pierre Gaultier de Varennes
    et de, 54
Lawrence, Charles (Governor), 65
Laws
    Act of Union (1840), 135, 238, 241, 251
    Act to Limit Slavery (1793), 141
    after Seven Years' War, 95, 98, 122
    Common School Act (1846), 246–47
    Constitutional Act, 1791, 19, 122, 131, 224,
        244
    Embargo Act (1807), 168
    funding for public schools (1807), 148
    government structure in 1830s, 224
    The Land Purchase Act (1875), 118
    Orders in Council, British, War of 1812, 168
    to promote business in New France
        (1690), 53
    Québec Act, 1774, 98–99, 122
    Rebellion Losses Bill (1849), 239–40, 251
    Slavery Abolition Act (1833), 215
    Stamp Act, 108
    Tea Act (1773), 106
    on women's right to vote, 244
Legardeur de St. Pierre, Jacques (French
    Commander), 62, 63
Longfellow, Henry Wadsworth, 71
Louisbourg, 61, 62, 78, 83, 84, 85, 105
Louis XIV (King of France), 30–31, 52
Lower Canada, 122
    Durham Report recommendations,
        236–38
    formation of colony, and House of
        Assembly, 122–23
    political conflict in 1830s, 135, 222–29
    political rebellion in 1837, 230–31
    population and immigration after War of
        1812, 200–201
    in War of 1812, 168, 171, 172, 183
    War of 1812 battles, 176–77, 179–81
Lower class people, life in 1800s, 140
Loyalist migration to British North America,
    19, 102–29
    American Revolution as cause of
        migration, 104–11
    challenges in new land, 112–19
    impact on residents, 120–26
    life in the backwoods, creating
        communities, 146–49, 152–55
    number of people, 130

Loyalists, 104
    Black Loyalists, 110, 115, 116–17, 154
    versus Patriots, 107–9
    views of American invasion in War of
        1812, 172, 174–75
Loyard, Father, 37

M

Mackenzie, William Lyon, 135, 225, 227, 229,
    233–35, 241
Macleod, Peter, 188
Madison, James (U.S. President), 170, 171, 172
Maitland, Peregrine (Lieutenant Governor of
    Upper Canada), 199
Manitoba, fur trade, 58, 160, 208–11
Manitoulin Island, 157, 242
Maple sugar production, 157
Maritimes, 105, 126
Marquette, Jacques (Father), 34
Mayhew, Jonathan (Reverend), 76
Mercantilism, 79
Merchant ships, French, seized by British, 79
Methodist Church, 158, 198, 207, 212–13
Métis, 160–61
    as Aboriginal people, 24
    Battle of Seven Oaks, 134, 209–10
    fur trade connections, 161, 208, 211
    origins of, and cultural identity, 160–61
    in War of 1812, 187
Michilimackinac, 90, 175
Middle class people, 140, 222
Mi'kmaq Nation, 67, 68–69, 120–21, 124–25
Military allies, with First Nations, 55
    between British and, 187
    between French and, 54–55, 62, 82
Military service
    impressment of American sailors, 167
    land grants to veterans, 195, 198–99
Military strategies
    in Seven Years' War, 79, 80–86
    in War of 1812, 174–75, 179–81
Minavavana (Ojibwe Chief), 88
Mississauga Nation
    impact of settlement after War of 1812,
        207
    land treaties, 92, 156
    territories, 24
    in War of 1812, 180, 181, 187
Mohawk Nation
    Loyalists in American Revolution, 111
    in Seven Years' War, 83
    in Six Nations of the Grand River, 11
    Thayendanegea and settlement, 156
    in War of 1812, 180, 184
Montcalm, Louis-Joseph de (Lieutenant-
    General), 83, 85, 86, 87
Montgomery's Tavern, Toronto, 234
Montréal
    French surrender to British, 86, 94
    fur trade, 28, 55, 58

immigration and population after War of
    1812, 200–201, 202
life in early 1800s, 139
parliament buildings burned, 239–40, 251
voting conflicts in 1830s, 223
in War of 1812, 180
Moodie, Susanna (author), 152–53, 204–5,
    232
Morris, Charles (British Naval Commander),
    66
Munro, John and Mary, 109
Murray, James (British General), 90, 95, 98

N

Nahnebahwequay (Catherine Sutton), 243
Napoleonic Wars, 166, 167, 186, 195
Natural resources, 24, 25, 26, 79, 80
Negro, 15, 141, 154. *See also* Blacks
Nelson, Wolfred, 230
Neutral French, 64, 126
New Brunswick, 31, 71, 112, 115, 126
New England, 42, 105
Newfoundland, 31, 144
New France. *See also* Canadien culture;
    French, in America
    alliance with Wabanaki Confederacy, 41
    conquest of. *See* Seven Years' War
New Orleans, settlement by Acadians, 71
Newspapers
    advertisements for Negro, 141
    public complaints, 187, 188, 213, 214, 232,
        243, 246
    role in politics, 77, 223, 225, 226–27
Niagara, in War of 1812, 179, 181, 184
Niagara-on-the-Lake, 175, 183
92 Resolutions, 229, 230
Nishiyuu walkers, 40
North America, and Treaty of Utrecht, 22–25,
    31, 34, 36
North West Company, 134, 161, 208–11
Notre-Dame-des-Victoires, 145
Nova Scotia
    Black Loyalists in Birchtown, 116–17
    land offer for Loyalist settlers, 105, 110,
        112, 116, 119
    Loyalist migration to, 112, 115, 126
    and Treaty of Utrecht, 31, 42, 64

O

Oath of Allegiance, 64–65, 95, 96
O'Brien, Mary, 215
Odawa Nation, 36, 89, 90, 121, 181
Ohio Valley
    American expansion in early 1800s,
        168–69
    conflict between French and British, 58,
        60, 62–63, 66, 77
    and Treaty of Niagara (1764), 93

Ojibwe Nation
    ancestor of Métis, 160
    fur trade, 35, 211
    land rights campaigns, 242-43
    movement around 1713, 36
    Seven Years' War, 82, 83, 88-90
    in War of 1812, 180, 181, 187
    written language, 207
Onondaga Nation, 11, 57, 61
Ontario
    First Nations land surrender, 121
    Loyalist migration to, 114-15, 127
    reserves for Six Nations, 156
    schools, 148, 245, 247
Oral history, defined, 35
Oro African Methodist Episcopal Church, 198
Oro Township, Simcoe County, Ontario, 198,
    215, 250
Ottawa, Ontario, 12, 98, 122, 241

P

Papineau, Louis-Joseph, 229, 230, 241, 244
Parr Traill, Catharine (author), 204-5, 206
Patriotes, 135, 229, 230-31, 233, 243
Patriots, in Thirteen Colonies, 107-9
Pemmican, 161, 208, 210
Pierpoint, Richard (Black Loyalist), 154, 182,
    199
Pioneers, 182
Plains of Abraham. See Battle of Plains of
    Abraham
Planters, from New England, 105
Politics in Canada, 1830s
    Durham Report recommendations,
        236-38
    economic conflicts, 222
    government structure, 224-25, 226-27, 229
    Lower Canada rebellions, 230-31
    religious views, 212-13
    Upper Canada rebellions, 233-35
    voting conflicts, 223, 233
Pontiac (Odawa Chief), 89
Population
    after War of 1812, 200-201, 202, 206
    of British North America, 19, 131
    of enslaved peoples, 141
    of First Nations, early 1700s, 55
    of New France and British colonies (1713-
        1754), 60
    reading a population graph, 202
    of Upper and Lower Canada in 1800s,
        134, 138, 250, 251
Post, Christian Frederick, 76, 78
Potawatomi Nation, 89, 90, 121
Poverty, 217, 222
Press gangs, 167
Prevost, Sir George (Commander-in-Chief of
    Canada), 172, 175
Primary sources, 6, 36, 56-57, 150-51
Prince Edward Island (P.E.I.), 31, 115, 118
Prisons, 142-43

Proclamation, 92
Protestants. See also Religion
    in Acadia, 66
    churches after War of 1812, 212-13
    clergy reserves for churches, 149, 222
    conversion of First Nations people, 158, 214
Pull factor, 105
Push factor, 105

Q

Québec, split into Upper Canada and Lower
    Canada, 122-23
Québec City
    early 1800s, 138
    fires in 1845, 144
    immigration after War of 1812, 201
    notice for Americans to leave (1812), 172
    rebuilding after Seven Years' War, 95,
        96-97
    surrender to British in Seven Years' War,
        74-75, 83, 85, 86
    walls of, and Porte Saint-Louis, 16-17

R

Racism, 117, 215, 237, 240, 247
Radisson, Pierre-Esprit, 27
Railway, 206
Rale, Sébastien (Father), 42-43
Rebellion, riots, protests. See also American
    Revolution
    political conflict in Upper and Lower
        Canada, 222, 230-35
    rebellion defined, 222
    Tories protest Rebellion Losses Bill,
        239-40
Red River area, Manitoba, 160, 208-11
Reformers, 225
    political conflict in 1830s, 225, 226-27,
        229, 230
    riots and rebellion, 233-35
    view of women's right to vote, 244
Religion. See also Catholic Church;
    Christianity; Protestants
    in Canadien culture, 52
    churches after War of 1812, 212-13
    clergy reserves, 149, 222
Religious freedom, 98
Representation, in government, 106
Reserves, 92, 156
Responsible government, 135, 227, 229,
    237-41, 251
Rideau Canal, 194, 196-97, 201, 206, 251
Roads, 118, 146, 149, 182, 195, 205
Robinson, William, 206
Royal Proclamation (1763), 92-93, 95, 98-99
Rupert's Land, 208
Russell, Peter (Upper Canada receiver
    general), 141

Ryerse, Amelia, 183
Ryerson, Egerton, 213, 229, 246

S

Saskatchewan, early fur trade, 58, 160
Saulteaux Nation, 160, 208
Saunders, Anne (Lady Melville), 118
Savages, 28, 143
Schaw, Janet, 109
Schooling. See Education
Seaver, William Rufus, 240
Secondary sources, 7, 36, 56, 125
Secord, Laura, 184-85
Segregation of schools, 247
Seigneurial system, 28, 48, 98, 122
Selkirk's settlements, 134, 208-10
Seneca Nation, 11, 78, 83, 89
Separatist movement, 97
Settlements. See also Communities
    displacement of First Nations peoples,
        156-57
    French and English in 1600s, 28-29
    impact on First Nations communities
        after War of 1812, 207
    in Maritime region, 126
Seven Years' War, 18, 74-101, 130
    Battle of Québec, 85-86
    battles over forts, 84
    causes of, 76-79
    French surrender, 86, 94-95
    impact on First Nations, 88-93
    impact on French, 94-99
    military strategies, 80-86
    names for, 75, 94
Shadd, Mary Ann, 247
Shanawdithit (Beothuk), 159, 250
Shawnee Nation
    fur trade, 58
    resistance to American expansion,
        168-69
    Seven Years' War, during and after, 78, 89
    in War of 1812, 187
Shelburne, Nova Scotia, 116-17, 119
Shingwaukonse (Ojibwe Chief), 242-43
Simcoe, Elizabeth, 114, 139, 145, 156
Simcoe, John Graves (Lieutenant-Governor
    of Upper Canada), 12, 114, 123, 139, 141,
    154
Sioux Nation, 55, 211
Six Nations Confederacy. See also
    Haudenosaunee Confederacy
    displacement and settlement, 111, 156
    of the Grand River, land claims, 10-11
    Iroquois groups as, 25
    in War of 1812, 179, 181, 187
Slavery
    Dawn Settlement, 216
    in early Canada, 15, 141
    of First Nations peoples, 37, 42
    outlawed, 141, 215
    and War of 1812, 182, 199

CREDITS

PHOTO CREDITS

Hemsworth, courtesy of Historica Canada. Heritage Minutes can be viewed at www. historicacanada.ca; 200: Library and Archives Canada, Acc. No. 1991-116-6; 201: Library and Archives Canada, Acc. No. 1983-47-44; 203: Toronto Reference Library, Baldwin 1832, Cholera bulletin. S; 204: Library and Archives Canada, Acc. No. 1970-188-2056 W.H. Coverdale Collection of Canadiana; 205: Archives of Ontario / F 1077-8-1-4-19 / End view of John's house, Canada, 1837, sketched by Anne Langton / Copyright Public Domain; 206: Exporail, The Canadian Railway Museum; fonds John Loye; 207: Victoria University Library (Toronto); 209: Library and Archives Canada, Acc. No. 1972-26-779; 210: Archives de la Société historique de Saint-Boniface, Collection générale de la SHSB, Série sujets, 1/304/36; 211: Library and Archives Canada, Acc. No. 1988-250-33; 212: Library and Archives Canada; 213 (top): Toronto Reference Library, Baldwin, JRR 252 Cab II, (bottom): Toronto Reference Library, Baldwin, JRR 2755; 214: © Design Pics Inc / Alamy; 216: Uncle Tom's Cabin Historic Site; 217: City of Toronto Museums & Heritage Services, 1978.41.40; 218: Toronto Reference Library, Baldwin, JRR 193 Cab III

CHAPTER 8 220–221: Musée national des beaux-arts du Québec; 223: Le Monde illustré, February 1, 1890 (Famille-sans-nom). From the collections of Bibliothèque et Archives nationales du Québec; 225: Library and Archives Canada, Acc. No. 1996-115-1; 226: The Vindicator, January 3, 1832. From the collections of Bibliothèque et Archives nationales du Québec; 228: Michael Stuparyk / GetStock.com; 229: Kyle, Fergus, c1876-1941, A Political Meeting in Lower Canada (reproduced from Kathleen Moore and Jessie McEwen, A Picture History of Canada, Illustrated by Famous Artists, Toronto: Thomas Nelson and Sons, [1938], plate 35 facing p. 78); 231 (top): McCord Museum M972.81.10, (bottom) Library and Archives Canada, Acc. No. 1992-566-6; 233: Library and Archives Canada, Acc. No. 1972-26-1384; 234: Library and Archives Canada, Acc. No. 1972-26-706; 235: Library and Archives Canada, C-001242; 236 (top): Library and Archives Canada, R9266-3063, (bottom) The First Council of Queen Victoria, 1838 (oil on canvas), Wilkie, Sir David (1785-1841) / Royal Collection Trust © Her Majesty Queen Elizabeth II, 2015 / Bridgeman Images; 239: McCord Museum M11588; 240: Mary Evans Picture Library / Alamy; 241: © Rolf Hicker Photography / Alamy; 242: Toronto Reference Library, Baldwin, JRR 2422 Cab IV Armstrong; 243 (top): Grey Roots Museum, (bottom): La Minerve, February 2, 1837. From the collections of Bibliothèque et Archives nationales du Québec; 244: The school house, its architecture, external and internal arrangements, with additional papers on gymnastics, the use of apparatus, school discipline, methods of teaching, etc., together with selections for public recitations in schools, Hodgins, J. George, 1857. Toronto Reference Library, Baldwin, 371.6 H57 BR; 245: Library and Archives Canada, nlc-16297; 247: Artis Lane; 248: Musée national des beaux-arts du Québec

UNIT 2 CLOSER 250 (top): Smithsonian American Art Museum, Washington, D.C. / Art Resource, NY, (bottom): Library and Archives Canada, Acc. No. 1954-153-1; 251 (left): Library and Archives Canada, Acc. No. 1983-47-44, (right): McCord Museum M11588, (horse and buggy icon): Yoko Design/Shutterstock.com

SOURCES

INTRO 5: Ann Harvey Nomination Letter, by Blanford Billard, http://www. isleauxmorts.ca/official_ah_nomination.php; 6: R.P. Gorham, "The Narrative of Hannah Ingraham: Loyalist Colonist at St. Anne's Point, October 1783." (Unpublished Manuscript, University of New Brunswick Archives & Special Collections, 1933); 7: Loyalist Women in New Brunswick, Hannah Ingraham, http://preserve.lib.unb.ca/ wayback/20141205153708/http://atlanticportal.hil.unb.ca/acva/loyalistwomen/en/ context/biographies/ingraham.html; 11: Six Nations Lands and Resources, Haldimand Treaty, October 25, 1784, http://www.sixnations.ca/LandsResources/HaldProc.htm; 15 (top): Archives nationales du Québec, Centre de Québec, Journal de Madame Bégon, P2, Rocbert de la Morandière, Elisabeth (Madame Bégon), Letter regarding her slaves, December 25, 1748, (top) Frank Mackey, Black Then: Blacks and Montreal, 1780-1880s, McGill-Queen's University Press - MQUP, 2004

CHAPTER 1 23: H.P. Biggar, ed., The precursors of Jacques Cartier 1497-1534: A Collection of Documents relating to the Early History of the Dominion of Canada, Ottawa: Government Printing Bureau 1911, 15-21. Original documents housed in the Milan Archives, Milan; 24: Peter Jones, History of the Ojebway Indians: With Especial Reference to Their Conversion to Christianity; with a Brief Memoir of the Writer, 1 January 1861, A.W. Bennett Publisher; 28: Emma LaRocque, PhD, Colonization and Racism, Aboriginal Perspectives, National Film Board of Canada; 28: Puritan preacher speaks about First Nations, 1609, from The Law of Nations and the New World, Green & Dickason, 1993, p. 18; 30: The Treaty of Utrecht, 1713; 32: Naomi Griffiths, "The Golden Age: Acadian Life, 1713-1748," Histoire Sociale I Social History 17 (1984); 34: Mark Haynes, The Forgotten Battle: A History of the Acadians of Canso/Chedabuctou, Trafford Publishing, 2004; 35 (top): The Treaty of Utrecht, 1713, (bottom): Peter Schmalz, The Ojibwa of Southern Ontario, University of Toronto Press, Jan 1, 1991, p.

35; 36 (fig. 1.20): Based on Helen Hornbeck Tanner, Atlas of Great Lakes Indian History, University of Oklahoma Press; 37: W.E. Daugherty, Treaties and Historical Research Centres, Research Branch, Corporate Policy, Department of Indian and Northern Affairs Canada, Maritime Indian Treaties In Historical Perspective, January 1983, https:// www.aadnc-aandc.gc.ca/eng/1100100028966/1100100028968; 38: Reuben Gold, Ed. Thwaites, The Jesuit Relations and Allied Documents. Travels and Explorations of the Jesuit Missionaries in New France, 1610-1791, Vol. LXVII. Lower Canada, Abenakis, Louisiana, 1716-1727, The Burrows Brothers Company (1900); 39: Portsmouth NH Commemorates the 300th Anniversary of the 1713 Treaty of Portsmouth with Speakers, Events, http://www.1713treatyofportsmouth.com/300.cfm; 41 (top): L.C. Green, Olive Patricia Dickason, The Law of Nations and the New World, University of Alberta, 1993, p. 119, (bottom) L.C. Green, Olive Patricia Dickason, The Law of Nations and the New World, University of Alberta, 1993, p. 119; 42: Reuben Gold, Ed. Thwaites, The Jesuit Relations and Allied Documents. Travels and Explorations of the Jesuit Missionaries in New France, 1610-1791, Vol. LXVII. Lower Canada, Abenakis, Louisiana, 1716-1727, The Burrows Brothers Company (1900); 43: John Francis Sprague, Sebastian Rale: A Maine Tragedy Of The Eighteenth Century, (1906), Kessinger Publishing, LLC

CHAPTER 2 49: David Kennedy, Thomas Bailey, The American Spirit: United States History as Seen by Contemporaries, Volume 1, Cengage Learning, Aug. 17, 2009; 50: Carolyn Podruchny, Making the Voyageur World: Travelers and Traders in the North American Fur Trade, University of Nebraska Press, 2006, p. 10; 53: Irene Ternier Gordon, Marie-Anne Lagimodière: the Incredible Story of Louis Riel's Grandmother, Heritage House Publishing Co, Jan. 1, 2003; 54: Continuation of the Report of the Sieur de la Vérendrye touching upon the discovery of the Western Sea (Amended to the Letter of M. de Beauharnois, [gov. of New France] of October 10, 1730); 55: Black Elk, Words That Speak, Native American Prayers, http://nativeamerican.lostsoulsgenealogy. com/prayers.htm; 57: George Edward Ellis, The red man and the white man in North America, from its discovery to the present time, Little, Brown, 1882; 58: Ken S., Fisher, Robin (eds.) Coates. Out of the Background: Readings on Native Canadian History. Irwin Publishing. 1988, p. 143; 60 (fig. 2.17): Based on List of French forts in North America. From Wikipedia, the free encyclopedia; 61: George Edward Ellis, The red man and the white man in North America, from its discovery to the present time, Little, Brown, 1882; 63 (top): Washington, George and Royster, Paul, editor, "The Journal of Major George Washington (1754)" (1754). Electronic Texts in American Studies. Paper 33, (bottom): Washington, George and Royster, Paul, editor, "The Journal of Major George Washington (1754)" (1754). Electronic Texts in American Studies. Paper 33; 66: John Mack Faragher, A Great and Noble Scheme: The Tragic Story of the Expulsion of the French Acadians from Their American Homeland, W.W. Norton & Company, pp. 288-9; 67: Stephen E. Patterson, "Indian-White Relations in Nova Scotia, 1749-61: A Study in Political Interaction," Acadiensis, XXIII, 1 (Autumn 1993), p. 30; 68: Naomi Griffiths, The Acadians, Creation of a People, McGraw-Hill Ryerson, 1973, p.37; 69: Gérard Finn, "Jean-Louis Le Loutre," DCB, IV, p. 455; 70: CMA, "Pohenegamook hosts the third grand youth rally 2014" from 2014 World Acadian Congress, http://cma2014. com/en/20-actualites/420-pohenegamook-hosts-the-third-grand-youth-rally-2014

CHAPTER 3 76 (left): The European Competition for North America, The British & American Colonial Perspective: A Sampling, 1699-1763, Early American Imprints, American Antiquarian Society, http://nationalhumanitiescenter.org/pds/ becomingamer/american/text1/europeancompetition.pdf, (right): Battle for a Continent Rumblings of War, Clashes in the Ohio Valley, CBC, http://www.cbc.ca/ history/EPCONTENTSE1EP4CH1LE.html; 78: National Humanities Center Resource Toolbox, Becoming American: The British Atlantic Colonies, 1690-1763, http:// nationalhumanitiescenter.org/pds/becomingamer/peoples/text3/indianscolonists.pdf; 80: The Papers of Benjamin Franklin, eds. Leonard W. Labaree et al. (Yale University Press, 1959-), #623187, http://nationalhumanitiescenter.org/pds/becomingamer/ american/text4/unionofcolonies.pdf; 82 (top): Wilbur R. Jacobs, ed., The Appalachian Indian Frontier: The Edmond Aitken Report and Plan of 1755 (University of Nebraska Press, 1967), pp. 7-8, http://nationalhumanitiescenter.org/pds/becomingamer/ american/text1/europeancompetition.pdf, (bottom): George Washington to Mary Ball Washington, July 18, 1755, The George Washington Papers at the Library of Congress, 1741-1799; 85: Report by Rear-Admiral Charles Holmes, Sept. 18, 1759, https://uwaterloo. ca/library/special-collections-archives/collections/holmes-rear-admiral-charles-report; 88 (top): Henry, Alexander, Alexander Henry's Travels and Adventures in the Years 1760-1776, R.R. Donnelley & Sons Company, 1921, p. 44, (bottom): Francis Parkman, The conspiracy of Pontiac and the Indian war after the conquest of Canada, Vol 2, Boston: Little Brown, 1870; 89: Burton, Mary Agnes (editor), Journal of Pontiac's Conspiracy 1763, Detroit: Published by Clarence Monroe Burton under the Auspices of the Michigan Society of the Colonial Wars, 1912, p. 38; 90: Henry, Alexander, Alexander Henry's Travels and Adventures in the Years 1760-1776, R.R. Donnelley & Sons

Company, 1921, pp. 78–80; 92: Library and Archives Canada, e010778430; 93: *Canada in the Making, Aboriginals: Treaties & Relations, 1764 – 1836: Pre-Confederation Treaties I*, http://www.canadiana.ca/citm/themes/aboriginals/aboriginals4_e.html; 97 (top): Thomas Thorner (Editor), Thor Frohn-Nielson (Editor), *A Few Acres of Snow: Documents in Pre-Confederation Canadian History*, Third Edition, University of Toronto Press, 2009, (bottom): From "Plains of Abraham re-enactment cancelled," *Toronto Star*, Tue Feb. 17 2009, http://www.thestar.com/news/canada/2009/02/17/plains_of_abraham_reenactment_cancelled.html

CHAPTER 4 105: Planter 2010 Celebration in Nova Scotia, http://planter2010.ca/proc/ns-proclamation1758oct12-bepost-1106.html; 109 (top): Mary Munro, Mary Munro to John Munro, undated letter. Letter. From Haldimand Papers, AddMss A748, (bottom): Janet Schaw, *Journal of a Lady of Quality*, June 1775, http://www.smithsoniansource.org/display/primarysource/viewdetails.aspx?TopicId=&PrimarySourceId=1011; 111: C. H. Parmelee, *Sessional Papers*, Volume 16, 1887; 112: Sarah Frost diary, 1783, http://preserve.lib.unb.ca/wayback/20141205161007/http://atlanticportal.hil.unb.ca/acva/loyalistwomen/en/documents/frost/sarah_frost.pdf; 113: Ann Mackenzie M.A., *A Short History of the United Empire Loyalists*, http://www.uelac.org/PDF/loyalist.pdf; 115 (top): Submission to the House of Commons in 1786, http://www.uppercanadahistory.ca/uel/uel7.html, (bottom): Historical Narratives of Early Canada, http://www.uppercanadahistory.ca/uel/uel7.html; 116: Dyott, William, 1761–1847; Jeffery, Reginald W. (Reginald Welbury), *Dyott's diary, 1781–1845: a selection from the journal of William Dyott, sometime general in the British army and aide-de-camp to His Majesty King George III*, A. Constable, 1907; 117: Memoirs of Boston King, Black Loyalist: Our History, Our People, http://epe.lac-bac.gc.ca/100/200/301/ic/can_digital_collections/blackloyalists/index.htm; 120: 1752 Peace and Friendship Treaty Between His Majesty the King and the Jean Baptiste Cope, https://www.aadnc-aandc.gc.ca/eng/1100100029040/1100100029041; 121: Siobhan Senier (Editor), *Dawnland Voices: An Anthology of Indigenous Writing from New England*, University of Nebraska Press, p. 40; 122: *Report on Canadian Archives*, Maclean, Roger & Company, 1891, p. Xxiii; 123 (left): Eric Bédard, *History of Quebec for Dummies*, John Wiley & Sons, May 30, 2013, (right): CBC, Canada: A People's History, p. 160

CHAPTER 5 138 (fig. 5.1): Based on Historical Atlas of Canada, Population and Economy, ca 1800; 139: Simcoe, Elizabeth, Robertson, J. Ross, *The diary of Mrs. John Graves Simcoe, wife of the first lieutenant-governor of the province of Upper Canada, 1792–6 : with notes and a biography by J. Ross Robertson, and two hundred and thirty-seven illustrations, including ninety reproductions of interesting sketches made by Mrs. Simcoe*, W. Briggs, 1911, pp. 94, 97; 141: Peter Russell letter to Matthew Elliott, York, 19 September 1801, http://www.archives.gov.on.ca/en/explore/online/slavery/peggy.aspx; 143 (left): John Woolstencroft, letter to the editor in the Colonial Advocate, December 22 1831, http://www.archives.gov.on.ca/en /explore/online/sharon_temple/need.aspx, (right): William Leete Stone, Life of Joseph Brant-Thayendanegea: Including the Border Wars of the American Revolution and Sketches of the Indian Campaigns of Generals Harmar, St. Clair, and Wayne; and Other Matters Connected with the Indian Relations of the United States and Great Britain, from the Peace of 1783 to the Indian Peace of 1795, Volume 2, Phinney, 1851, pp. 482–483; 144: Father Pierre Frechette writing to Bishop Hubert, (1786 - Fort Detroit, QC) pp. 213–214: reproduced from Letter of Pierre Frechette, parish priest, to Bishop Hubert, April 24, 1786, Archives de l'Archidiocese de Quebec, 7cm, Etats-Unis, Vol V, 46. Correspondence with Detroit; 145: John Ross Robertson, *The Diary of Mrs. Simcoe*, William Briggs, 1911; 147: Mary Alice Downie and Barbara Robertson with Elizabeth Jane Errington, Eds., *Early Voices: Portraits of Canada by Women Writers, 1639–1914*, Dundurn, p. 35; 149: *Social Studies 10*, Our Land: Building the West, Chapter 2, The Struggle for Reform in the Canadas, 1815–1840, http://myriverside.sd43.bc.ca/cross/files/2014/10/READINGS-for-chart-on-Oligarchies-and-Reformers-in-Upper-and-Lower-Canada-ygw2mr.pdf; 153 (left): Susanna Moodie, Roughing It in the Bush, London: Richard Bentley, 1852, (right): Catharine Wilson, "Reciprocal work bees and the meaning of neighbourhood," *Canadian Historical Review*, Volume 82, Issue 3, University of Toronto press, p. 3; 154 (top): Petition of Free Negroes, 1794; 155: Charlotte Gray, *Canada: A Portrait in Letters, 1800–2000*, Doubleday Canada, Limited (2004), p. 23, (bottom): Peter Baskerville, *Ontario: Image, Identity, and Power*, Don Mills: Oxford University Press, 2002, p. 54; 157: Hanipaux letter to superior, 1846, Lonc and Topp, *Letters from the New Canada Missions*, Vol. 6-1, pt. 1: pp. 391–392; 161: NAHO, Métis Women: Strong and Beautiful, National Aboriginal Health Organization, 2011

CHAPTER 6 168: Tom Holmberg, The Acts, Orders in Council, &c. of Great Britain [on Trade], 1793–1812, American State Papers: Documents, Legislative and Executive, of the Congress of the United States. Class I.: Foreign Relations. Selected and edited under the authority of Congress. Washington, DC: Gales and Seaton, 1832–1861; 170: Henry Clay (Author), James F. Hopkins (Editor), Mary W. M. Hargreaves (Editor), *The Papers of Henry Clay: The Rising Statesman*, 1797–1814, Vol. 1, University of Kentucky Press, 1959, p. 450; 171 (top): J. F. C. Fuller, *Decisive Battles of the U.S.A.*, 1776–1918, Bison Books, 2007, p. 103, (middle): Stanford History Education Group, Beyond the Bubble, The War of 1812, https://beyondthebubble.stanford.edu/assessments/war-1812, (bottom): Thomas Jefferson to William Duane, 4 August 1812, http://founders.archives.gov/documents/Jefferson/03-05-02-0231; 172 (top): Announcement of the expulsion of United States citizens from Quebec City, 1812, McCord Museum, M6606, (bottom left): PBS, The War of 1812, Personal Journals from the War of 1812, http://www.pbs.org/wned/war-of-1812/essays/personal-journals-war/, (bottom right): Canadian War Museum, War Experience, http://www.warmuseum.ca/war-of-1812/explore-history/the-canadian-war/war-experience/; 174: Canadian Museum of History, Hull's Proclamation, 1812, http://www.canadashistory.ca/Magazine/Special-Feature--War-of-1812/General-Correspondence-The-Words-and-Wisdom-of-Si/July/Hull-s-Proclamation; 175: Sir Isaac Brock, *The Life and Correspondence of Major-General Sir Isaac Brock, K. B.*, Simpkin, Marshall & Company, 1847, p. 150; 183: R. Taylor, The Burning of Newark, December 1813, http://www.warof1812.ca/burningofnewark.htm; 184 (top): Historica Canada, Laura Secord, from the Heritage Minutes collection, https://www.historicacanada.ca/content/heritage-minutes/laura-secord, (bottom): Mona Holmlund, Gail Youngberg, Margaret Eleanor Atwood, *Inspiring Women, A Celebration of Herstory*, Coteau Books, 2003; 187 (top): Randy Boswell, "'Red-Haired Man' remembered for pivotal role in War of 1812," *Postmedia News*, June 17, 2012, (bottom): Andrew Shankman, ed., *The World of the Revolutionary American Republic: Land, Labor, and the Conflict for a Continent*, NY: Routledge, 2014, p. 258; 188: James Careless, "Tallying the winners and losers of the War of 1812," *Postmedia News*, December 12, 2012; 189: Morris Zaslow, *The Defended Border: Upper Canada and the War of 1812*, Toronto: Macmillan, 1964, p. 331

CHAPTER 7 195: Jean S. McGill, *A Pioneer History of the County of Lanark*, T.H. Best Printing Company, Toronto, 1968 and subsequent printings; 197: William N.T. Wylie, "Poverty, Distress, and Disease: Labour and the Construction of the Rideau Canal, 1826–32," *Labour / Le Travail* Vol. 11 (Spring, 1983), pp. 14–15; 199: Steve Pitt, *To Stand and Fight Together: Richard Pierpoint and the Coloured Corps of Upper Canada*, Dundurn, 2008; 201: Marjorie Kohli, *The Golden Bridge: Young Immigrants to Canada, 1833–1939*, Natural Heritage, 2003, pp. 40–41; 203: Charlotte Gray, *Canada: A Portrait in Letters, 1800–2000*, Doubleday Canada, Limited, 2004, p. 35; 205 (left): Catharine Parr Strickland Traill, *The Backwoods of Canada: Being Letters from the Wife of an Emigrant Officer, Illustrative of the Domestic Economy of British America*, C. Knight, 1836, (right): Susanna Moodie, *Roughing It In The Bush*, London: Richard Bentley, 1852; 206 (top): Catharine Parr Traill, The Backwoods of Canada, CBC, *A People's History* Volume 1, 2001, p. 221, (bottom): Charlotte Gray, *Canada: A Portrait in Letters, 1800–2000*, Doubleday Canada, Limited, 2004, pp. 65–66; 207: Charlotte Gray, *Canada: A Portrait in Letters*, 1800–2000, Doubleday Canada, Limited, 2004, p. 50; 210 (top): CBC, Battle at Seven Oaks, Canada: A People's History, http://www.cbc.ca/history/EPCONTENTSE1EP6CH5PA3LE.html, (bottom): Pierre Falcon, "Chanson de la Grenouillere," 1816, http://www.mhs.mb.ca/docs/forkssevenoaks/introduction_sevenoaks.shtml; 213 (top): John Strachan, D.D., A Sermon Preached at York, Upper Canada, Third of July, 1825, on the Death of the Late Lord Bishop of Quebec, Kingston: Printed by James MacFarlane, 1826, http://anglicanhistory.org/canada/strachan/mountain_sermon1826.html, (bottom): Ryerson's response to Strachan, published in 1826 in the Colonial Advocate, a reformist newspaper, p. 15, http://static.torontopubliclibrary.ca/da/pdfs/37131052104536d.pdf; 214 (top): Letter #124, https://www.trentu.ca/admin/library/archives/78-008%20letters%20100-149.htm, (bottom): Ireland Park, Great Famine History, http://www.irelandparkfoundation.com/famine-memorial/great-famine-history/; 215 (top): Alexandra Vinci, MA Thesis, *A Study of Race-relations between Blacks and Whites Over Issues of Schooling in Upper Canada, 1840–1860*, University of Toronto, 2011, https://tspace.library.utoronto.ca/handle/1807/25680, (bottom): Karolyn Smardz Frost, *I've got a home in Glory Land*, Farrar, Straus and Giroux, 2008

CHAPTER 8 222: Claude Corbo, Alexis de Tocqueville's visit to Lower Canada in 1831, http://www.ameriquefrancaise.org/en/article-466/Alexis_de_Tocqueville%E2%80%99s_visit_to_Lower_Canada_in_1831.html; 225: CBC, The Colonial Regime and the "Family Compact", http://www.cbc.ca/history/EPISCONTENTSE1EP7CH2PA1LE.html; 227: John Sewell, *Mackenzie: A Political Biography of William Lyon Mackenzie*, 2002; 229: CBC, The 92 Resolutions, http://www.cbc.ca/history/EPISCONTENTSE1EP7CH2PA4LE.html; 230: Mitch Abidor, The Patriotes Rebellion, https://www.marxists.org/history/canada/quebec/patriotes-rebellion/introduction.htm; 232: Susanna Moodie, edited by Charles Forbes Fothergill, *Palladium of British America, and Upper Canada Mercantile Advertiser*, Vol. 1(6), 1839; 233: CBC, Canada: A People's History, p. 230; 237 (top): Durham Report, http://www.thecanadianencyclopedia.ca/en/article/durham-report/, (bottom): The Durham Report and Its Solutions, https://slmc.uottawa.ca/durham_report; 238: The Durham Report and Its Solutions, https://slmc.uottawa.ca/durham_report; 240: CBC, Canada: A People's History, p. 253; 241: CBC, Canada: A People's History, p. 254; 242: James Rodger Miller, *Skyscrapers Hide the Heavens: A History of Indian-white Relations in Canada*, University of Toronto Press, 2000; 243: *La Minerve*, 2 February 1837, http://collections.banq.qc.ca/ark:/52327/278148; 244 (top): *The Provincial Statues of Canada*, 1849, p189 12 Vict. Cap 27, (bottom): Directeur général des élections du Québec (DGEQ), Right of Québec women to vote and to stand for office, http://www.electionsquebec.qc.ca/english/provincial/voting/right-to-vote-of-quebec-women.php; 246 (top): *Gleaner and Niagara Newspaper*, 9 July 1825, (bottom): Egerton Ryerson, An early editorial from the *Christian Guardian*, founded by Egerton Ryerson (1829), http://library.ryerson.ca/asc/archives/ryerson-history/; 247: *Provincial Freeman*, 6 Oct. 1855